VOICES FROM THE ANCESTORS

VOICES FROM THE ANCESTORS

Xicanx and Latinx Spiritual Expressions and Healing Practices

EDITED BY LARA MEDINA AND MARTHA R. GONZALES

THE UNIVERSITY OF
ARIZONA PRESS
TUCSON

The University of Arizona Press
www.uapress.arizona.edu

© 2019 by The Arizona Board of Regents
All rights reserved. Published 2019

ISBN-13: 978-0-8165-3956-7 (paper)

Cover design by Leigh McDonald
Cover art: *Fruta Amarga* by Emilia García

The ornament that appears on the title page and throughout the text is *Word In Xochitl*, which was designed by Lilia "Liliflor" Ramirez exclusively for *Voices from the Ancestors* to serve as a guide for oral, written, and visual presentation. Inspired by various Mesoamerican glyphs, it is said that the scroll signifies speech, oral tradition, or song. The scroll represents the wind, the tongue, or the word. In Xochitl, the flower, is the synthesis of nature representing joy and beauty. This visual illustration is a gentle reminder of the importance of oral traditions, a new contemporary scroll signifying documentation and the preservation of our ancestors.

Library of Congress Cataloging-in-Publication Data are available at the Library of Congress.

Printed in the United States of America
♾ This paper meets the requirements of ANSI/NISO Z39.48-1992 (Permanence of Paper).

We dedicate this work to all our loved and respected colleagues who have transitioned over into the spirit world since we began this work three years ago.

We especially remember Elisa Facio and Luis D. León for their contributions to the study of Latinx spirituality and religious studies. May their spirits soar in peace, love, and light!

CONTENTS

ACKNOWLEDGMENTS

We first want to thank the contributors to this anthology for their deep sharings of experiences and practices that offer them much healing. We could not have done this work without you. These writings from the heart contribute to our collective efforts to heal, understand, and reclaim ancestral wisdoms.

We thank the anonymous reviewers who highly recommended the book and editor Kristen Buckles and the support staff at the University of Arizona Press for their enthusiasm and assistance throughout the project. We are grateful to the artists who have created the visual art and symbolic language so integral to the process of healing. And we thank those contributors and Trinity University in San Antonio, Texas, and the Department of Chicana and Chicano Studies at California State University, Northridge, who financially supported the inclusion of visual art, and Sybil Venegas for her curatorial insight.

We offer blessings to our elders, our *maestras* and *maestros*, and our mothers, aunties, and grandmothers who have kept these ways alive and have passed them down to us. We are grateful for the inspirations brought about by our experiences, research, creative endeavors, and the spiritual circles we are part of, which also inform these writings. This text is an offering to all our ancestral lineages we carry within us, without whom we would not be here, and to the seven generations to come.

VOICES FROM THE ANCESTORS

Introduction

This is a collection of Chicanx/Latinx[1] wisdom writings, wisdom based on our oral traditions, our research, our intuitions, and our lived experience. Wisdom inspired by, and created from, our personal trajectories on the path to spiritual *conocimiento*.[2] It is spiritual wisdom that has reemerged over the last fifty years as we advance in our efforts to decolonize our lives, our minds, our spirits, our

---

1. We are aware of differing opinions on the spelling of Chicanx/Latinx, all of which have varying degrees of merit; however, the spelling of Chicanx/Latinx challenges us to think beyond the heterosexual gender binary of distinct male and female identities and sexualities. Our use of *x* allows room for the awareness that male/female sensibilities and energies exist in all humans, regardless of their sex or sexuality, and that there are more than two genders. The inherent existence of male/female complementary energies in all people is fundamental to Mesoamerican epistemology. Chicanx might also be spelled Xicanx, with *X* implying an Indigenous consciousness as central to one's identity. However, we have maintained the spellings of these identities as written by each contributor (e.g., Chicana, Latina). We are not suggesting the entire Spanish language be changed to reflect gender neutrality, but rather we are addressing the spectrum of identities, specifically in the Chicanx/Latinx context in the United States.

2. Gloria Anzaldúa (2002, 541–42) wrote that *conocimiento* is "the inner exploration of the meaning and purpose of life . . . a form or spiritual inquiry . . . reached via creative acts—writing, art-making, dancing, healing, teaching, meditation, and spiritual activism."

bodies.[3] Yet this wisdom goes back many generations, to when our ancestors understood their interconnectedness with one another, with all nature, and with the sacred cosmic forces and viewed the human body as a microcosm of the universe (Lopez Austin 1988; Carrasco 1990, 52–54, 65–70). Reclaiming and reconstructing our spirituality based on non-Western epistemologies is central to our process of decolonization, particularly in these most troubling times of incessant Eurocentric, heteronormative patriarchy, misogyny, racial injustice, global capitalist greed, and disastrous global climate change. The contributors to this volume believe that it is time our wisdom be shared with our peers, younger generations, and allies, as we carry medicine in reclaiming and reconstructing the ways of our Indigenous and African ancestors[4] and in rethinking inherited/ imposed religious beliefs or in learning from diverse faith traditions.

3. In the late 1960s, the Chicano movement for civil rights brought forth a consciousness critical of Christianity as the religion of the oppressor, and among many Chicanx activists, an intentional return to Indigenous spirituality was set in motion. The cultural legacy of Christianity, particularly Catholicism, has remained embedded in Latinx cultures, yet many people affected by the Chicano movement have continued to seek out Indigenous spiritual philosophies and practices. Fortunately, Latinx who remain Christian and who pursue theological studies produce a significant body of work reconstructing Christianity through a liberative, feminist, and queer lens. We are fortunate to have some of these theologians as contributors to this volume.

4. As Elisa Facio and Irene Lara eloquently state in their introduction to *Fleshing the Spirit: Spirituality and Activism in Chicana, Latina, and Indigenous Women's Lives*,

> Moreover, as 'Chicanas,' we acknowledge the multiple strands of our Indigenous or mixed-race ancestries, recognizing the historical and political contexts of (neo) colonialism that have led to many Chicanas [and Latinx] becoming detribalized Indigenous women. This means that although many Chicanas [and Latinx] know we have Indigenous [and African] genealogies and experience the transcultural *sobrevivencias* of Indigenous practices, including healing knowledges in our families, some may not have a direct generational link to a specific tribal identity or land base, while others do. Hence, for some Chicanas [and Latinx], to state they are Indigenous is considered redundant, while for others to identify as Xicana or Chicana Indígena is to explicitly claim their indigeneity in the face of racist (neo) colonial powers who benefit from cultural erasure, amnesia or denial. (2014, 15)

Furthermore, as do Facio and Lara, we recognize the ongoing tensions among many Native and African people of North America who challenge Xicanx or AfroLatinx identities as appropriated identities removed from the historical experience of being "Indian" or African American in the United States and the ongoing consequences of that history. Yet, we believe that the distorting and the silencing in the U.S. educational system of

It is important to state that none of the writings in this book are considered protected ceremony meant not to be shared with cultural outsiders. Ceremony is when a community gathers with recognized spiritual elders and, according to long-established, traditional ritual protocol, generates collective spiritual energy through prayer, song, dance, rattle/drum, and other offerings to honor or help transform the need at hand.[5] Ceremonies carry protected knowledge in Indigenous communities; thus, what we share in this book lies more within the realm of healing practices. Many of the essays use the terms "ritual" or "ceremony" to describe their practice, but they do not include protected knowledge. Some of the writers indicate that the rituals they share are to be done within community, which we refer to as communal ritual. Our use of ritual implies less long-established protocol yet are ways "undertaken with intention and belief that grow[s] powerful through repetition and connection" with spirit sources (McCampbell 2002, 33). We have received permission from all the contributors to share these healing practices, as they have received permission from their teachers, or the authors themselves are the creators of these healing ways. Many contributors are now considered elders in our communities.

The wisdom offered here appears in a variety of forms, in reflective essays, poetry, prayers, guidelines for healing practices and communal rituals, and visual art. We learn from one another's reflections on our experiences, through poetic language, through direct guidance, and through imagery. The visual artwork has been chosen for the spiritual and cultural inspiration it offers, and we recommend that each image be mindfully reflected on to receive the embedded medicine. As Laura Pérez (2007, 6) writes in her extensive study on the political spirituality within Chicana art, "The artwork itself [is] altar-like, a site where the disembodied—divine, emotional, or social—[is] acknowledged, invoked, meditated upon, and released as a shared offering."

---

the complete histories of Chicanx/Latinx/AfroLatinx people and Native Americans prevents an understanding of the shared histories of "genocidal constructions" and of the treatment of Indigenous and African people in Mexico, Latin America, and the Caribbean islands that has led to the detribalization of mixed-race Chicanx/Latinx/Afro-Latinx (Rodríguez 2014; Menchaca 2001). As Anzaldúa (1987, 86) advised all of us in *Borderlands / La Frontera*, "Before the Chicano can have unity with Native Americans and other groups, we need to know the history of their struggle and they need to know ours . . . each of us must know our Indian lineage, our afro-*mestisaje*, our history of resistance."

5. See Mehl-Madrona (2003, 116–19) for a discussion on ceremony.

Some of us walk the Red Road, staying close to the path of Indigenous wisdoms and traditions, while others of us integrate Indigenous ways with diverse spiritual traditions (e.g., Buddhism, Santería, Christianity), which can be called *nepantla* spirituality (Medina 2011, 2014) or remain primarily Christian but with a feminist and liberationist lens. We offer our medicine for healing the deep historical and generational trauma resulting from colonization that began more than five centuries ago and the wounds that fester due to the current consequences of neocolonialism, inherited or learned dysfunctional behaviors, and the impact of racialized poverty.[6] As one of our elders, Dr. Concepcion Saucedo Martinez, states, "Health is considered a community responsibility with an understanding that our actions or inactions affect our wellbeing as well as the wellbeing of the entire community" (Carrillo et al. 2017, 177).

Our work here centers on healing the fragmentation of our "bodymindspirit" (Lara 2014, 119), begun through the imposition of Western Christian epistemology, so that we can in turn heal the traumas endured in many of our families and in our communities. However, the healing is not limited to personal/familial/community work but also involves transforming the educational institutions many of us labor in. We realize that spirituality is an essential component of educating the whole person.[7] Among Indigenous Mesoamericans, shaping the face and the heart, in *ixtli in yollotl, cara y corazón*, the distinct character of the person, played a central role in forming educated, responsible, and visionary community members. Spirituality is a major aspect of one's face and heart, as spirituality is a way of life deeply aware of one's relationship to self, to others, and to the sacred source of life and death, the Creator / the Great Mystery, Ometeotl, Olodumare, Hunab Ku, Pachamama, the Sacred Cosmos.[8] How we live within

---

6. According to the National Latin@ Network, one in three Latinas experience domestic violence, and 63 percent of victimized Latinas experience multiple acts of victimization. Furthermore, "Domestic violence in Latina communities is NOT traditional" (National Latin@ Network 2016). According to the 2016 Joint Economic Committee of the U.S. Congress, the poverty rate for Hispanics (23.6 percent) is more than 10 percentage points higher than the rate for non-Hispanics (12.9 percent) and 14 percentage points higher than the rate for non-Hispanic whites (10.1 percent) (Senate Joint Economic Committee 2016).

7. For further exploration of spirituality in secular education, see hooks (2003), Delgado Bernal et al. (2006), Rendón (2009), Ritskes (2011), Facio and Lara (2014), Medina (2006), and Hernández-Ávila (2006).

8. The Great Mystery offers a generic name for the diversity of Indigenous and African languages that name the pure sacred cosmic energy through which all life comes

"all our relations" reflects our face and heart, our character, and directs our choices on the path we choose in life.

The banishment and criminalization of our ancestral ethical and ceremonial practices that ensued with colonization disrupted and silenced Latin American, Caribbean Indigenous, and African knowledge systems that centered our relationship to the sacred cosmic forces, the natural world, the ancestors, the land, and one another as well as the knowledge embedded within ritual practices and ways of acting in the world.[9] Those of our ancestors who were convinced or forced to deny their Indigenous and African lineages became separated from the bodymindspiritnature web of consciousness. The Maya ethic of *In Lak' ech / Somos uno / Tú eres mi otro yo /* We are one was disrupted but did not vanish. This central ethic has returned to hold a primary place in our understanding of interconnectedness and reciprocity, both foundational Indigenous and African values essential for balanced living.[10]

To further decolonize our understanding of how Christianity has maintained such a strong influence over nations and tribes of people in the Western Hemisphere into the present day, it is important to acknowledge the violent history

---

into being. A few examples, in Nahuatl of Mesoamerica, Ometeotl names the divine duality (male and female) present in all creation. Olodumare, in Yoruba of West Africa, names the supreme deity, "the Prime Mover, the Ultimate Source, the First Cause" (De La Torre 2004, 34). In Quiché of the Maya, Hunab Ku names the "Grand Architect of the Universe" (Rodríguez 2014, 176). And in Quechua, Pachamama names the feminine creative power to sustain life on earth. We use the term "the sacred cosmos" to name the sacredness of the universe in which humans are part. There are many definitions for spirituality. A common thread is relationality, or our interconnectedness. See essays in Facio and Lara (2014); see also Pérez (2007) and Delgadillo (2011).

9. Unlike Eastern spiritual knowledge/epistemology that was welcomed in the United States beginning in the 1960s with the practice of yoga, spiritual knowledge from the South and the Caribbean has rarely been acknowledged or validated by the European American culture in the United States, except for a short period of time by practitioners of "metaphysical religions" in the later part of the nineteenth century who sought healing from *curanderos/as* in the Southwest (see Hendrickson 2014). A more recent interest in Mesoamerican knowledge has been made popular through the work of Don Miguel Ruiz, in his several publications on Toltec wisdom. For example, see *The Four Agreements* (Ruiz 1997).

10. See Malidoma Patrice Somé (1993) on African values expressed through ritual and Rodríguez (2014) for these Maya concepts. Chicano activists and artists who, beginning in the 1960s, were returning to Indigenous knowledge emphasized this Maya ethic, particularly Luis Valdez in his work with Teatro Campesino; see Valdez (1994).

of the church as an institution whose ideological hold on its adherents has been established through a long history of violence, genocide, and epistemicide. We identify its birth as an institution when in 312 CE, Constantine defeated his rival at the Battle of Milvian Bridge, on the Tiber in Rome, for rule of the Roman Empire.

While receiving a visitation in a dream from the Christian god, Constantine was instructed to carry the Christian cross "before him as divine protection." Constantine ordered his armies to replace "the traditional pagan standards with ones displaying a cross, topped with a wreath and the first two letters of Christ's name" (Brownworth 2009, 14). With control of the Roman Empire at stake, "by wielding the cross and sword, Constantine had done more than defeat a rival—he had fused the church and the state together" (14). Shortly after his triumph in 313 CE, Constantine issued an edict of toleration legalizing Christianity throughout the empire. This calculated shift in favoring the Christian god to gain the political support of a growing Christian community and an influential ecclesiastical class instigated the first wars of an imperial church against non-Christians and their practices. "Pagan sacrifices were banned, sacred prostitution and ritual orgies were outlawed, and temple treasuries were confiscated to build churches" (17). In the following decades, high-ranking church officials gathered together to suppress divergent theological views among the existing ecclesiastical communities and determined "what it meant to be a Christian, and defined what the true (orthodoxy) and universal (catholic) church believed" (19). And in the following century, edicts were issued ordering the persecution, banishment, destruction, and defacement of non-Christians, or pagans, their temples, healing centers, libraries, and ritual practices. Marble and stones were taken from temple complexes to build Christian churches over the same sites formerly dedicated to the deities of the pagan social order (Rassias 2000). Banished traditions included the consultation of the Delphic Oracle, the most prestigious and authoritative oracle throughout the Mediterranean delivered exclusively by womxn.[11]

The ancient commercial port city of Alexandria, Egypt, founded in 331 BCE, where the Nile flows out to the Mediterranean Sea, was a target of the early church fathers. Their "toxic combination of anti-pagan imperial legislation and aggressive actions against pagans destabilized the city" (Watts 2017, 52). The

---

11. We are choosing the spelling *womxn* to encompass a broader and more fluid range of gender identity.

materials gathered in Alexandria's sacred spaces, libraries, and centers of learning, by which the population flourished, contained knowledges from ancient Mesopotamia, Babylon, and Syria, from Persia, India, Greece, and from the Egyptian culture that had flourished along the Nile, and further south, for centuries. The intellectual and spiritual belief systems, often one and the same, of Alexandria's inhabitants were thus varied and rich in distinct cultural traditions and histories, positioning this great cosmopolitan city as a major center of learning. Philosophers, temple priests and priestesses, officiators of ritual practices in the home, and keepers of wisdom traditions passed down for generations posed a threat to the messianic message of salvation only through Jesus Christ preached by proselytizing Christians throughout the city. Philosophers, in particular, could with ease and confidence question the claims of the young belief system, itself debated in the variant views of the diverse Christian communities and communes living throughout the region (Raju 2012). For the city's Christian elite, a war against the pagan world meant the destruction of houses of wisdom and learning and the suppression of divergent views on questions the church wished to monopolize, questions concerning the immortality of the soul or life after death, "correct" sexual behavior and expressions of desire, and gender roles in private and public arenas (Raju 2012; Warner 2013). Accordingly, in 392 CE, a riot by Christian mobs resulted in the looting and destruction of the Serapeum, Alexandria's most sacred temple and library and the city's "most important center of scholarship" (Watts 2017, 13). A lasting impression of early Christian state-sanctioned violence against "paganism" and womxn in particular is the murder of a most learned womxn: the philosopher and teacher Hypatia of Alexandria, daughter of the mathematician Theon. Widely respected by her peers and male city officials who sought her counsel, she was "Alexandria's leading thinker for nearly thirty-five years" (2). In the spring of 415 CE, the Bishop of Alexandria, who would come to be canonized as Saint Cyril by the church,[12] negotiating for power within the city, allowed for the provocation of a Christian mob to accuse Hypatia of witchcraft,[13] violently attacking and murdering her in public. "They shredded her clothes and her body with pottery fragments, tore out her eyes, dragged her corpse through the streets of

12. Many of the church's early saints committed horrendous acts of violence against people who posed a threat to the church (Warner 2013; Raju 2012).

13. Cyril and his loyalists believed it was Hypatia's counsel to Governor Orestes that prevented him from coming to terms with Cyril and his political ambitions in the city (Watts 2017).

Alexandria, and then burned her remains" (Watts 2017, 3). The public, horrific murder of Hypatia, who sought to intervene through her teaching and influence for the well-being of Alexandria by embracing "the idea that a philosopher needed to play a public role in the life of her city," was felt throughout the empire (61). Her murder, and the systematic murder of many other pagans, would serve as a dire warning to womxn and men of all sexual orientations and practitioners of non-Christian faiths now outlawed throughout the Roman Empire (Raju 2012; Watts 2017; Rassias 2000).

In the following millennium, the Holy Roman Catholic Church instigated armies to fight the "holy" Crusades, beginning in the eleventh century and lasting through the fifteenth, and when convenient, mobilized mobs to wage local battles against heretic Christian sects throughout Europe, enriching its coffers and intellectual holdings by sacking and looting towns, cities, and villages in the process (Raju 2012). The birth of Islam in 610 CE and its rapid consolidation of commercial trade routes, its intellectual, mathematical, scientific, and medicinal wealth, and its tolerance for difference in spiritual belief systems, stands in sharp contrast to the feudal European Christian world. The political and intellectual authority and commercial success of Muslim caliphates flourished throughout the Islamic world, in Egypt, Persia, and India, and in the great cities of Al-Andalus, Timbuktu, and Baghdad. By the fifteenth century, the Christian monarchs King Ferdinand II of Aragon and Queen Isabella of Castile joined their kingdoms with the church to fight a series of wars against the caliphate of Al-Andalus on the Iberian Peninsula. The results of these "holy wars" were the destruction of Muslim and Jewish temples of worship, the burning of libraries, the closure of public bathhouses central to the hygiene of the population, forced conversions, exile, and torture or execution under the infamous Inquisition. Nine days after Queen Isabella and King Ferdinand completed the holy wars "over Muslim political authority in the Iberian Peninsula," they granted Christopher Columbus "the royal authorization and resources for his first voyage overseas" (Grosfoguel 2013, 79). In the fall of 1492, when Columbus arrived in the Caribbean, he and his conquistadors embodied, as agents of the church and state, a one-thousand-year-old tradition of waging war and genocidal and epistemic violence against non-Christians as a means of instituting and maintaining religious, political, economic, and ideological domination.[14] By 1496, the

---

14. For further reading on the relationship between religion, conquest, and race, see Maldonado-Torres (2014).

Taino populations of the Caribbean had been drastically reduced by enslavement, starvation, viruses, and murder, producing "the stunning reduction in their numbers [as] the most shocking immediate repercussion of European contact" (Deagan and Cruxent 2002, 24). By 1518, approximately 90 percent of the Taino had been exterminated, issuing in the importation of enslaved Africans to replace their labor. At minimum, 750,000 enslaved Africans would be brought into the Latin American colonies of New Spain during the first three centuries of Spanish control of this region (Palmer, n.d.).

In this context, the advanced mathematics, astronomical observations, agricultural genius, and advanced herbal medicine and surgical practices of Indigenous civilizations were dismissed and marked for destruction. For example, the cultural imperatives that guided the planning and building of Inca, Toltec, Maya, Nahua, and Zapotec (among many others) architecture, as well as the many ritual celebrations inspired by the celestial bodies and agricultural cycles that had been passed on from generation to generation, were eradicated. Initially, this destruction destroyed the complex sedentary societies of the Caribbean (Deagan and Cruxent 2002, 24). Profound understandings of the human body holding spiritual energies correlating to the spiritual energies in the universe were deemed irrelevant. The knowledge and ways of our ancestors were deemed either ignorant or demonic (Rodríguez 2014). Whether Indigenous people were even human was put up for legal debate in 1537 (Menchaca 2001). The honoring of female cosmic energies as fundamental to sustaining life came to be supplanted by the male, omnipotent, personified Christian god. The closure of temples and the destruction of sacred sites throughout Christian Europe, prior to 1492, was replicated in the "New World" as colonizers destroyed or buried sculptural and painted representations and sacred sites of female sacred cosmic forces, such as Coatlicue, the Mother Goddess and her daughter, Coyolxauhqui at Tenochtitlan, the Goddess at Teotihuacan (Pasztory 1997, 85–94), Ixchel at Cozumel, and womxn honored at Xochitécatl in Tlaxcala (Puche 2001). Indigenous womxn, considered subhuman, were coerced into unwanted sexual relations and violently raped. Womxn who refused to comply were subjected to violent beatings or put to death by dogs (Kellogg 2005), "the colonizer's weapon of mass destruction," by which *joyas*, or third-gender males, were also murdered en masse (Miranda 2010, 258). In the perversity of their worldview, colonizers forced the Christian baptism of Indigenous womxn before demanding sexual favors from them (Townsend 2006). "The frequency of sexual violence and the willingness of military leaders such as Cortes and Pizarro to distribute

Indigenous women among their close lieutenants suggest that conquerors indeed used 'the phallus as an extension of the sword'" (Kellogg 2005, 60).

Bartolomé de las Casas (2011, 11–12) documented how the steel weapons and armor of the conquistadors were used to commit mass murder in villages, towns, and cities of Indigenous peoples, all of whom were victims of the Christian conquistadors' genocidal mania:

> They entered the villages and spared neither children nor old people, neither pregnant women, nor those with nursing infants. They made bets to see who could, with a single sword stroke, slice an Indian in half, spill his entrails, or cut off his head. They ran swords through a mother and child at once, or flung infants into rivers, laughing and making fun. They pulled babies from their mothers' breasts and swung them by the feet to smash their heads on rocks. They split open women's bellies and hacked them apart as though butchering lambs.

By the close of the sixteenth century, the Indigenous population in central Mexico alone decreased from twenty-five million to one million due to genocide, lack of immunity to European viruses, and slavery (Carrasco 1990).

Even following their forced or willful conversions to Christianity, both in the Americas and in Europe, womxn, although acknowledged as capable of finding salvation within the church and equal to men in this regard, were still restricted to positions of servant, housewife, and mother and were forced to obey and be subject to men in matters of everyday life, as the people must obey and be subject to the church and its male authorities. Only independently wealthy womxn or those dedicating their lives to Christ could find some modicum of relief from the oppressive conditions of having to live under the rule of men in practical matters (Warner 2013). Sor Juana Inés de la Cruz, in sixteenth-century Mexico, chose religious life to escape the control of male authority in matrimony, yet the church patriarchs ultimately silenced her because she "challenged both secular and religious worldviews that were used to exclude and undermine the full humanity of women and non-Spaniards of her day" (Yugar 2014, 99). Misogynistic and homophobic violence culminated in the genocide of thousands of womxn and third genders deemed outside of Catholicism. "Jews, Christian non-conformists, woman-centered folks spiritualists known as witches and 'sodomites'" were tortured and put to death by the Inquisition from the fourteenth to the nineteenth centuries throughout Europe and in the "New World" (Williams 1986, 132).

According to Walter Williams (1986, 132), homoeroticism, accepted and considered quite normal within the Roman Empire prior to the adoption of Christianity, came to be seen as heretical and mortally sinful "due largely to Church dogma, and to political opportunism." Furthermore, "Spain appeared to be at the forefront of this persecution . . . where the Inquisition reached sadistic extremes in its suppression of sexual diversity" (132). Europe's declining population due to the bubonic plague and Spain's own depleted population due to its centuries-long war against Muslims gave church officials a reason to condemn sexual acts not serving the interest of biological reproduction, or "any non-reproductive sexual act (usually a same-sex act but sometimes anal sex between a male and a female)" (132). The condemned often had their properties and wealth seized by the church. By the time of the conquest of the Americas, sodomy and homoerotic practices were considered the "abominable sin," with conquistadors chronicling and fatally punishing those persons among the native populations practicing same-sex relations (137). According to Deborah Miranda (2010, 260), in Spanish-occupied lands "gendercide" accurately describes the violence that took place in the Americas toward third-gender people, in which colonizers destroyed their significant roles in spiritual leadership while planting homophobia (and female subordination) in the minds and values of native peoples. Violence toward the female gender, and gender nonconforming people, extends itself well into the twenty-first century, most notably today in the United States through the attacks of the Republican Christian Right against womxn's reproductive rights, our health care, and LGTBQ individuals.

This collection of writings is our effort to address the ancestral wounds perpetrated by these histories of violence on our psyches, bodies, and spirits. It is our effort to share and document how the spirituality of those presumably "conquered" has survived, and it is a step toward restoring the respect and honor that third-gender and transgender members of our communities held before colonization. It is our effort to heal historical trauma affecting our lives today. Our work also seeks to honor the fluidity of gender and the complementary feminine and masculine energies in all of us that correlate with the fluidity and duality of the sacred cosmos, which are core teachings of Indigenous and African epistemologies.[15] We were inspired by the publication of *Fleshing the Spirit: Spirituality and Activism in Chicana, Latina, and Indigenous Women's Lives*, edited by Elisa Facio

---

15. For an excellent discussion on these Mesoamerican and African Indigenous concepts, see Marcos (2009) and Oyewumi (1997).

and Irene Lara (2014), both of whom are among the contributors to this volume.[16] The collection of essays and poetry in *Fleshing the Spirit* provides readers with the invitation to enter into the personal spiritual consciousness of Chicanx/Latinx/Indigenx womxn and how they use their consciousness for self-healing and for the empowerment of those they teach, raise up, and challenge. *Fleshing the Spirit* planted the seed for us to invite Xicanx/Latinx/AfroLatinx womxn to share more specifically their spiritual reflections, healing practices, and insights that would further our collective learning as we return to holistic epistemologies based on interdependency, reciprocity, balance, fluidity, cyclical movement, the natural environment, and respect for the ancestors. The response to our call was exceptional and affirmed our vision to document and share just a small portion of the richness that brown and black racially mixed womxn have cultivated to heal personal and communal wounds. As racially mixed womxn, we emerge from the borderlands, from the spaces between cultures, racialized identities, languages, and epistemologies.[17] We are shaped by Western thought and culture and thus suffer from the wounds of fragmentation, while we also benefit from institutions of Western "higher education." Many of the contributors hold doctorates in the humanities and social sciences and are published scholars. Others are professional artists, cultural workers, teachers, and organic intellectuals. We invited a few select male allies specifically because they acknowledge their feminine spiritual energies and actively seek healing from colonization. We do not understand ourselves within the Western paradigm of individuals fighting for our private spaces in which to survive, nor are we dependent solely on pharmaceuticals for healing. We strive to live according to communal values in our own families and in our communities and workplaces. We strive to reclaim our plant medicines and our relationship to the land we inhabit, to honor our bodies and sexual orientations, to conduct ritual and to participate in protected ceremony, and to create art, all ways to ensure healing. Our literary and visual artists and scholars have guided us in reconfiguring and reclaiming icons of female deities that reflect the centrality of sacred female energies at work in the universe and in our own self-understanding (Anzaldúa 1999; Elizondo 1980; Castillo 1996, 2014; Gaspar de Alba and López 2011; Gonzales 2012). Tonantzin-

---

16. Elisa Facio passed into the spirit world August 30, 2018, and we are eternally grateful for her anima and scholarship, which enriched so many.

17. Our work has been highly influenced by the borderlands theorizing of Gloria Anzaldúa. For a select list of her publications, see the references.

Guadalupe, Coatlicue, Coyolxauhqui, Tlazolteotl, Pachamama, Yemayá, and Oschún, among others, play central roles in the representation of the divine at work in our lives. We have learned to see these icons through decolonized eyes, as reflected in much of Chicanx/Latinx art. (See plates 3 and 10 for two examples of our sacred icons reimagined.)

Important to us and to our contributors is that we rely on higher and deeper sacred energies and our ancestors, "known and unknown," to guide us through our lives and that we enact our rituals and create art in order to access these sacred energies. As Marta López-Garza writes in her contribution on house blessings, we "accept the existence of the divine, that we live among spirits, and that those who have passed on remain with us in some form."[18] This spiritual work serves as a testament to our willful refusal to accept the negative energy of the times that we live in and the ongoing marginalization of all peoples of color. Ritual, ceremony, and art carry power: the power to create, the power to transform. As medical doctor Lewis Mehl-Madrona (2003, 7) writes in *Coyote Healing: Miracles in Native Medicine,* a principle in the work of traditional healers is:

> The healing power of spirit and the spiritual dimension in our lives, including the role of ritual and ceremony in catalyzing change, in connecting us to nonphysical energies, in giving us a view of ourselves as capable of more than we had previously thought, and by enfolding us in the comfort of the Divine.

In our collective willingness to share, we acknowledge the importance these spiritual expressions and practices play in pointing the way to healing possibilities. Contextualized within our everyday lives, this collection of writings also reveals how we are keeping and remaking culture. Culture changes, shifts, and transforms over time. What we offer here is cultural knowledge—our cultural capital that has assisted us in overcoming traumas, in celebrating significant transitions in our lives, and in connecting with our ancestors and the natural world. A well-known *dicho* in Latinx cultures is "la cultura cura," the imperative that culture heals.

For years now, womxn scholars, in their attempts to be inclusive, have misidentified or misrepresented or have not managed to properly capture the spiritual experience of Xicanx/Latinx womxn. And AfroLatinx womxn have mostly

---

18. See López-Garza in part 3, "Creating Sacred Space."

been left out of the narrative. We offer this collection as a first of its kind and add it to the body of texts written by Xicanx/Latinx scholars and practitioners discussing spirituality.[19] In our return to non-Western spiritual epistemologies, some of us are fortunate to be able to talk with our elders who know their original ways and can teach us what they can. Some of us turn to maestras from Latin America and the Caribbean who travel here to teach us, or we travel to the motherlands to learn from maestras there. We receive the stories, the medicine, the danza that they carry; we participate in ceremony, in communal ritual; we share oral tradition; we research, read, paint, dance, drum, and sing. We learn about the knowledge that our bodies carry, the medicine of the plants that help us heal. We learn about the significance of the elements—air, earth, fire, water—and how essential it is to integrate them into our lives, and we realize their natural presence in our bodies. We learn that spirituality is a way of life, a tool, and ultimately "oppressed people's only weapon" (Anzaldúa 2000, 98).

Spirituality includes the profound understanding that we are not alone, "that we are spiritual beings in physical bodies," cocreators of this world, connected to one another and to the Source of all. Our Mesoamerican and Caribbean Indigenous beliefs teach us that death transforms us so that we can (from the spirit world) continue to renew the living. We pray in a different way now. Some of us retain the prayers of our childhood, taught to us by our loving elders, prayers that honor God but no longer hold "him" to the rigid image of a white man in the heavens. Some of us alter the prayers so that the divine is female, and heaven is our cocreation here and now on this earth. Our prayers have changed as we have learned to honor the sacred directions, the elements, Grandmother Moon, Madre Tierra, the orishas, Pachamama, and our ancestors. While this volume holds more than one hundred contributions from eighty-five contributors, it represents only a small fraction of the varied spiritual traditions practiced by Chicanx/AfroLatinx/Latinx in the United States. Indeed, a work representing the many traditions would require a much longer volume beyond the scope of this work. We recognize that our contributions are minimal on the experience of Indigenous and African peoples in the Caribbean. We invite other scholars to keep pushing past barriers, both

19. Select texts include Anzaldúa (1999, 2015), Isasi-Díaz and Tarango (1988), Castillo (1996, 2014), Medina (2004), Pérez (2007), Delgadillo (2011), Gonzales (2012b), and Facio and Lara (2014).

institutional and personal/social, that keep us from one another and prevent us from sharing our traditional knowledges.

The prayers, poems, healing practices, *consejos*, and critical spiritual reflections in this book come from deep places. Some have been passed down in families, most often through the womxn, from elder female members, keepers of knowledge. Some have emerged from the intuitions of the contributors themselves or, as our respected elder Inés Hernández-Ávila states in her morning prayer, from "the awareness that has become me." We begin this collection with Inés's "Sunrise Prayer," that through heartfelt imagery we receive teachings on how to awaken in gratitude and align our body, mind, will, and spirit to the healing elements of the universe and the healing we receive as we listen to our hearts. Gracias, Inés, for providing us with this opening blessing! We are affirmed in our purpose here by your words:

> For my remembering,
> powerful
> beautiful memory
> brings us home to ourselves
> gives us strength, courage, *firmeza*
> Memory heals
>> *Memory of ourselves as original peoples of this hemisphere*

Poeta Gloria Alvarez also blesses the opening of our work, with her poem "... Keeping It Real ..." And real is exactly what our contributors offer. Strength, wisdom, power, purpose, and joy are transmitted through Alvarez's passionate *palabra*. Gracias, Gloria, for your anima! The "Prayer to the Orishas," by Martha R. Gonzales, praises the presence of the orishas as reflections of the divine natural forces within the human experience. These words of gratitude and humility move us to receive the blessings of the Great Orishas at work in the world.

What follows is an overview of the topics addressed in this book. Morning prayers and prayers to the sacred directions comprise two of the most important traditions passed down to our peoples. Morning prayer is when we greet the life force, as learned from the winged ones, the birds, who are the first to greet the new dawn. Prayers to our ancestors and to the sacred directions include teachings on ethical ways of living, on maintaining relationships of reciprocity with one another and our environment, and on mindfulness of the life cycle. Practices for creating sacred spaces in our homes are rooted in traditional ways of welcoming and honoring the sacred in our intimate spaces. Reclaiming our power to bless our newborns and young children is vital to the process of decolonization and to ensuring and sanctifying their place in our families and in this world. Creating art in a variety of forms as a spiritual practice affirms what artist Amalia Mesa-Bains (1993) stated many years ago: "Art is about healing, making art, viewing art, heals."[20] Assisting our dying and communing with our deceased occur in many ways, and here our contributors share their intimate experiences with *la muerte* and the spirit world. Dreaming offers us another opportunity to connect with the "life of spirit, moving, traveling, visiting, healing, being with loved ones."[21] Private and communal practices for holistic health care, either through self-*limpias, el temazkal,* or protective objects, are essential for our balanced living as we face the many challenges in our lives. The fragmentation resulting from the disruption of traditional rites of passage is being healed through the re-creation or creation of communal rituals that reconnect ourselves, our young ones, and our elders to our sacred cycles in life. The stages of our life cycle and the honoring of our great losses require ritual that affirms and/or heals where we find ourselves on our journey. Meditation, also fundamental to balanced living, can be a simple breathing and/or visualization practice or a more involved practice of creating a Medicine Wheel on which to meditate.

Medicinal foods for ourselves and for the spirit world remind us of the reciprocal relationship between our consumption and our bodymindspirit. Many *comadres* in this publication offer their consejos and experience in the section "Mother-Child Bonding." Moon ceremonies have returned to reestablish our relationship and rejoin our cycles with Abuela Luna, Grandmother Moon. Our sexualities are anointed, and our sexual traumas must be healed. Prayers and songs to be shared hold space here as does our relationship to land and plants. Activism and teaching are both viewed as spiritual practices, and reflective essays offer examples of how they can be integrated. Talking circles show us how listening and holding space for one another serve as traditional ways to resolve conflicts, find solutions, and support one another on our paths. And we close this collection with evening prayers to honor all that has come before and all that will come!

---

20. Interview in film *La Ofrenda: The Days of the Dead* (Muñoz and Portillo 1989).
21. Hernández-Ávila in "Sunrise Prayer," part 1.

We intend this text to be used with care, respect, and thoughtfulness in the classroom, in community settings, with friends, or privately by oneself. We ask that non-Indigenous-identifying people honor the cultures, knowledges, and peoples represented here, and if the healing practices are utilized, that they be done so with utmost respect and not for commercial purposes. We ask that this text serve an enlightened purpose as we move forward together.

Lara Medina and Martha R. Gonzales
To All Our Relations
Ometeotl
Ashé!

1

MORNING PRAYERS

Sunrise Prayer

INÉS HERNÁNDEZ-ÁVILA

"cantemos con alegría que al cielo le está gustando,
a la santísima cruz las gracias le estamos dando"[1]

Buenos días, Señor y Señora del Universo
Gracias, Siempre Gracias

In the mornings we welcome the new day, the sun as it rises to take its place in
the sky.
The colors of life lift up the solitude of night that we share with our mother
Moon.
We hear singing throughout the expanse of the sacred embrace that holds us.

La canción del tzintzontle nos llama
Sometimes mockingbird serenades us through the night *con gusto,* heralding
our dreams.
We sing back from every cell and fiber of our being.

We wake from dreamtime, from our nightlife of spirit, moving, traveling,
visiting, healing, being with loved ones. We give thanks for these visits, to the
dreams that guide us and fill us with joy. We give thanks to the dreams that help
us foresee, to the dreams that send messages, sometimes puzzles, to intrigue us.

For the dreams that are troubling we ask for help, we place these dreams in
the hands of the Supreme Being, we offer some moments to contemplate the
meaning of what we have been shown. We allow our *conciencias* guided by our

---

1. *Alabanza Conchera.*

hearts to wonder. *Ofrecemos incienso para ayudarnos contemplar.* Sage, cedar, copal, angelica.

El sol nace cada mañana
llega del regazo de la Madre y Padre Tierra
los dos son llenos de amor para nosotrxs

May each new day
be a day of gratitude, compassion,
forgiveness, resurgence
We rise as the sun rises we rise
to give light
to be light
We must begin with ourselves

I. *El Oriente Mi Cuerpo*
Enséñame, cuerpo mío, mi cuerpo sagrado
como cuidarte mejor
como vibrar con la vida
Como llenarme de la energía del sol,
la tierra, la luna,
toda la naturaleza
Show me how to cleanse
the home of my spirit
My spirit home
My body
I make teas of white sage to purify
Manzanilla to help me sleep
I bring in to the house where my spirit home lives
Rosemary, lavender, *laurel*
flowers whose aromas send up my prayers

"*recibe estas flores con gusto y anhelo*
que son escalones que llevan al cielo"[2]

---

2. *Alabanza Conchera.*

Pido bendiciones para cada uno de mis órganos

Cada músculo

Hueso

Articulación

Célula

Cada gota de mi sangre

Bathing we give thanks to the precious water

for the cleansing we receive

Mi cuerpo adorado

Many years ago, when I was young

I placed you sometimes

where you were degraded,

violated unspeakably

Places not tender

not loving

not full of *cariño*

Por eso I ask your forgiveness always

Spirit of mine heal your home my body

Guardian spirits heal me

Help me to find joy

To find laughter

To know love

II. *El Norte Mi Conciencia*

"*Gracias a la vida,*" canta Violeta[3]

Gracias for the awareness that has become me

For the knowingness life has gifted me

For the lessons

tropiezos

milagros

de la vida

For my remembering

powerful

beautiful memory

brings us home to ourselves

---

3. "Gracias a la vida," song by Violeta Parra.

gives us strength, courage, *firmeza*
Memory heals
    Memory of ourselves as original peoples of this hemisphere
Memory imposed can kill us
Memory enforced can drain us of our life force
  assaults engraved
    terrifying moments implanted
      encoded
    into our beings over the centuries
  the generations
    within communities
      families
        nations
How to tell the true memory from the lie
Our *conciencias* guides us
We must nurture and grow our *conciencias*
Like we would our loving plants, our medicine plants
we recognize for their power, generosity, wisdom, teachings
Gracias to all the pensadorxs de corazón who have taught me
My *conciencia* my medicine
My *conciencia* guided by my heart healer of my spirit wisdom

                      III. *El Sur Mi Voluntad*
                      The South My Will
                      I will to will thy will
                      The Runes say this
                  It is beautiful to know other traditions
                    to respectfully learn from them
                    and then the *Conchero* prayer
                  adapted to reflect our ancient past
                    "*Santo Diós Santa Diosa*
                  Líbranos Señor y Señora de todo mal
                    Santo Diós Santa Diosa
              Hágase Señor y Señora su Santísima Voluntad"
      I do not fear the will of the Supreme Being Mother-and-Father
      I unite my will to the will of the Great Spirit of the Universe
                      I am a part of this Great Spirit

We are part of this Great Spirit
the collective of us all
all of life
I will do my part
to nurture peace kindness love
We will do our part
Siempre
Siempre

IV. *El Poniente Mi Espíritu*
The West My Spirit
I must remember
   We must remember
      Why we chose to come
         To this earth
           In this life
         To take a body
      Why we chose our parents
     What we came to do
We must remember
   I must remember
      I am SpiritLight
         LuzEspíritu
My Spirit is a Wise One
   Our Spirits are Wise Ones
      We must remember
         I must remember
      It is about honoring
   Cherishing
Nurturing
   Calling on my spirit
      Calling on our spirits
         To help me
           to help us
              remember
     What we already knew before we arrived

Once remembering, once knowing, then protecting
What belongs to me, what belongs to us

We did not come from nothing
We came from something
We came from Spirit
We Are Spirit
And we will continue.

V. *El Centro Mi Corazón*
The Center My Heart
Ayy corazón de mi corazón
You are the Altar of My Being
You bring me together
You make me whole
You speak to me
Always
I listen
I listen
Listen to your heart
Listen to our hearts
Our hearts will lead the way
Our hearts will cleanse and bless
Our Hearts will find the Words that Heal
Our Hearts tell the Stories of our Precious Selves
Stories We Must Remember
We Must Remember.
For the generations
We Must Sing.

*"cantemos con alegría que al cielo le está gustando,
a la santísima cruz las gracias le estamos dando
las gracias le estamos dando."*[4]

4. *Alabanza Conchera.*

. . . Keeping It Real . . .

GLORIA ENEDINA ALVAREZ

. . . That's why we need to reach into the earth with our words coursing through our hands . . . so that they can return once more, new but old, with the strength, the knowledge, the wisdom that is witness, purpose within action, within love, colors the vibrations, the music of time . . . face up . . . *cara, corazón y manos* . . . that's what the antiguas would say, face, heart, and hands!!!

Prayer to the Orishas

MARTHA R. GONZALES

Now I bring you to the Lady and her true power, the sea.
— MIGENE GONZÁLEZ-WIPPLER

Awakened by Dawn
and the peaceful sounds
of the Sea's consistent movement . . .

¡Maferefun[1] *Obatala!* Thank you for my breath today, for the dream,
may your many blessings collectively move humanity toward a more loving,
humble and peaceful dream in this world; may I live this day and every day
with an inspired heart.

¡Maferefun Yemaya!
Great Mother of All Life,
Keeper of Intelligence,
Guardian of Mothers to Be,
I come before you, as I am,
to swim in and receive the blessing
of your soft salt waters,
to bask in the great peace
of your embrace Mother.

---

1. An expression of thanksgiving and praise.

On your altar I offer sweet watermelon,
melao de caña,
and seven silver coins
in gratitude for life, for love, for all of it.
That I be worthy of and not betray
the gifts which you have bestowed upon me.

¡Maferefun Olokún!
Firmament of the Oceans,
Great Orisha of the Abyss,
bless me with stability
and accept in exchange
these offerings of
flowers, candles, sea water,
these writings
and the intentions with which I carry
myself in the world.

2

HONORING THE SACRED DIRECTIONS

INTRODUCTION

Offering up prayers to the sacred cardinal directions is an old way of praying shared across cultures and time. The practice of honoring these sacred directions was disrupted in the Americas when agents of the church and state sought to do away with all Indigenous ritual observances interpreted as being directed toward multiple gods, for which there was no place in the monotheistic tradition of the colonizers. This simplistic interpretation led to the destruction of scientific knowledges that had guided the lives of Indigenous peoples of this hemisphere for hundreds, if not thousands, of years. The ritual practice of honoring the sacred directions acknowledges the forces that constitute the world we inhabit and ourselves as integral energetic units in a binding reciprocal relationship with the cosmos. In honoring the sacred directions, we honor the four quadrants of the earth from where distinct people hail, with each being equal and integral to the existence of the next, and we honor the upper realm, the sky, and the lower realm, the earth, and the center point, where the directions converge and balance is achieved. Each of the cardinal directions offers us a lesson, as well, and correlates to the full life cycle: new beginnings and infancy in the east, earth-centered knowledge and childhood in the south, integration and application of this knowledge and adulthood in the west, peaceful and grateful completion in elderhood in the north.

Each of the directions also correlates to specific elements that together constitute the fabric of our very being: fire, water, air, earth. These elements make all life possible on our planet. Each of the elements carries energies that are also within us. We must develop relationships with the elements and integrate them into how we live—to embrace the transformation of fire, the stability of earth, the renewal of water, the sustenance of air. But we must also remain flexible enough and strong enough to work through their opposite energies: destruction, eruption, inundation, and deprivation, respectively.

Honoring the directions and the elements is a form of prayer containing a map of that which constitutes our human condition and the powers of the natural world, which humanity is bound to and ultimately powerless against; it is a reminder of our fragile and ephemeral human existence. In honoring the directions and the elements, we acknowledge ourselves in time and place—our histories, our ancestral lineage, our coming together as a people or as a community; these teachings for right living have held communities together for generations.

In "As the Ceremony Begins . . . ," Sara H. Salazar, in beautiful verse, shares that in order to commence a ceremonial healing, one invokes the directions "for protection and guidance, always beginning in the east and following their hearts to the left." Depending on the tradition, or the prayer, four to seven directions (north, south, east, west, sky, earth, and center) are honored and called on to assist in grounding ourselves, our intentions, in prayer and for the medicine this practice can provide.

While there are similarities between the prayers offered here, note the differences.[1] Lara Medina offers a teaching from Calmecac, in Los Angeles, speaking to the way traditions are passed down in Chicanx community circles that emphasize teachings for the well-being of community life. These teachings offer directions for a *right* of way of living, or ethical action, in the world, of walking with good character.

Martha R. Gonzales and Lara Medina

---

1. Corresponding elements to the directions may differ depending on the Indigenous culture.

As the Ceremony Begins . . .

SARA H. SALAZAR

As the ceremony begins, the healer and the wounded warrior womxn
call in the seven directions for protection and guidance,
always beginning in the East and following their hearts to the left,
They invoke the energies of the East,
where the spark of the rising sun welcomes new beginnings;
West, the place of great expanse, the setting sun, and letting go;
North, where fire collides with ice and our compass surely points;
South, the land of our ancestors that is continually warmed by the sun;
Above, the home of the sun, moon, and stars which map our destinies;
Below, the resting place of our ancestors and motherland for all;
Center, the space of reflection and remembrance of the divine within.

Honoring the Sacred Directions

LARA MEDINA

I first learned to honor the sacred directions in 1990 from Calmecac, a group of Chicanx/Latinx mental health professionals, teachers, and social workers in Los Angeles that, beginning in the 1970s, taught our communities Indigenous values and communal rituals to honor our youth. Veteran members included Becky Bejar, Ana Luisa Espinosa, Norma Pendragon, Melinda Garcia, Linda Villanueva, and Jerry Tello.

I was taught that each direction holds the energies of a sacred element and also correlates to a stage in the life cycle. In the Nahua tradition, we begin by facing the east, then turn to our left (as our heart is on our left) to face the west, then turn a three-quarter circle to face the north, then a half circle to face the south. Return to the center and raise arms or gaze up to the sky, and then kneel down to touch the earth. The following prayers may be said to honor each direction.

We face the East and give thanks for the sunrise, for new beginnings, for new life. We are grateful for the gift of Fire that lights and heats our universe, for the Fire in our hearts that stirs our passions, our creativity, our *tonalli*, or divine Fire within, for our artists and for our warriors of all genders who fight for justice.

We face the West and give thanks for Water, for the nourishment and cleansing that Water offers, for our womxn, for adulthood, when we integrate the lessons we have learned from our ancestors and make them our own, when we refine our character, our *cara y corazón*.

We face the North and give thanks for Wind that reminds us to pay attention to our environment, to all the elements, to the ancestors and all our relations. We pray for our elders, for the completion of the life cycle, for the fulfillment of our intentions, and for those who have passed over into Spirit.

We face the South and give thanks for Mother Earth, Madre Tierra, for the stability and strength that she offers. And for our children, for the stage in life when lessons of justice and compassion are learned, when the ethical teachings of our ancestors are imparted to form our face and heart, cara y corazón.

We return to the center, where wholeness and balance are achieved. We look up into the vastness of our existence and we affirm our place within the sacred cosmos; we kneel with humility and touch the earth. Help us to be mindful of our interconnectedness to all that is, in Tloque Nahuaque, knowing when to accept, when to challenge, when to let go, and always to walk in balance.

To All Our Relations, Ometeotl

3

CREATING SACRED SPACE

INTRODUCTION

Creating sacred space is fundamental to nourishing our holistic sense of self and for reminding us who we are.[1] Altars, or shrines, feed our spirit and psyche as they make visible our intent of bridging the physical and the spiritual realms and of sustaining the relationship between the two. The practice of altar and shrine making has roots among our ancient Indigenous ancestors of Mesoamerica, Latin America, the Caribbean, and Africa, as well as among the Indigenous cultures of Europe. From the domestic shrines of our diverse ancestors, where effigies were gifted with herbs, incense, and foods, to the immense ceremonial platforms of advanced civilizations, such as the Toltec, Mexica, Zapotec, and Maya, to the contemporary home altar honoring ancestors and cosmic forces and holding symbols of what is most important to us, the altar or shrine serves as the axis mundi, or sacred center, of our lives. For womxn who have been denied religious authority in patriarchal religions, home altars are sites of autonomous spiritual agency where we control what symbols, objects, and memorabilia represent our deepest selves and the teachings and memories we wish to pass on.

---

1. For visual reflection, see plate 5, *Mujeres poderosas* by Ofelia Esparza.

Despite historical periods of spiritual domination and increased secularization that diminish the importance of creating personal sacred space, the tradition of altar making persists. The complexity and rich layers of *nepantla* are visualized in these axis mundi. For practitioners of Santería, Vodou, and *curanderismo*, the construction of elaborate shrines oftentimes has existed in the shadows due to the exclusion of these spiritual paths from mainstream understanding. The late twentieth century witnessed a reclamation of altar making by Chicanx/Latinx artists such as Ofelia Esparza, Amalia Mesa-Bains, Yreina D. Cervántez, Linda Vallejo, Ester Hernandez, Carmen Lomas Garza, and Yolanda Garfias Woo, who symbolized their feminist, Indigenous, and mestiza consciousness in their altar constructions. They reminded us of our role as "modern temple keepers" and of how "the domestic altar serves as a juncture where history lives" (Mesa-Bains 1993, 5–6). Exhibitions of womxn's altars in museums and galleries led many of us back to the significance of creating personal and communal sacred spaces where we communicate our desires, our commitments, our histories, and our sacred sources of sustenance.

Altars can take a variety of forms as there are few rules (with exceptions depending on the tradition) other than choosing and cleaning a functional space for the altar, blessing the chosen space, working with intention, choosing objects, symbols, and/or images imbued with meaning, and creating a sense of balance in the arrangement of the objects. Altars might be located not only in living spaces but also in public spaces, again depending on the tradition, such as businesses, restaurants, grocery stores, bars, and even on the dashboards of vehicles. Wherever located, the altar blesses the space and announces a spiritual presence overseeing the activities at hand. Once created, altars become either passive or active sites of healing energy. Once created, a passive altar exists but with little subsequent interaction from the altar maker. The energy around the altar becomes static. In contrast, an active altar is regularly cleansed and fresh flowers and herbs offered, candles lit, objects cleansed or rearranged, and prayers said or silent reflections occur. The healing energy is activated. Quoting Doña Chole Pescina in Austin, Tejas, who maintained her altar for more than fifty years, "It's an ancient tradition, and you can't get away from it, wherever you go . . . *mi altarcito* helps me to live" (Turner 1986, 41).

In this section, we open with Sara H. Salazar's poetic imagery of a *curandera* tending to her altar. We are then gifted with the wisdom of Ofelia Esparza, a third-generation *altarista* from East Los Angeles who in 1980, at Self Help

Graphics and Art, reintroduced altars as *ofrendas* for annually honoring our dead during Días de los Muertos. Since that time Ofelia has created public altars, or ofrendas, in numerous museums, galleries, and schools, both nationally and internationally. Here, she shares her childhood formation in creating domestic shrines and how shrines continue to empower her family. Describing her personal family altar in the intimacy of her living room serves to inspire and captivate our spiritual imaginations. In a subsequent contribution, Ofelia and her daughter, Rosanna Esparza Ahrens, guide us in creating shrines of self-realization that invite us to reflect on our higher self and to move forward in realizing it through writing, intention, affirmations, and imagery. Contributor alba onofrio offers us powerful musings on her salvation found within the "cosmology and on-going benefaction of Our Lady of Guadalupe." Her ritual practice of building queered altars in honor of the Divine Feminine calls us to "acknowledge our spiritual authority as healers and co-creators."

Healing childhood traumas has center focus in Susy Zepeda's offering of "Creating an Altar for the Healing of Our Younger Self." Susy guides us in journeying to painful pasts and shows us how the altar created with prayerful mindfulness can reach back and heal the parts of ourselves that inherited intergenerational trauma. In "Little Altars," Martha R. Gonzales reveals the intimate relationships she maintains through her altars with her ancestors, spirit guides, and the orishas. Reciprocity characterizes these relationships, as her offerings given from a place of love are reciprocated with abundant blessings of well-being, magic, and belonging. These *mujeres* unveil the creativity as well as the responsibility in the altar-making tradition.

This section closes with thoughtful guidance from Marta López-Garza on house blessings. Blessing our homes, work spaces, hotel rooms, etc., is important because, as Marta writes, the spaces "we live in, love in, work in need to be supportive spaces that will embrace our lives and nurture our hopes."

Lara Medina

The Curandera Prepares for Healing . . .

SARA H. SALAZAR

The curandera prepares for healing and transformation
with ritual and invocation.
She gathers bundles of any herbs that grow around her feet—
rosemary for remembrance,
sturdy sage for strength,
lavender for security—
and tenderly wraps each bundle with a piece of cloth.
Gifts from the earth.

She then invokes the seen and unseen elements and
welcomes Fire, Water, Earth, Air, and Ether.

She constructs an altar for forgiveness and renewal, and everything in between,
by burning small fragrant chunks of copal and
lighting candles to Coatlicue, Coyolxauhqui, Quetzalcoatl, Tonantzin,
the goddesses and gods of our ancestors,
and La Virgen and Her son, too.

She always leaves room for the ancestors.

My Home Altar

OFELIA ESPARZA

I am known for creating public altars to honor the dead during Días de los Muertos. A majority of my *ofrendas* have been built at Self Help Graphics and Art, where I first began with community altars more than thirty-five years ago. I learned this tradition from my mother, who always had altars, not only for Days of the Dead but also for other feast days and celebrations during the year. Most of these celebrations stemmed from Catholic observances, yet they were imbued with traditional Indigenous rituals that were indistinguishable to me as a child. *Nacimientos* were the most elaborate and most inspiring to me, where my mother's creative spirit nurtured my own and brought me close to nature. I was fascinated by her imaginative creations, which I later assisted her with. And much later, I recognized that in my mother's way of preparing food, in her faith and devotion in creating her altars, and in her hopeful way of looking at and enjoying life, was the life of a strong, spiritual woman.

These early experiences and images have been my greatest influences in forming my own spiritual journey and in leading my aesthetics in creating multifaceted altars. Altars imbued with colors, flowers, photos, and many objects, creating an array of vignettes, not only tell the story of my loved ones but also reflect my devotion and faith in honoring my ancestors and nurturing my own spirituality. My home altars are similarly designed but on a much smaller scale. They are displayed year-round on small surfaces in my living room and bedroom, on a bookcase in my work space, and in my small garden areas. Some of my garden altars are on small ledges with only a few collected items, or they are made up of items hanging overhead in a mobile or from a tree. Invariably, these change throughout the year. I consider all these compositions altars, for they serve as a place for reflection, contemplation, meditation, and prayer, and, most importantly, they provide me with an intimate space for my intentions. These altars reflect my spiritual Indigenous roots, yet I embrace other cultural modes of ritual as well.

My outdoor altars, where I spend the most time, are the more personal spaces for me. These are intimate, sacred spaces where I do my gratitude rituals and celebrate nature's gifts, including my own animals and plants (*mis yerbas*). These altars are free and organic and do not take any prespecified form. I do include organic representations of the four elements—water, fire, wind, and earth—although not necessarily all in one altar space.

I will note in more detail my largest space for an altar. It is in my living room on a vintage dining-room sideboard that belonged to my mother. This is my family altar, since it is largely a shared space and is the focal point upon entering my home. The scale of the altar is dictated by the small space I have available and can be reduced or expanded at any time. Here I have to mention that this altar is not unlike those my mother had in our home or unlike those found in many homes when I was a child (and still found today) except that they were always very simple, small displays dominated by photographs, one or more *veladoras*, religious images, and/or statues. These altars were held on a small space all year, not necessarily as a Days of the Dead altar.

Below is how I have created my altar, starting with a piece of furniture, in this case my mother's old five-foot buffet piece. On this I have created various tiers, or levels, with boxes and small footstools to hold the many photographs of my family members who have passed. This has become the template for all my altars, from the huge ofrendas to the very small, even miniature altars.

Next, I like to cover some of these tiers with small woven mats or textiles, unless the surface is presentable as is. Otherwise, I will use small keepsake doilies crocheted by my mother or from my collection.

The photographs are the most important element in the altar, and I have many. I prefer using old black-and-white photos in vintage-style frames whenever possible. The more recent photos are added, sometimes temporarily or for specific occasions. And, of course, an image or statue of Our Lady of Guadalupe is a permanent element of the altar.

Then, the other objects are placed on the altar in an aesthetic composition that is important to me. These are votives and personal mementos of my mother, my sister, my husband, my father, and others. I was taught that handmade ofrendas are especially meaningful, so there are artifacts created by my children or by me. I welcome any small ofrenda from my grandchildren or great grandchildren. I enjoy adding these small details that give life and add color to the altar, like the figurines of animals, birds, and bears (important to my family). Here is where details are in flux, but the basic elements do not change often.

The altar extends on the wall behind, where the larger photographs are displayed and are surrounded by a collection of various crosses, most of them gifts. Also mounted on this wall is a collection of various-styled angels from different countries, some of them handmade. A few of my hummingbirds, symbols of my loved ones' spirits, hang over the altar.

On the special days of Days of the Dead, the Feast Day of Our Lady of Guadalupe, and Christmastime (and other times, when my children just wish to) this altar is bedecked with fresh and handmade flowers. There are also lighted candles, incense, and handwritten cards for birthdays or anniversaries. For the most part, this is a semipermanent altar, a space for our family to honor and remember our family. I love to talk about the family members in the photographs, about their mementos and their lives, especially to the children. I take any opportunity to do this, just as my mother did for me throughout her lifetime. I got to know about my ancestors through my mother's stories. I even felt that I knew them, some of them intimately, even though I had never met them.

Thus, I am passing on this tradition to the next generations. I believe this is also true for the many people I talk to and teach about ofrendas, and for those who view the altars I create in public places, with the intention that they will recognize the importance of their own family legacy. Through honoring my ancestors and making altars all these years, I have become a more spiritual woman. I believe there is no set measure of size, space, time, or other specification for making a home altar. What is important to me is the intention and the significance given to the altar in my daily life. I have come to feel the connectedness of mind and spirit guiding me in all that I do, whether it is building ofrendas, making art, working with plants, preparing food, or teaching others. I am also sustaining my focus on the sacredness of life and death and on all living things that connect us to a meaningful, mindful way of living a spiritual life.

Shrine of Self-Realization

ROSANNA ESPARZA AHRENS AND OFELIA ESPARZA

Creating a shrine for self-realization requires deep inquiry into who you are as your higher self. In the creation process, you must allow the thoughts, words, and images to come forward without judgment as you construct your personal shrine.

ELEMENTS OF SHRINE: Poem, Affirmations, Intention, Symbols, Container for the Shrine

POEM, MY NAME: Allow yourself to imagine your name as its own entity, with attributes that you can see, taste, feel, smell, and hear. You also want to describe the energy that emits from it. Remember, you are allowing the words, images, and sounds to come forward. Do not decide the shape or the size of your name before you write, allow it to flow as you write.

MY NAME PROMPTS: What does your name sound like? What does it look like? What does it feel like? What does it taste like? What does it smell like? Describe the energy it emits. From these prompts you can start to create a poem where your NAME comes into form. Have fun with it—this is for YOU. Decide whether you want to arrange the poem in the shape of your name or in a standard writing format.

AFFIRMATIONS: I AM, I TRUST: Affirmations are inner truths about who you REALLY are, not necessarily who you experience yourself to be. Choose three to five affirmations from the list below or create your own that you want to manifest during this self-realization practice. Stay away from saying "I can" or "I will." This is not about a promise to yourself or your abilities, this is about WHAT IS. This is powerful language that activates true self-awareness, above your conscious experience. So choose three to five affirmations you want to focus on. Every morning when you wake, say them out loud. You can record yourself saying them. It's helpful to hear your own voice telling you wonderful truths about who you REALLY are. Say them at least three times, then whisper them. You can whisper them to yourself throughout the day.

AFFIRMATIONS

1. I am the architect of my life; I build its foundation and choose its contents.
2. Today, I am brimming with energy and overflowing with joy.
3. My body is healthy; my mind is brilliant; my soul is tranquil.
4. I am superior to negative thoughts and low actions.
5. I have been given endless talents that I begin to utilize today.
6. I forgive those who have harmed me in my past and peacefully detach from them.
7. A river of compassion washes away my anger and replaces it with love.
8. I am guided by Spirit.
9. My relationships become stronger, deeper, and more stable each day.
10. I possess the qualities needed to be successful.

INTENTION: A CLEAR GOAL/PURPOSE FOR YOUR PRACTICE: So now you have empowered your NAME and you have chosen affirmations or statements of TRUTH about your true self. Now you are ready to SET AN INTENTION for your self-realization journey. Setting an intention and writing it down helps to DIRECT the MIND. Your intention may change as you move through your journey.

SYMBOLS: IMAGES THAT REPRESENT INTENTION: Symbols are excellent reminders of your intention. Placing symbols in a shrine with clear intention activates the purpose and brings the intention to the forefront of the mind. Symbols only carry the energy you intend for them. You give them meaning. When you are before your shrine and you see the symbols you placed on it, you are immediately reminded and brought to the place you are realizing for yourself. Arrange the poem, affirmations, intention, and symbols in a box or other container for display in your private space for self-reflection and self-realization!

Reclaiming Our Mother, Reclaiming Ourselves

ALBA ONOFRIO

In my long *caminata* of decolonizing my religious practices and reembodying my direct communion with the Divine, the offerings of Gloria Anzaldúa and the analysis of AnaLouise Keating on spiritual activism and revisionist myth-making have been my scripture. They remind us that our spiritual practices are political, and therefore we are called as *la raza*, as the intertwined Afro-Indio-Anglo children of these colonized lands, to go back to our past to move forward to our future.

We must first collect the scattered pieces of our stolen cultures, languages, histories, and religious traditions, and then we must sort, discard, reclaim, and re-create ourselves in the images of the Sacred we seek. By acknowledging our spiritual authority as healers and cocreators, we are able to take the best of our past and weave new ancient practices on the loom of our sharpest political analyses. And in doing so, we carve out sacred spaces for our aching diasporic bodies to find spiritual identity and home in the powerful legacies of our many ancestors.

As a mixed-race, queer Latinx who has been othered from many religious spaces, I have found salvation in the cosmology and ongoing benefaction of Our Lady of Guadalupe. She offers an embodiment of the Divine that resonates with my soul. She occupies a contested, liminal identity of both divine and human. She appears as an Indigenous woman; she speaks the language of the people

(Nahuatl), and yet she is also the Mother of the Creator and Giver of Life. Most importantly for me, Guadalupe appeared on this continent to the subjugated people of a conquered land and spoke power and truth at a time of unspeakable death and domination.

She commands a legacy of providing uncompromising refuge, deep accompaniment in suffering, and healing care for all those who seek her—without coercion or condition. And though her narrative has long been assimilated by Christian hegemony and her image often co-opted by the forces of heteropatriarchy, deeper truths of Guadalupe's identity can be found in her ancient origin stories written in Nahuatl, in the embodied practices of her devoted followers, and in the recovery of her image by feminist recreations of her in a multitude of marginalized bodies.

In my ritual practices, I build queered altars and re-form religious rites that center and honor the Divine in the name of Guadalupe-Tonantzin. My altars to her always include the following items:

- multiple interpretations of her image (both traditional and feminist/queered)
- symbols of each of the four elements: water (preferably from a living source—river, ocean, etc.), fire (a candle), earth (preferably a living potted plant), and air (ideally copal, but also symbolized in incense or feathers)
- offerings: food and drink, flowers, rocks/crystals, poems, photos of ancestors, children's offerings, and any other treasures
- words or images offered up in prayer or representations of prayer requests

Lastly, I submit this prayer in place of the traditional Hail Mary, in recognition of the intertwined history and complex relationships that many of us carry from the Christian tradition. It is a *grito* of rebellion against the forces of Christian evil that subjugated, raped, missionized, and then baptized our Amerindian and African ancestors. This stolen prayer is re-membered in deep gratitude for our ancestors who found a way to the Divine in spite of colonization and in honor of the Divine who finds her way back to us still.

Ave Maria, Guadalupe-Tonantzin,
all Creation is in Thee.
Beloved are Thee, most Divine
and blessed are we the fruit of your love.

Santa Lupita, Madre de Dios,
care for us, *tu gente*,
now and at the hour of our death.
Amen.

Creating an Altar for the Healing of Our Younger Self

SUSY ZEPEDA

Here I share teachings by Estela Román (2012), via Pablo Alvarez, on creating an altar for the intentional healing of our younger self, *para la sanación de la niñez*.

When writing my qualifying exams, I went into complete isolation to figure out how to move forward. The violence of academia had triggered my traumas. I was at a crossroads. At that time, I was engaged in intensive intellectual work, diligently reading and writing about injustices, race, and decolonization, yet I needed to reconnect my heart and spirit to my mind, to align and find balance again. I was blocked; there were emotional barriers. *Mis aires estaban muy presente*. I was feeling uprooted and experienced paralysis on the left side of my face. My spirit *hermano*, Pablo, through dialogue and deep listening, guided me to raise an altar specifically for my childhood. To acknowledge and "touch the pain" (Hahn 1992). To relive, relieve, and breathe into what I had experienced as a child—a nonbinary, queer, feminist, brujx child—who lacked language. Creating a sacred altar became the way I unraveled the violence I had grown up with and had silently adopted as my own—domestic violence, sexual violence, and unspoken intergenerational violence. I had internalized the harm and thought it was my responsibility.

Full of *tristesa*, fear, and grief, in the process of raising this altar I realized I had abandoned my younger two-spirit/queer self. *La habia dejado en su miedo*. I lovingly spoke and sang to my younger self while bringing together rebozos with vibrant colors, photos, toys, and sacred elements to honor myself and to call for the return of my spirit (Gonzales 2012a, 25–39). *Llamado a mi alma, recordando mi niñez.* I let my younger spirit know it was safe. I was ready to walk with my whole self in harmony and love, *empezar a caminar en armonía.*

Pablo had initially visited Estela Román, a *maestra* we now share, in Temixco, Mexico, in 2003 and received her guidance in building sacred *altares para la sanación de los niños.* He recalls "the way she taught me was to flow along with my unknowing" while building the altar. Pablo guided me to find a space where I could build an altar, clean it with a wet wash towel, light a candle, and place water on it to prepare the space to create. He guided me to burn sage or copal and include the four elements—water, earth, fire, and air—on the altar.

This altar to my *niñez* became a space for me to cry, to have *llanto,* to release the deep *abandono* and *tristeza* I felt in my heart. I later realized that through creating this altar I was healing a generational cycle of abandonment in my family lineage, particularly on my paternal side. I began to pray not only for the healing of my younger self but also for the healing of my father, *mis tíos,* and my grandfathers. And now, with that same reflection, I pray for my nephew and future generations.

I offer these guidelines for creating an altar for the healing of one's younger self:

- Set your intention for *sanación* (healing).
- Say a prayer or words to guide the building of your altar. For example, ask for permission from the land and acknowledge the original peoples, the directions, and *Creador/Creadora* (Creator) and/or Universe.
- Visualize with your mind's eye the sacred items, dimensions, colors, and energies your altar will hold.
- Decide the direction of the altar. East—new beginnings / masculine; west—the feminine / sanación; north—elders / ancestors; south—the youth / next generations (Facio and Lara 2014).
- Clear the energy of the space. For example, take a small table, wash it with water, and offer sage or copal.
- Place a container of water and a candle on the altar space. Light the candle while holding your intention in your mind and your heart.
- Continue to burn copal or sage. Cleanse yourself and the space/location you are in.
- Be in ceremony with the sacred smoke and offer a prayer for the heart of your younger self. For example, you can ask for courage and strength to

revisit the past, your trauma, with the intention of healing wounds and of forgiving yourself and anyone else who caused you harm. Be careful, go one memory at a time so you don't overwhelm yourself. Always ask for help.

- Call on your ancestors to guide your journey. Add sacred items on the altar that belonged to or remind you of the land of your family/ancestors, your relatives and relations.
- Let the altar rest and allow some time for sacred energy to build.
- Continue to gather sacred items, items that you associate with your childhood, gifts offered to you that remind you of your worth. Reflect on your purpose for building the altar, gather the sacred items that speak to your intention and spirit, allow for the flow of the unknowing, guided by your creativity and your connection with the Creator as you build. Include a photo of yourself as a child.
- Gather herbs that call to you, such as rosemary and lavender. Let them be medicine for you.
- Be in ceremony as you create the space. Allow yourself to be present with your whole heart for the duration of this journey. You may experience grief, sadness, and joy as you allow yourself to be guided and as you search for and honor sacred items. Take deep breaths, and when it feels difficult, remember your intention and that you are not alone. You can journal, sing, pray, and/or sit with your altar daily, as a way to release and call your spirit back. Ometeotl.

Little Altars

MARTHA R. GONZALES

He sits by my doorway, protector of my home, surrounded by his offerings: a candle, tobacco, a bottle of rum, flowers, toys, and candies, along with Ogún and Ochosí. Whenever I travel, I usually buy him a gift first; he is always on my mind, for through the *caracol*, his cowrie shells used in divination, he has spoken words of such beauty and profound meaning to me, they have changed my life. I love Eleguá, and I do my best to let him know so.

My home is a series of little altars, there is at least one to two altars in every room: to the Great Goddess in her various guises, to the agricultural mystery rites, to Yemayá, Oschún, and ErosPsyche, to San Lázaro / Babalú Ayé, and Asklepios.[1] These sacred spaces remind me of my work in this world, remind me of my interconnection with all living beings. They ground me, provide peace in my home, remind me that I am loved and am love itself, and my mundane domestic acts become sacred little rituals, for these altars require attention to keep the flow of energy moving in my life. They bless my home with their presence, make it a place filled with well-being and magic; they make me want to be home.

---

1. Asklepios is the god of healing and health in Greek antiquity. Therapeutic centers where the healing arts were practiced included an incubation stoa, or sacred space, "where patients passed the night. . . . During their sleep, Asklepios came to them in a dream and healed them miraculously or gave them therapeutic advice" (Pandermalis, Eleftheratou, and Vlassopoulou 2015, 62–65).

Dressed in white, the last altar, which is also the first, located in the final room of my home, is the one to my ancestors, spirit guides, and Obatalá. On it sits a set of clear glasses, each glass filled with water and one tied with a blue ribbon, as I've been instructed to do, a small lit candle, white fragrant flowers, preferably narcissus for Obatalá and hyacinth during the spring. This altar completes the circle, without it I can do no work with my other altars; for first and foremost, the ancestors, guardian spirits, and guides are acknowledged and fed. On special ritual occasions, a small plate of food is offered here first, before anyone else present is served. They are honored for the blessings they bring to my life, for the protection and guidance they have always bestowed on me, even when I lived unaware of their presence.

Bendiciones de casa (House Blessings)

Life and Spirit in Living Spaces

MARTA LÓPEZ-GARZA

Bendiciones de casa (house blessings) have been a part of my entire life in some form or another. I watched as a child those around me who in various ways practiced and lived their lives spirituality and culturally, such as through making altars, lighting candles, praying, burning incenses, copal, and herbs, and entreating the services of saints. These practices were performed by priests, family elders, and family acquaintances. As a young adult, I lost sight of the spiritual dimension of living and working spaces. It was not until later in my life that I realized I was carrying ancestral memories within me. Once I acknowledged what I held within, I was open to learning more, to expanding my understanding of space and energy, to learning from many teachers and from many ceremonies by Chicanas, Indigenous elders, and peers.[1] Beyond that, I learned several spiritual traditions' sacred practices from a number of powerful teachers and mentors from diverse mystical and spiritual cultures.[2]

I do bendiciones de casa[3] for family members, friends, and acquaintances. I do this because the dwellings we live in, love in, work in, need to be supportive spaces that embrace our lives and nurture our hopes. The world is often in turmoil, and life is uncertain; therefore, it is essential to have one's own space

1. Gracias a Estela Román, Ofelia Esparza, Lara Medina, Yreina Cervántez, *y mis abuelas* Manuela Ronquillo Garza and Juanita Andazola López.

2. Thích Nhất Hạnh, Raven Lee, Ana Gonzalez, among others.

3. At times referred to as *limpias de casa.*

as affirmative and as secure as possible. Therefore, the meaningfulness of ben- diciones de casas, which have been a global tradition since ancient times, is generally for the purpose of asking for the grace of the Divine / the Universe (or however one calls that higher/deeper power within us and around us) and for that blessed entity to enter our dwellings, nurture our souls, and bring security and comfort to those living and passing through our homes. Certainly, ben- diciones de casa have played a part in Mexican and Indigenous and Catholic rituals for centuries. So within that larger context, I have taken what feels right for me within my spiritual understanding, and I fashion it according to the specific occasion. For example, for a *limpia de casa* I conducted a few years ago, I arrived with my sacred objects and prayers from the mixture of religious and spiritual traditions I follow. However, when we prepared for the bendición, I realized that the parents of one of the individuals were strongly Catholic, so I applied primarily rituals and prayerful words that accommodated their beliefs, along with everyone else's involved.

GUIDELINES

There are at least three stages, or parts, to the bendición de casa: (1) pre- bendición, (2) the bendición itself, and (3) post-bendición. How you approach a limpia de casa depends on the spiritual and/or religious precepts to which you adhere. For example, if you are a practicing Buddhist, rely on those teachings. What I offer are suggestions for house blessings that encompass that which grounds me best, and that is a combination of Catholicism and Indigenous practices along with a mixture of Eastern traditions. The basic premise of giv- ing a bendición de casa is that we accept the existence of the Divine, that we live among spirits, and that those who have passed on remain with us in some form. The Divine and the spirits (you may consider them angels or saints) help protect and watch over our homes and important spaces. How you manifest that awareness depends on your cultural journey, your spiritual path. As long as you listen to your heart and act without desire to harm others, then bendiciones are truly sacred and powerful ceremonies.

It is also important to note that there may be occasions when you are not in an effective spiritual and/or mental "space" to successfully perform a bendición. Be attuned to those times and reflect on whether you are able to conduct this ceremony at that time.

PRE-BENDICIÓN

SELF: To prepare for the bendición, you must first prepare yourself. This entails centering, focusing, praying. This self-blessing can include the sign of the cross, Reiki symbols, or any other protective blessing. By doing this, you will create a blessed vessel (yourself) and a safe space.

GATHER YOUR IMPLEMENTS: Implements refer to those items you will use in the bendición, including religious objects such as crosses, singing bowls, and holy water and/or organic materials such as shells, crystals, stones, herbs, and flowers. Also feel free to bring candles and copal or dried sage to light during the house blessing. These are just a few examples of the tools you can avail yourself to, keeping in mind that these implements should be items you hold spiritually dear and that are sacred to you. Prepare and clean your implements by either blessing them with the sign of the cross, saging, or salted water.

I also recommend that you set your sacred implements outside during a full moon to receive that special monthly lunar energy. Return items to their customary place promptly early the next morning.

BENDICIÓN DE CASA

1. Prepare/bless the space. Ask the ancestors and spirits of the land and the home to accept your presence, to accept the bendición. Thank them by honoring the four directions and the accompanying elements. Ask for help with the bendición.[4]

    Above all, it is important to apply whatever practices you feel from your heart and are right for you. At all times, respect and give thanks to the ancestors from where that ceremony comes.

2. Bless those in attendance with sage and copal. You can give each participant a role for the ceremony, such as assisting in building the altar and helping to sage/smudge the space.

3. Perform the bendición itself.

    a. Scan the home/dwelling, feeling for energy fields, which can be sensed as positive/light or negative/heavy. Even note when there is no

---

4. Refer to part 2, "Honoring the Sacred Directions."

detection of energy at all. You may begin the ceremony at one of the strongest positive vibration spaces.

b. Light the sage and have up to four people help cleanse/bless the entire home, room by room, including all nooks, cabinets, closets, and electrical outlets, preferably moving in counterclockwise direction. Use sage and healing plants like rosemary, which extract and absorb negative energies. Chanting, praying, singing, and/or playing drums or other musical instruments go well with the smudging. In the areas where you feel positive and uplifting energies, give thanks to the energy/spirits.

c. Cleanse/bless the outdoors/gardens the same way—offering prayer, smudging, thanking the spaces, the plants, the animals.

d. Offer final overall gratitude to the house, land, and spirits/angels/deities for welcoming those now living in the space.

e. Seal the openings of the home (i.e., doors, windows) at the end of the ceremony. This practice varies from culture/tradition to culture/tradition and is an important element to the cleansing. For example, in Western cultures, holy water is sprinkled on the thresholds and window sills to seal the blessings and protect the dwelling and inhabitants. Among the Buddhists in Thailand, the same practice takes place with mustard seeds or white paste.

POST-BENDICIÓN

Post-bendiciones entail cleansing yourself, the tools you used, and those who worked with you. Gather everyone in a circle and place implements in the middle. Sweep burning incense/copal/sage over the implements in order to cleanse them. Have participants take three deep breaths. In prayer, thank the spirits and the Divine for their blessings and their protection of the home and the participants of the ritual. Offer the ceremony for the benefit of all beings, and, lastly, thank all in attendance for their participation.

May you find peace and fulfillment in this ceremony.

4

BLESSINGS FOR BABIES
AND YOUNG CHILDREN

INTRODUCTION

Blessing our newly born babies is one of the most important ritual acts we can do in our process of decolonizing our spirituality. Most of our *gente* have been Christianized over the generations; thus, most of us are familiar with the misguided belief that babies are born with "original sin" that is transferred through the parents during their act of sexual intercourse. Catholicism under the theology of Augustine of Hippo (354–430 CE) imposed this doctrine very early in the development of Christianity. While Roman Catholicism no longer places inherited guilt or direct sin within babies, official dogma states that as descendants of Adam and Eve, babies inherit "the fallen nature" of the first couple, which resulted from their disobedience of God's command not to eat of the tree of knowledge. Some of the more theologically conservative Protestant traditions continue to teach that sin and guilt actually reside within a newborn. The Catholic tradition of a male priest baptizing a baby to ensure the baby's salvation and the receiving of divine grace was understood as being absolutely essential for the child to have a place in the Christian heaven. Without this ritual, the child would be condemned to hell in the event of his or her death. Later on in Christian theology (1300 CE), the souls of unbaptized infants could enter into limbo, a liminal state of existence allowing for hope in the mercy of

God to save these children from life in hell (Kelly 2000). Theologian and priest Matthew Fox (2000) challenged the doctrine of original sin with his teachings on "original blessing," present in all humanity, including infants, for which he was eventually restrained from teaching. Fox was ultimately expelled from the Dominican order of the Catholic Church in the late twentieth century. However, original blessing remains an alternative perspective that has not been officially condemned.

Sixteenth-century missionaries in Mexico relied on a rapid formula of baptism for the sake of Christianizing hundreds of Indigenous people at one time; however, ambiguity about the meaning of one's baptism among "the converted" remained pervasive (Morales 2001). As Jorge Klor de Alva (1993) points out, for Indigenous "converts," baptism ensured one's entrance into the new society and the new town center and sacred community symbolized by the church building and the lesser concern was entrance to heaven. During subsequent periods of colonization, the absence of clergy in rural communities led the church to grant womxn the authority to baptize. *Rezadoras* and *curanderas* were and are frequently called on to baptize newborns with prayers and blessed water.

In great contrast to the dogma of original sin, traditional Nahua beliefs teach that babies are born with *tonalli*, a divine vital force, an inner heat located in the head that must be ignited or warmed by laying the baby next to a domestic sacred fire for four days following the birth. Tonalli connects one to the sacred cosmos from the moment of conception, providing an individual vigor, heat, and the ability to grow. Disconnection from one's relationship to the sacred in the natural world or engagement in unethical behavior can cause one to lose tonalli. Frightening events and psychotropic substances that result in dreaming also cause the tonalli to leave the body and travel (Ortiz de Montellano 2001). Tonalli can be reinstated through ritually addressing one's *susto*, engaging in ethical behavior, or reviving one's relationship to the sacred cosmos. Ritual cleansings, prayers and songs, self-acceptance and compassion, and reflective time in nature are helpful for reigniting one's tonalli.[1]

Decolonizing our spirituality requires that we understand and honor our own sacredness that we receive from the source of life, or sacred cosmic energy. Blessing our young ones shortly after the birth and again later with family and friends gathered is a powerful act of decolonization that offers gratitude

---

1. See part 10, "Holistic Health Care," for ritual cleansing practices.

for creation and communicates our unconditional love to the baby. As poet Gloria Enedina Alvarez states in the prayer that opens this section, "a miracle exchanged through eyes" is our birthright.

Understanding our given name also aids in the decolonizing process. Naming ceremonies for Indigenous peoples traditionally acknowledge "the sense of power inherent in a name or in the person performing the act of naming" (Miranda 2010, 260). In the Mexica tradition, names were/are given depending on the day and time of birth in consultation with the spiritual leader who interprets the sacred 260-day calendar. While the majority of Chicanx/Latinx continue to carry names of Spanish origin, many of us choose to name our children using ancestral Indigenous languages. Xochitl is a popular name, meaning "flower" in Nahuatl. I chose Ixchel for my daughter's middle name, referencing the Maya goddess of medicine and midwifery. Regardless of our tradition, it is important to explain the meaning or reasoning of the names we choose for our children in our blessing rituals, and to them later as they grow.

Many of the elders in our families continue to adhere to the importance of infant baptism in the Catholic tradition, although some Protestant traditions wait until the child chooses baptism on their own (Aponte 2012). Either way, the practice offers "not only entrance into the church but also as affirmation of a family and a culture [and] is a very solidifying event" (Aponte 2012, 84). Yet, for those of us who feel the need for a ritual beyond the confines of a church baptism, which can be held if close family members feel it is essential, the church baptism can be followed by a communal ritual at home, preferably outside. In this section, I offer the ritual I created for the blessing of my daughter, Marisol, when she was one year old.

Also in this section, traditional baby catcher Patrisia Gonzales offers us a "A Little Baby Prayer" as one example of words of beauty and love that can be said to welcome a baby into our world. As she notes, "There are many moments in birthing when prayers may be offered."

Mónica Russel y Rodríguez penned a most welcoming poem for me and my daughter before she was even born, calling her to join the circle of womxn waiting for her arrival! Gathering in ritual circle to mark the significance of pregnancy and birth is womxn caring for womxn and claiming our authority to bless each other and our children.

In "Planting the Umbilical Cord" by Jennie Luna, we are called to honor the sacredness of the initial tie that linked us to our mothers. In this ritual, the cord is buried at the time of puberty, symbolically releasing the young person from the full protection of their parents and reaffirming their connection to sacred Mother Earth. As Jennie states, "There are many Indigenous rituals around the umbilical cord." Burying the cord can take place shortly after the birth or the cord can be safeguarded in a medicine bundle or special memory book. I buried my own daughter's cord a few months after her birth, under an avocado tree on the land of her great grandmother.

Lara Medina

Life Arrives

GLORIA ENEDINA ALVAREZ

always from an immortal kiss,
pieces taken from doubt,
a miracle exchanged through the eyes . . .

la vida arriba

siempre desde un beso inmortal
retazos de duda robados
milagro á traves de los ojos

A Home Baptism

LARA MEDINA

To respect the Catholic elders in our family, we asked my good friend, who is a feminist-minded Catholic priest, to baptize our young child in the church. Later that day, I created a ritual at home in our backyard to further nourish our spirituality and to proclaim the Indigenous values and symbols we would teach alongside Catholicism.[1] First, I laid a large canvas cloth on the grass, and then I created a mandala of the four directions, rimmed and sectioned with flowers and filled in with large dried corn seeds, with a smaller circle of soft cornmeal in the middle of the mandala. A large candle and *un sahumerio de copal* were placed in the east, the direction of new beginnings and sacred fire. In the west, I placed a glass bowl of water. In the south were small percussion instruments (rattles, a Peruvian windpipe, a miniature drum). In the north was a handful of colored feathers. When the ritual began, we placed our child in the middle of the mandala, where she sat during the ritual, happily playing with the cornmeal.

After welcoming everyone present who was standing around the mandala, the four friends I had chosen, one for each direction, opened the ritual by offering prayer and words of wisdom related to their assigned direction and its corresponding element and cycle of life. A trio of *mujeres* serenaded us at different moments in the ritual. *Los padrinos* then entered the mandala and picked up

---

1. The ritual language can use gender-neutral pronouns and can provide the opportunity to emphasize the freedom the child will have to choose their gender.

our child. My partner and I followed with the bowl of water. We explained the meanings of the first and middle names we had chosen for our child, and then we blessed our baby with the water. We publicly asked los padrinos to guide our child throughout their lifetime. The *abuelos* present were then invited to enter the mandala and bless our daughter and us and our compadres with water. The abuelos chose their own words for their blessings. Abrazos were warmly exchanged, and music concluded the ritual as we thanked everyone for being present.

A communal ritual utilizing cultural symbols, ritual actions, and prayers reflecting our spirituality is a powerful act of decolonization for everyone present. The elders felt particularly empowered as their authority and role in the family was honored. The peace and comfort of the ritual seemed to soothe our daughter, who remained fascinated with the cornmeal!

A Little Baby Prayer

PATRISIA GONZALES, TRADITIONAL BABY CATCHER

Breath of Life, Life Makers, Life Formers
To the flower beings, the sacred flower pot,
We give thanks to All that is above and below, to the Four Winds that carry all
    living beings
Aliento de la Vida, we offer thanks for this sacred bundle given to us.

From the Celestial Gourd, Sieve of Medicine
You have come a long way
The Midwives in the Skyworld threw their rebozo shawls in the sky for your
    protection.

We present you . . .
Grandmother Moon, Grandmother Earth
Bright Star, hear our baby's name . . .

Child, may you have a Good Road, a Green, Flat Road, a Dream Road
You have been in the spirit world of the womb
May you stay in this human world
May you have a beautiful blanket
May you have flowers and good words

May you be a hard worker
May you be kind and upright
May you live with a straight, strong spine
With your feet firmly planted.

From your first baby breath to Creator's breath, we promise to take care of you
and love you.

There are many ways to welcome a baby and many moments in birthing when prayers may be offered. Prayers vary based on family, communal, and Indigenous teachings. This small prayer is only one offering of words.

The Mujeres Circle

MÓNICA RUSSEL Y RODRÍGUEZ

I call to you, come together in the Women's Circle
I call to you, come together *mujeres* to celebrate
Come together as a community and as a family
Let us share the sage to cleanse our auras of the difficult and heavy feelings that
    have fallen on us
Let us share the circle's power to give us renewed energy
Come together to share your gifts of love and support for Lara and *la nena*
Come together to celebrate and affirm life
Come together, come to the circle.

On behalf of all of us, I welcome you to the circle
Your presence here makes the circle complete
Each of us has an equal place in the circle
Together, as a circle, we ask the grandmother spirit, the mother spirit, and the
    comadre spirit to join us.
Together, we ask the sister spirit, the daughter spirit, and the *sobrina* spirit to
    join us.
We welcome these family spirits and family feelings to our circle and they make
    our circle complete.

We are here for each other and for the difficult times and the celebrations.

We are a circle community which shares and commemorates change: birth, life, puberty, difficult transitions, marriages, and loss.

Today we celebrate the coming birth of Lara's baby and we celebrate the ways in which that affirms us as a community.

As a circle we are affirmed as an enduring community with the arrival of *la nena.*

She is a blessing and she will make our circle complete.

She will join our community in resistance, in celebration, and in creation.

She will add to our community, she will change the circle.

This will then ensure our continuation as a community.

We are here to celebrate Lara as our friend, our intellectual colleague, our *compañera en la lucha para justicia,* our sister, our *comadre.*

Lara, we form a circle around you in celebration of the many relationships we have with you.

Today we ask Lara to become her support, to let us share her joy and her burden of being a mother.

Lara, we are here to affirm our roles as *las tías* of your *nena.*

Lara, we are here to affirm our roles as *las comadres* with you.

And we welcome *la nena, nuestra sobrina.*

We welcome you to our circle.

You will be born with the spirit of the grandmother and you will complete the circle.

We welcome you, you will be our daughter.

We welcome you, you will be our *sobrina.*

We welcome you, you will be our sister.

—CIRCA 1993, LOS ANGELES

I wrote this piece while belonging to a *mujeres* circle in Los Angeles in the early 1990s. In writing this, what was compelling to me was the idea of change as radical inclusion and how in embracing others we ourselves necessarily change. This prayer for our pregnant friend and her soon-to-arrive baby was also a call to the group to affirm that inclusion. While this was written for the occasion of a birth, I also wanted to think of the "you" in this call as each of us being members of a community. Years later, I also named my daughter Marisol. This is not entirely coincidental. It is a call, then, to my own daughter and her entry into a sisterhood.

I am aware now of how gender binary this call to the mujeres circle is, but I think the sentiment remains. I would hope the idea of radical inclusion imagines all genders. The reality that we need resistance, particularly by way of inclusion, is still so necessary.

Planting the Umbilical Cord

JENNIE LUNA

My mother saved my umbilical cord for more than fifteen years, and when I was past my fifteenth birthday and well into my puberty years, she decided to host a garden gathering in our backyard to plant my umbilical cord under a tree gifted to her by my grandparents. Growing up, my mother always told me that I would never have to worry about my fertility because she had a pomegranate tree in the backyard. This fruit is symbolic of a woman's fertility, and as long as this tree grew and bore fruit, my fertility would be secure. Bringing my family together around the new tree to be planted was a way to honor my life by giving back that umbilical cord, the original connection to my human mother, and offering it to my earth mother. Burying the umbilical cord during my teens also symbolized the second separation between mother and child. As a child enters puberty, the parent begins to release their child to the adult world where they must make their own decisions. The child years are over, and it is time for the young person to grow into their own adulthood.

There are many Indigenous rituals around the umbilical cord. Some parents will coil it and let it dry, and the cord becomes part of a medicine bundle or pouch that the child carries with them throughout their life. Some parents choose to keep it in a baby book, while others might discard it. My mother's ritual is just one of many possible ways to honor that sacred cord that was our connection to our first tree of life, the placenta. This placenta was attached to our mother and gave us blood, nourishment, and life. Whatever one decides to do with the umbilical cord, the sacredness of that cord should be recognized and honored.

Parents should choose a fruit tree, rose bush, or yerba with meaning they would like to impart to their child. Some examples include the pomegranate or avocado tree for female and male fertility, respectively; a sage plant for continued health and medicine; or a special flower bush that symbolizes a beautiful path for their life. Any plant or tree is acceptable and will have meaning because it will grow from the prayers planted with the umbilical cord.

Gather family and friends to help and to witness the planting of the umbilical cord and the tree. Parent(s) should recount the birth story of their child and share their prayers, hopes, and dreams for their child. The planting will now hold the memory of these words and prayers. Relatives and friends should share in this talk-story and recount their memories of the child and impart wisdom to them as they enter adulthood. This moment can include lighting copal and/or sage to call in the ancestors and ancestral memory or singing any songs anyone wants to offer. The goal is to create sacred, grounding space to share and to give energy to the young person who is entering puberty and adulthood. This ritual is to honor the bonds to *familia* and also to recognize the rite of passage to adulthood. Once the tree is planted, a meal should be shared to celebrate the planting of the umbilical cord and the tree. A commitment is made to care for the tree and for one another.

5

CREATING ART AS SPIRITUAL PRACTICE

INTRODUCTION

Art making follows the Mesoamerican tradition of *in xochitl in cuicatl / flor y canto* / flower and song, art, beauty, and truth, as privileged modes for communing with our sacred sources and our sacred selves.[1] The intentional act of creating art, regardless of its form, enables the artist to enter into a space of silent meditation or heart-full communication with fellow artisans. The process of creating invites the artist to take a journey into the self, to feel what moves us, what tantalizes us, what inspires us to live, whether it be through writing, painting, embroidering, sculpting, sewing, or moving the body to rhythms of the earth. Art heals. Art heals our wounded or just plain tired spirits. Art restores our psyche, our spirits, and our bodies to a balanced state of being.

Mesoamerican ancestors believed that our distinct character, *in ixtli in yollotl*, face and heart, was shaped by how each of us integrated the traditions and teachings into our lives and made them our own. Art making was and is an important aspect of shaping our distinct character.

The *tlacuilo*, or divinely inspired artists of ancient Mesoamerica, live among us today. Chicanx/Latinx consciousness has been shaped largely by our artists,

---

1. For visual reflection, see plates 1–11.

through a symbol system and a metaphorical language that have restored much of our Indigenous ancestral wisdom. In this section, we are graced with the insights of Xicana feminist visual artist Yreina D. Cervántez, a *veterana artivista* from the Chicano movement who continues to inspire us with her layered iconography "imbued with memory and the profound wisdom discovered in the language of our ancestors." We receive a glimpse into her creative, spiritual process of art making, meant for us all to look deeper into our own sources of inspiration and, as she says, liberation! Her watercolor *Canción y Cura* (plate 3) and poem honor Tlazolteotl, protector of midwifery, healers, the *temazkal*, and overall regeneration.

Dora Xochitl Lopez-Mata and her mother, Maria Eva Mata, offer an intimate sharing of their familial tradition of *bordar y tejer*. Passed on from Dora's great-grandmother to her grandmother, to her mother, and then to Dora, embroidering and crocheting are art forms that allow for reflective solitude or communal bonding. As they state, they are "womxn who carry medicine in their hands."

Esther Díaz Martín also shares her inherited tradition of bordar, as learned from her mother. Embedded within the embroidery instructions were life lessons drawn from the stories her mother shared as they embroidered together. Years later, Esther has turned to bordar to listen deeply to herself as she navigates the complexities of her life. Her detailed description of the process of bordar offers inspiration to turn to this art form as a spiritual practice.

"Luz de luz," penned by Gloria Enedina Alvarez, speaks to the fluidity and illumination within the process of creation. Her prayerful words seem to speak directly to the act of bordar, as the hands, hearts, and minds of *mujeres* stitch their stories, their lives, their art into offerings of love.

The act of gifting love through the gifting of one's art expresses the passion and compassion that Margaret "Quica" Alarcón invokes through her art making and shares with us in "The Gift of Art." Taking us on a journey through the highlights and lowlights of her training as a young artist, she offers us a glimpse into the deep healing power of art shared with those who saw her for the artist that she is! For Quica, love inspires expression and her art expresses her love.

To close this chapter on art as spiritual practice, Eddy Francisco Alvarez Jr. explains intimately how creating the fabulous "being fabulous" is sacred "queer world-making moments" in the face of heteronormativity. Deeply reflecting on the influences of his spirituality, Eddy remembers a *mezcla* of domestic spiritual traditions he witnessed as a youth and his joyful interactions with his own cre-ative imagination "that make you belong or that glitter your world in ways that respond to the violence and dysfunction around you." He shares how sustaining an art practice for finding inner peace is a loving reminder to us all "who need a place to start."

Lara Medina

On Creating Art / Flor y canto

YREINA D. CERVÁNTEZ

I have incorporated the use of Mesoamerican glyphs in my artwork for some time. These are not mere designs or decorations but powerful symbols imbued with memory and the profound wisdom discovered in the language of our ancestors. These glyphs have become part of my own personal and collective visual vocabulary. They represent legacy reclaimed and translated into a contemporary, Xicana, feminist iconography that speaks to a community moving toward liberation. They are the "spirit glyphs" referred to by scholar Laura E. Pérez (2007, 22), the glyphs inscribed in our hearts.

My art is oftentimes a *mezcla*, a layering of past, present, and future, pieced together with the shards of knowledge I have collected. I reflect on what it must have been like more than five hundred years ago for the Native Mesoamerican scribes/*tlacuilos* who, after experiencing violent processes of colonization and assimilation, were forced to forsake their religion, abandon their own sacred texts, and nearly relinquish their distinctive way of communicating, which was eventually displaced/replaced by the written Spanish/European language and alphabet. Within that imposed language manifested the tension and juxtaposition of two opposing worldviews and aesthetics.

What a challenge it must have been for these tlacuilos to continue their important work, finding ways to renegotiate their vital role as scribes in colonial New Spain, by becoming innovators and interpreters for the "postconquest" codices, and, even so, preserving and salvaging ancient knowledge in this way.

Centuries later, I and many other artists inspired by the ancient Mesoamerican symbols and *amoxtli* are determined to decipher their meaning for our own time. It is a testament to the enduring power and message of transformation in the glyphs.

My image *Canción y Cura* is about healing the body, spirit, and mind by invoking the positive forces through ritual and ceremony and by calling on the powers of Tlazolteotl, a sacred feminine force for the Mexica, or Aztec. Tlazolteotl provided support and inspiration to midwives and all healers. She is associated with the lunar aspects. She was also revered as the "goddess" of the *temezkalli*, or sweat lodge—a purification ceremony. Most often referred to as the goddess of sensuality or sexuality, Tlazolteotl as Great Mother has many dimensions. In her book *Red Medicine Traditional Indigenous Rites of Birthing and Healing*, writer and healer/midwife Patrisia Gonzales states, "Tlazolteotl is an energetic function and process that undergirds all healing and regeneration, from plant to human life" (2012b, 94). She also expresses, "Through the symbols of Tlazolteotl, we access the metaphoric mind surrounding birth and regeneration that is woven across Mesoamerica, threaded into sayings, purification practices, murals and ceremonies" (93). In my painting, the *curandera*, or healer, is making offerings and songs to all who need healing. *Curar, curar y curar.*

MAPA
territory of imagination and creation
The body reveals its own wisdom
cherished,
corazón / heart of the earth
Mi tierra firme
cuerpo de Mujer,
This is my sacred ground
no one can desecrate it.
Curar, curar y curar.

Bordar y tejer es medicina

DORA XOCHITL LOPEZ-MATA AND MARIA EVA MATA

We (my mother and I) come from a long line of strong *mujeres*, womxn who carry medicine in their hands. *Medicina* that allows us to stay together. We were hesitant to share our ritual with others, as it has been passed down among the mujeres in our family. However, from many of the *platicas* during our ritual, we have learned the importance of preserving this tradition and sharing it with others. My mother was the one who came up with new *bordados*, or patterns, for crochet and later taught them to the other womxn in our family. For my mom and me, this ritual is sacred because it is personal and it means a lot to us. Her mother taught her these skills, and my great-grandmother taught my grandmother. The art of *tejido*, or crochet, is disappearing. Therefore, my documenting this practice and my mother sharing her knowledge with me is a way of ensuring that our ritual does not end with my generation. For both of us, writing about it is a way of documenting and attempting to preserve our cultural and spiritual tradition.

Our family ritual consisted of the mujeres getting together in our house to engage in bordado (embroidery) and tejido. However, our ritual has been modified due to migration. Now, my mother and I are the ones to continue this tradition here in the United States, and we practice our ritual in an intimate way. As we sit down together in the outdoor area and set up to engage in bordado and tejido, our ritual begins by getting our materials together, our *aros* (embroidery hoops), *hilos* (threads), *tela* (cloth), and *aguja* (needle). We enjoy this preparation because it gives us peace and it is something we do to bond with each other as we begin to make our art. The final creation will show the work of our hands and the love between us.

Bordar y tejer es medicina as it was a way for the mujeres in our family to challenge gender roles by offering a means of support and a way to contribute to the well-being of the household through selling and trading the items. At times, my mother and I sell our work at community events. This ritual is not easy, as it takes time and patience. However, as mujeres, it has been a way to heal and to find a spiritual connection to our ancestors through our bordado, as many of the things we create are part of our Días de los Muertos altars. For my mother and me, bordado provides us with guidance, and practicing this ritual is a way of nurturing our bodymindspirit.

Aprender bordando

Embroidery as Meditation and Knowledge Making

ESTHER DÍAZ MARTÍN

Mi mamá me enseño the practice of *bordar*, or embroidery, when I was a young girl. In her usual way, she weaved her knowledge in *anecdotas*, or stories, about my ancestors and about her childhood. Mi mamá would go on about the way things were done *antes*, while also recognizing the things that have changed and, more generally, that change is part of life. "*Las cosas tienen que ir cambiando*." With these words she gave me permission to adapt *mi forma de bordar* and the trajectory of my life in accordance with my own judgment and desire.

We began by studying a finished model, *la muestra*. Mi mamá would show me a *servilleta*, which is typically used for setting out tortillas or bread on the dining table. There, the embroidered artwork adorns everyday *convivencia*. She would explain the different *puntadas*, or stitches, some simple and some advanced. Then she would demonstrate *como se le hace*, the specific techniques of placing the fabric on the embroidery hoop and stretching it to a desired tautness. The fabric must stay in place but also have enough flexibility so that it can be worked on comfortably. In choosing the color and thickness of the thread, we consider both the quality of the fabric and how the finished piece will be used or displayed. Many of these decisions require trial and error. It is impossible to really know what something will look and feel like until you actually try it out.

In the process of instruction, my mother would recall *dichos* with some element of *costura* in them: "*Recuerda que primero pasará un camello por el ojo de una aguja antes que un rico entre al cielo*."

There is always a first step, *una puntada facil*: pass the needle through the fabric from the underside of the canvas up. We strive to show neatness in both the display side and the underside of the piece. An orderly underside demonstrates that we worked following a carefully planned method, respecting the availability of materials and established techniques. An experienced *costurera* will always check out the underside of a *bordado* to get an idea of how much care and method were put into the work. Following established methods teaches us to stay organized, work steadily, and stay focused on a series of connected steps. As we sew a new stitch, we hold extra thread out of the way *'pa que no se te enrede*, to avoid tangles. When the inevitable *enredo* occurs, carefully work backward or clip off the error until you find a viable restarting point. Be patient. It may take many days, weeks, months, or even years to complete your project. Step back and acknowledge your progress, "*ya terminé la ramita, ya terminé una hoja, ya terminé una flor.*"

Some twenty-plus years after my first lessons, I again picked up the practice of *bordar* while working through graduate school. Perhaps I was inspired by the texture of *servilletas* and *manteles* that I studied over the course of *sobremesas* at my mom's and at my *suegra's* tables. Each stitch that grazed my fingertips was a record of their daily work, time, thoughts, and *sentimientos* as they worked their *proyectos*.

In the process of developing my own practice of *bordar*, I found in it guidance for contesting patriarchy within academia. This stemmed from an episode when a professor, who was fond of calling me and my female peers "hijas," critiqued a draft of my work by suggesting I wrote it as if "hacking away with a machete." Instead, he suggested, I should strive to write like a skilled assassin, killing my target with the quick jab of a stiletto heel to the neck. Rejecting his violent metaphor, I offered him the process of *bordar*: study the models, prepare a flexible canvas, concentrate on the step at hand, edit errors, and acknowledge your progress.

As mi mamá says, "*Es cosa de mucho afán.*" Keep in perspective that great works take commitment, diligence, and time. Your work should complement life and bring you relief, not burden you or keep you from your other *quehaceres*.

Bordar is meditation that allows me to disconnect from the anxiety of "*el trabajo que no se ve*"—the work of teaching and writing—and to connect to the tangible work of my hands, vision, and creativity. While pulling each *puntada*, I become aware of thoughts, worries, and other echoes occupying my mind. I connect these to the metaphors I find in the process of *bordar*. By weaving this practice with the work of my academic profession, I honor the technologies passed down by my mother and my grandmothers and I find in their knowledge guidance that is not grounded in violence and competition but in creative love and humility.

PRACTICAL GUIDELINES

You can find the materials you need at a craft store or at your local swap meet / *pulga* / *remate*. *En el remate*, you can usually find a vendor who carries a variety of prestamped fabrics, needles, and threads, and the know-how she is probably willing to share. As you gain some experience, you may also choose to draw your own design, or *muestra*. Choose an appropriate fabric, preferably a natural fiber like cotton, an embroidery needle of a conformable size, a wooden embroidery hoop, and a sharp pair of small embroidery scissors.

The process of *bordar* is simple: Place the fabric on the embroidery hoop, thread the needle, pass the needle through the fabric, and repeat, repeat, repeat, repeat. . . . To learn how to do different *puntadas*, you may find a family member willing to teach you or you can access instructional videos on the Internet. Some search words include "bordado," "bordar," "puntadas para bordar," "punto de cruz," "embroidery stitches," and "cross-stitch."

Be prepared to learn from your mistakes as you experiment with fabrics and threads of different qualities. Most importantly, pay attention to what you are learning about yourself in your process of *bordar*. Do you need to finish one project at a time or do you like to have several projects of varying complexity going at the same time? How quick were you to choose a project? Did you foresee the potential complications? What thread colors drew your eye and why? What memories do these colors bring up? How generous are you with your work? Do you keep enough *bordados* for yourself? As you engage in your work, tune in to thoughts, ideas, and feelings that are brewing in body and mind. Reflect on your creation!

Luz de luz

GLORIA ENEDINA ALVAREZ

Oraciones bordadas nitidas al fondo
Corredizas y constantes
De luz a luz
    She of the waters
    In a limitless blue
    Free and constant
En azul ilimitado

    Light of light
    From light to light
La de las aguas
Multitudes de formas
    Precious liquid is your altar in
    Multitudinous forms

Luz a luz
Vidas a ella
    Light to light
    At her hem
    Lives to her
    Claim murmurs of peace

Vidas a ella
A su bastilla
Clamán murmuros de paz
   Stitch prayers neatly below

The Gift of Art

I have always been particularly close to my family on my mother's side, and since I was a child I have prepared gifts to give them on Christmas. One year, I collected all the Nescafé coffee jars my parents had gone through that year, for all my *tíos* and *tías* and my grandparents. Using liquid lead, I wrote each person's name and drew outlines of personal icons on the jars, then used stained glass paint to color them in. One of my tíos loved reptiles, so I painted a snake on his jar. On another, a ball of yarn and two knitting needles, another a butterfly, and so on. I then filled each person's special jar with chocolate kisses or licorice or some favorite candy. I glued a circular piece of red felt on top of each bright red plastic lid to cover the word "Nescafé." On Christmas morning, we placed all twelve individually wrapped jars in a decorated cardboard box and exchanged our gifts when we gathered at my grandparents' house. I could feel the warmth during that "season of giving" every time I gave each carefully crafted handmade gift.

I was the first grandchild in our family and always felt special, cared for, and cherished by my family. My mother was nineteen when I was born, and for a time we lived with my grandparents and all my mother's sisters and brothers. Therefore, sometimes it can be very difficult for me to talk about the sexual trauma that I experienced during my first year of college. I was eighteen that summer. I came home and contemplated suicide. My father caught me before I could build up the nerve to use the revolver I had found. I saw the look on his face and realized that the pain of hurting my family felt as great as the pain of rape.

My introduction to Red Road ceremonies and making *papel picado* became a foundation for my healing. My tío Pablo had built a sweat lodge at his home in El Sereno, around 1988, and the Lakota sweat lodge ceremony was a powerful experience for me. I had also started taking papel picado classes with Olga Ponce Furginson, at Plaza de la Raza, along with my mom and my tía Margaret. The sweat lodge ceremony helped me to stay humble and grateful while the cutting of paper helped me to move away from the urge to cut myself or self-mutilate. Giving the gift of space that allows one to be heard and to create can be a powerful healing force for anyone who is ignored in society, especially for women of color and those who are abused.

When I later pursued art as a career by attending ArtCenter College of Design in Pasadena, I was expertly trained, but my voice in my creative expressions had no place in the art world. When the women of Mujeres de Maiz found me in 1997, they saw my work as important and significant. I was able to converse with these women and my community using the language of art. This creative sharing literally saved my life. It was comforting to know that my work was understood and that I was not alone. Helping Mujeres de Maiz publish zines filled with women's voices that are traditionally marginalized in the arts gave me a purpose that would help to heal me. My ability to create art and bring meaning and beauty to the world helped me recover what was still precious inside me after years of feeling that this violent, polluted system had "chewed me up and spit me out."

The artwork I practice now can be described as healing sculptural mobiles. The process involves layering oilcloth with the "purity" of *amatl* paper, cutting and sewing it together to produce something awesome in the light of day, revealing shadows, suspended in time. The meditative cycle of layering, cutting, and re-creating helps me to make something beautiful in the world. My process is cerebral, instinctual, and intentional. It is inspired by ancient aboriginal symbols, ceremonies, and practices and involves the exploration, discovery, and release of feminine trauma. In the adoption and modification of images, culture is reinterpreted and passed on with the hope of offering something meaningful and beautiful to future generations.

In Christmas 2012, I used graphite and re-created an old damaged picture I had of my father and me in Acapulco. With the help of my mother, I carefully framed the rendering. My brother, his wife and kids, my parents, and my *novio-esposo* gathered that Christmas morning. When my father opened the gift in front of us, he began to cry. I never expected this response. The entire experience made us all cry and I felt the real gift of that moment. I was four when my parents were married and he's the only father I've known. He never treated me in a way that made me feel like I wasn't always "his" precious baby girl, so I love my father dearly.

For me, love is a verb that inspires expression. The process of making art soothes my soul and becomes a time when I can play and converse with the ancestors. But the most powerful healing moment in art making is when it becomes a meaningful gift for someone I love.

Joto Rituals for Healing, Self-Love, and Social Justice

EDDY FRANCISCO ALVAREZ JR.

As a politically and spiritually conscious *joto*, I believe spirituality, as others have written, is about an authentic relationship with the self, others, the world, and creation and is a commitment to social justice (Medina 1998, 2004). My own sense of spirituality comes from my Mexican, Chicanx, Cuban, working-poor, queer historical memory, my aesthetics, and my personal and corporeal sense of self. My spirituality and healing practices are rooted in my *jotería*. How I perceive and negotiate the world is anchored in my queerness, and therefore my practices are always informed by this—by joterías, *mariconerías*, and the fabulous as sacred, something we as queer people have had to work hard at—being fabulous—in the face of a Western society that deems us deviant and wants us dead. We choose to be fabulous as resistance to social and physical death, as an "act of making and narrating self" (Hyatt 2012). What may seem like pagan rituals and prayers to some, for jotería, are sacred: dancing, touching, dressing up, putting on makeup, watching or performing in a drag show, these are sacred spaces and queer world-making moments for me. My spirituality is lodged in and emerges from a place between contradiction and consciousness, multiple dualities, and layers of knowing and being that manifest themselves in different ways daily in my life. My spiritual practices are also rooted in the lingering remnants of my Catholicism, instilled in me since I was a child. Although I no longer claim Catholic as an identity, much of the ritualistic aspects of the religion are present within me still. My mother's and father's ways of praying and offering stay with me. For example, my father was a lover of the rosary, and so am I. My mother prayed to *la Virgencita* and believed that "*el que da, dios le da*," a person who gives, receives back from God. My mother's way of practicing Catholicism is a theology of justice and kindness, I believe. I follow these practices and insights as I place objects on my altar. Growing up, my Cubana grandmother had an altar to Santa Barbara in the house, which she always kept clean and clothed, with water and an apple. While she never accepted the Afro-Cuban syncretism, I know Changó was with us—always. Now my own altar and its upkeep are part of my daily practice. Xicana feminist understandings of La Virgen de Guadalupe also inform my spiritual practice. The following rituals, prayers, chant/songs, recipes, and meditations are part of my tradition and of how I practice. I follow them as practical or practicable guidelines.

Praying to La Virgen de Guadalupe, Coatlalupe, Tonzantzin
Praying to my queer ancestors
Making and maintaining altars
Dancing, alone or in a group, at home or at a club or party
Writing poems, prayers, academic articles, essays, letters, and love notes
Making art (especially collages)
Walking on the beach or making contact with bodies of water
Spending time with loved ones
Reading Gloria Anzaldúa, Audre Lorde, or other womxn-of-color feminists
Teaching, especially using pedagogy that encourages deep self-reflection in
    response to texts; seeing the classroom as a space of possibility; building
    community with my students

Gloria Anzaldúa (1999) writes, "I write the myths in me." Her essay "Tlilli, Tlapalli / The Path of Red and Black Ink" from *Borderlands* has been instrumental to me. Her ideas about the life of writing and the sacred creative process are ones that resonate with me. As a child, making art, writing, dressing up, using my imagination were ways of constructing an alternative world, as kids in general do, but as a queer kid, the imagination functions to create ways that make you belong or that glitter your world in response to the violence and dysfunction around you. I remember drawing and cutting out fashion designs, writing stories, and dressing up in mom's clothes or rags, and all those things, those memories I carry in my body, are part of my spiritual practice and inform how I see the world. Creating—the act of creating, making, piecing together—makes me feel good. I chose to go into academia because I love to write, and it is not exactly how I imagined, but I do get to write, and when I am immersed in those moments, whether I am writing a formal article or something more personal like this essay, it is a privileged moment of spiritual growth for me. Through art making, I find peace with myself, even if I am not happy with the piece or it isn't what I had conceptualized. The process is the important part. Handmade collages are especially healing. Something about slowly cutting and pasting, assembling the cutouts, choosing the colors, then gluing, the art is a palimpsest, a montage, and it holds the layers of me, of where I am at the moment, but also the intention for where I want to go. It is also a way to save memories and turn them into art.

I don't always get to practice these things in the way that makes me feel energized and cleansed. So, in many ways, this essay is also for me, to remember and to continue on the path, but also for other jotería, feminists, artists, writers, and lovers who need a place to start.

6

CREATING ART THROUGH
PROSE AND POETRY

INTRODUCTION

The writing and recitation of poetry, *flor y canto*, is a key feature of Xicanx culture. The poets of the Movimiento period wielded poetry as a means to speak truth to the community, to invoke knowledges and lifeways that survived the genocide and ethnocide of colonialism.[1] Poetry appeared, and the cadences of Chicanx/Latinx poetry flourished, in self-published magazines,[2] chapbooks, and publications by university presses, and it was on university grounds where the first three-day Festival de Flor y Canto was held.[3] Throughout the 1970s, 1980s, and 1990s, Xicana and Latina womxn wrote poetry, prose essays, and short stories fervently, publishing through smaller presses,[4] with a few breaking

---

1. I'm thinking specifically of Juan Felipe Herrera, U.S. Poet Laureate, and Jose Montoya, Lucha Corpi, Lorna Dee Cervantez, Pat Mora, among many others.

2. *Con Safos Magazine* featured poetry along with a vocabulary list of Caló, documenting the language of Mexican American working-class barrio youth.

3. Recordings can be viewed on the University of Southern California Digital Library website (http://digitallibrary.usc.edu/cdm/landingpage/collection/p15799coll79).

4. Kitchen Table: Women of Color Press, Third Woman Press, Aunt Lute Books, Calaca Press.

through to the world of New York publishing, ensuring a place for themselves within the literary production of Xicanx and Latinx culture and broadening the scope of Xicanx/Latinx studies itself, as well as other disciplines. The poets and prose writers included in this selection write from this tradition, itself part of a much older Indigenous tradition of composing songs and sharing them in public.

In "Mujer Jaguar PRESENTE!" Gloria Enedina Alvarez writes, "The words grow out of the heart and flow along the ways of our lifeblood." A lifelong poet, Alvarez speaks to the existential necessity of language to our experience here on earth. This use of poetry to speak to this philosophical truth is in line with the tradition of the "sages of ancient Mexico," who found "it the best means for communicating the essence of their thought and intuition" (León-Portilla 1992, 70). Many of the first forms of recording human thought in symbolic language were utilized for preserving wisdom, science, and knowledge related to the cosmos in the attempt to illuminate life and its meaning. The composition of poetry following this ancient Mexican tradition speaks to poetry as a path to come into a more intimate and complete relationship with the self, to decolonize ourselves, if you will, of "the sterile word play that, too often, the white fathers distorted the word *poetry* to mean" (Lorde 1996, 37).

In addition, poetry was and continues to be composed in honor of the Divine, of godhead, in honor of the many blessings this world has to offer. The writers, aware of the power of words, offer up their verses in the forms of *conjuros* and incantations. A conjuro, or conjuring, is a means to invoke a divinity, to call forth energies to intercede on one's behalf, a form of release. Xánath Caraza's "Fuerza ancestral" is a litany offered to the feminine forces of creation. She speaks to the strength of womxn in each of her stanzas, invoking the energies necessary to lead a strong life. In "Canto Ocelotl / Jaguar Incantations," visual artist Yreina D. Cervántez calls up the spirit of the jaguar to transport us to a place of ancestral memory, of ancestral wisdom, "back to the Land of the Red and Black"—a way of keeping history and ancestral knowledge, the place that can make us whole, the heart of our continent. "Canto Ocelotl" also addresses the struggles of the Maya people against neoliberalism, the denouncement of a cruel and necrophilic system. Claudia A. Mercado, in "On My Relative's Skin," acknowledges the animal's spirit from whose skin the drum she is singing with is made of, as she reflects on the medicine the tradition of singing with a drum offers her—herself a microcosm of the universe, "breaths birthing *canciones*."

Writing as a transformative process challenges the writer to put their thoughts down on paper, egging the writer on into a dialectic conversation with themselves. Journaling, as a consistent practice, then, can be about growth, for journaling is an embodied act, as Lauren Frances Guerra affirms in her meditation on writing, "Latinx Liberation." As Chicanx/Latinx womxn, we have had to write ourselves into existence, to create our own literature. In "Writing Is as Necessary as Air to Me," Xánath Caraza powerfully states, "Our writing is a part of human history." Writing affirms the decolonial imperative for a multiplicity of voices bearing witness to the conditions of our world across time and space.

Martha R. Gonzales

Mujer Jaguar PRESENTE!

GLORIA ENEDINA ALVAREZ

. . . The words grow out of the heart and flow along the ways of our lifeblood . . .
bathed in the healing light of *nana luna* . . .

. . . Words are wings
Are shadows
Are bile and rain
Fire and snow with
Honey of the day
From night to noon . . .

. . . Palabras son alas
Son sombra
Son hiel y lluvia
Fuego y nieve con
Miel de día
De tarde a noche . . .

Fuerza ancestral

XÁNATH CARAZA

Fuerza de mujer
Delicada
Que fluye en aguas rojas
Pensamientos concéntricos
Fuerza que renace
Se enreda en las copas de los árboles
Cihuacóatl

Fuerza creadora que canta
Que despierta
Que guía entre el oscuro laberinto
Que susurra al oído el camino extraviado
Que invita a vivir
Tonantzin

Latidos de obsidiana
De fuerza incandescente
De humo azul
Corazón de piedra verde
Frente a ti están

Otras vibraciones femeninas
Yoloxóchitl

Fuerza de mujer que fluye
Entre las páginas
De poemas extraviados
De signos olvidados
Entre galerías
De imágenes grabadas
Poesía tatuada en la piel
Xochipilli

Corazón enardecido
Que explota
Respira
Siente
Vive
Tlazoteótl

Montañas de malaquita
Áureo torrente matutino
Que recorre los surcos
Del cuerpo
Coatlicue

Fuerza femenina ancestral
Sobre papel amate
Que se entrega
A los intrínsecos diseños
De las frases dibujadas
Coyolxauhqui

Pensamiento de jade
Que se evapora con la luna
Que se integra a los caudalosos blancos ríos
Tonantzin

Fuerza de mujer
Del lejos y cerca
De arriba y abajo
Del dentro y de fuera
De ciclo eterno
Fuerza dual
De cielo de granate
Cihuacóatl, Tonantzin
Yoloxóchitl, Xochipilli
Tlazoteótl, Coatlicue
Coyolxauhqui
Guirnaldas de flores blancas las celebran
Plumas de quetzal adornan las cabelleras
Las abuelas creadoras cantan
Al unísono en esta tierra
Fuerza femenina, ancestral

—POEMA INCLUIDO EN CARAZA ET AL. (2012)

Writing Is as Necessary as Air to Me

XÁNATH CARAZA

I need to write every day. *Necesito escribir todos los días.* I need to release my hold on time, as if in meditation, and write. Being a *mujer* is something that motivates me a great deal, as I truly believe that as women we need to be heard and seen more. We need more female writers. This certainly keeps me engaged. Also, I feel that I need to respond to the world in the form of a poem or short story about what I have seen, experienced, or witnessed. Our writing is part of human history. It reflects our times, our life, the political atmosphere, the beauty of a sunset, but also a war and its effects. All these elements motivate me. As a writer, I think we have the responsibility to discuss what is occurring in the world. Words are powerful and we need to use them wisely.

Writing is as necessary as air to me. This creative process is a priority in my life, of which I am mindful. I welcome what comes from my hands. When I write poetry, I simply sit, opposite my computer screen, and my fingers proceed. I allow ideas to come to life on paper or within the computer. On a different day, I edit. Some days, ideas on paper are simply ideas, but usually these become a poem. I always remember what Louis Reyes Rivera told me, "Never be afraid of the inner sounds you hear."

My journeys are present in my work. Not just physical journeys but internal, spiritual ones—they are deeply reflected on and often appear in a short story or a poem. Occasionally, I connect the geography and the space with the subject or mood of a poem. For instance, in *Sílabas de viento / Syllables of Wind* (2014), each poem is dated, and a location signals where it was written, working as an umbilical cord throughout the entire book. In *Ocelocíhualt* (2015), the opening poem, "Espuma sangrante / Bleeding Foam," is a poem I wrote in Acapulco, Guerrero, Mexico, on October 11, 2014, almost a month after the disappearance of the forty-three students from Ayotzinapa. This poem is dedicated to them. "Landing in St. Louis, MO," written on November 24, 2014, honors Michael Brown and shares my experiences of that historic evening at the airport. *Donde la luz es violeta / Where Light is Violet* (2016), my latest collection, is about my journey in Italy in the summer of 2015. Having spent two months in Italy, I mindfully wrote every day, at least a poem per day. Some days, I wrote four or five poems. The concluding poem was scripted on the plane returning home.

Ultimately, I must write every day. Writing is as necessary as air to me; *escribir es tan necesario como el aire que respiro.*

Canto Ocelotl / Jaguar Incantations

YREINA D. CERVÁNTEZ

Heart of the Mountain
Mountain of Sustenance
YAX HAL WITZ NAL, First True Mountain Place
First Mountain of Creation

Guardian,
at the womb of La Madre Tierra
Little Spirit,
Canto,
Ocelotl
Penetrate the hearts of our enemies

Copal burning
Nagualito transforming
Transport us on your flowery back
Back to the Land of the Red and the Black
Más allá
the realm of the ancestors

At the center,
Corazón Sagrado

Heart of the Mountain/Heart of the Earth
We are made whole

My mouth is filled, I taste cool jade
Replenished
At the center,
the place where we are made whole

On My Relative's Skin

CLAUDIA A. MERCADO

In the direction of the Sun
I begin
Tobacco falling like rain
Prayers
On my relative's skin
I strike the tight stretched hide
Breaking the silence
Piercing through time and space
Beating rhythmically
Cells awaken
The ancestor web
Nourishing my *corazón*
Mirroring the stars in the cosmos

On my relative's skin
I drum
A hypnotic *ollin*
Running like the four-legged
Across the fields, prairies and mountains
Breaths birthing *canciones*
Emerging from beneath the pounding hooves

Mantras de mi Corazón
Channeling visions for healings
Hands in rapture
Spirit in motion
Invoking a reflection of the source
Inside you and me

Latinx Liberation

A Meditation on Writing

LAUREN FRANCES GUERRA

Writing is an embodied act that possesses both spiritual and political power. Preparing myself to write often means the clearing of physical space on my desk, mental space in my mind, and emotional space in my heart. I find that through the act of clearing space, creative energies are better able to move and flow. I light my candle to La Virgen de Guadalupe-Tonantzin. I know that she is with me as she continues to look after all her people. I turn on the music that suits my mood— some days it is rap, some days it is classical, and some days it is salsa. With this ritual, I am then ready to begin working. May this mediation inspire and affirm that you are not alone in the struggle for liberation. Pa'lante!

From early on, I understood the power of words. Words could build up or tear down with deadly precision. I also began to notice how for many women of color, writing was a tool for survival. Not a luxury but a necessity.

I realized my responsibility and my authority to speak up. Undoubtedly, this has been one of the greatest gifts of education: to think critically and to trust in my experience. When I sit down to write, I am ever aware that I am not writing for myself but for a much bigger purpose.

There are days when the words pour right out on to the page like a raging river. Other days, I have to squeeze them out, drop by drop. In both cases, it is a part of the writing process. Nobody said it was easy. At my core, I hold on to faith in a Creator who loves all of creation beyond measure. I believe in the Spirit as a source of perseverance and inspiration—continuing to breathe new life. This same Spirit has been present from the beginning and sustains the earth's many creatures. I also hold on to belief that my ancestors possessed infinite wisdom about divinity, which is known by many names and which we may encounter in many forms.

When I write, I call on the wisdom of Latinx authors whose writing changed the course of history. I ask for their guidance and their way with words. Across time and across geographic space, Latinas have fought to be heard in a world that seeks to keep us silent. We have fought to protect our lands and our sacred knowledge and to keep our culture alive. They tried to bury us, but they didn't know we were seeds.

I call on the fierce womxn whose words have transformed me forever. From Sor Juana Inés de la Cruz: I ask for her poetic brilliance and ability to speak well of God. She embraced her intelligence as a precious gift bestowed on her. From Marcella Althaus-Reid: I ask for her unapologetic way of articulating unspoken desires. She recognized how our bodies, our sexuality, and our experience of the Divine are in fact inseparable. From Gloria Anzaldúa: I ask for her resilience in a world that continually sought to divide her in two. She, like so many of us, inhabited multiple worlds freely. She honored the beauty and ambiguity of the Borderlands.

Most importantly . . . I ask the countless unnamed womxn whose daily lives are a testament to love and justice for their communities. Calling to these women, I approach the writing task at hand. *Seguimos en la lucha, palabra por palabra, juntas.*

7

CREATING ART THROUGH DANZA

INTRODUCTION

Brown bodies of various ages, sizes, and genders, adorned in ceremonial garments or *trajes* and feathered headdresses, or *penachos*, all claiming public space
to dance, drum, and pray, are acts of decolonization of the spirit and the body.
Danza, or Mexica ritual dance, offers a return to a non-Western epistemology
that understands the power of dance, music, song, color, the body, and the drum
to lift one's prayers and gratitude to creation. *In xochitl in cuicatl,* flower and
song, drumbeat and dance, remain primary ways to commune with the Divine.

The roots of Danza Azteca lie in ancient Mesoamerica, with a resurgence
of its visibility among Chicanx people in the late 1960s and early 1970s due to
the teachings shared by visiting Mexican *danzantes* Andrés Segura and Floren-
cio Yescas. These *maestros* crossed political and cultural borders specifically to
teach "indigenous dances and spirituality to Chicanos/as throughout the United
States" in an effort to reverse the spiritual conquest begun in 1521 (Ceseña 2009,
83). Their commitment to teach danza nourished the desire erupting among
Chicanx to claim their Indigenous ancestries and construct their Chicanx Indigenous identity in resistance to the ongoing legacy of colonization. As María
Teresa Ceseña eloquently states, "Chicano danzantes took what they were given
by danza as clues about how their ancestors might have been, and more importantly, who they as Chicanos wanted to be" (81). Danza inspired the works of

numerous Chicanx artists, poets, musicians, teachers, and cultural workers, all dedicated to the construction of cultural pride and political empowerment for the Chicanx people as an original people of this continent. From danza came exposure to the Nahuatl language and Mesoamerican spiritual philosophy, opening the gates further to profound ancestral knowledge.

The attraction to danza has continued to expand with danza groups or circles now existing throughout the United States, where a critical mass of Chicanx reside. A turn to one's Indigeneity has not subsided in Chicanx communities but has increased as more of us seek healing from historical trauma and choose to live our lives in balance with the universe and all our relations. While being a danzante is not essential to claiming Indigeneity, for many Xicanx it is a pathway to understanding and to experiencing themselves as Indigenous people.

Now commonly seen at community cultural events, danza has become familiar to many North Americans, yet still the profound spirituality and cultural identity underlying danza remain not fully understood. As María Figueroa writes, "How does one describe feeling the presence of the divine once your bare feet caress *la madre tierra* during an *ofrenda*? How does one explain that each step is a word, a syllable composing spiritual language?" (2014, 40).

In the sixteenth century, Fray Diego Durán (1971), in Mexico, wrote about the great civility of the Mexica people, as he observed the following:

> In each of the cities, next to the temples, there stood some large houses which were the residences of the teachers who taught dancing and singing. These houses were called Cuicacalli, which means House of Song. Nothing was taught there to youths and maidens but singing, dancing, and the playing of musical instruments.... Attendance at these schools was so important.... The Houses of the Dance were splendidly built and handsomely decorated, containing many large, spacious chambers around a great, ample, and beautiful courtyard, for the common dance.... Young people took great pride in their ability to dance, sing, and guide the others in the dances. They were proud of being able to move their feet to the rhythm and of following the time with their bodies in the movements.... The dance they most enjoyed was one in which they crowned and adorned themselves with flowers. A house of flowers was erected for the dance on the main pyramid at the temple of the great divinity Huitzilopochtli. They also erected artificial trees covered with fragrant flowers where they seated the goddess Xochiquetzal. During the dance some boys dressed up as birds, and others [dressed] as butterflies descended [from the trees]. They were richly decked with fine green, blue,

red, and yellow feathers. These youths ascended the trees, climbing from limb to limb, sucking the dew of the flowers. (289–96)

The pride and enthusiasm for communal song and dance documented by Durán resonates with the affection and passion that the contributors to this chapter carry in their hearts and bodies as they reflect on the power of danza in their lives.

Luis Salinas, in "Queering Mi Palabra," reveals the power of danza to liberate their queer body, mind, and spirit. Participating in a circle "where we were all equal members . . . [and] my queerness was not an issue" enabled Luis "to discover new possibilities . . . to decolonize the policing of my body." Through their beautiful narrative, we are able to accompany Luis on their journey to dance as a "queer Paloma . . . without judgment."

Issa Linda Arroyo also opens her world of danza as she recounts the story of her journey back to herself through danza. "I soon knew without a doubt in my mind that danza had opened its doors to me." Offering an intimate gaze into the protocol required in her role as Malinche, the sacred fire carrier, unveils the ethic of loving responsibility she carries into all her relations. For both Luis and Issa Linda, danza emerges from their hearts, bodies, and minds as they honor the directions, the elements, the sun, the earth, and the ancestors and as they become the paloma, the deer, the mariposa . . . the shooting stars. And making the trajes for danza, as described by Patricia Juárez, emerges from the deep spiritual communion she has with sacred cosmic energies, speaking and inspiring her to create her garments, or her "wearable prayers."

Lara Medina

Queering Mi Palabra

LUIS SALINAS

When we dance, we touch the essence of who we are and experience the unity between spirit and matter.

—THE FOUR-FOLD WAY

I led my first *danza* at the summer solstice ceremony. I had been dancing for two years, but I did not know many danzas. At the solstice ceremony, I led "La Paloma," a danza that gave me the courage to first dance during practice after two months of observation. People would ask me, "Why aren't you dancing?" I would shrug and look down, feeling my face red hot with embarrassment. Hilda, our *maestra*, would say, "*Dejenlo, el tiempo le dirá cuando.*" I remember the rattles, my body moving left then right, spreading my arms like wings, feeling the air as I twirled left then right again, with freedom to embody la paloma, while looking around at others to not lose my steps. As time went by, I understood danza as more than exercise, as a way of life that teaches spiritual and physical discipline, builds character, creates community by respecting others: their danza, their *palabra*. Palabra in Spanish means "word," yet palabra within danza is more than a word, it is the expression and energy that comes from the heart, and it is transmitted outward with and for the community. Palabra connects the body, mind, and spirit to express or create sacred prayers through our voices, dances, and art.

When I attended my first practice, I was separated from my spirituality. I had not found a community that could accept all of me, including my queer self. But in this new space with elders, families, college students, youths, professionals, activists, day laborers, and queer/trans folks, we were all equal members. The community's greeting ritual took place at every practice. As people walked in, they would walk around the imaginary danza circle, stopping to greet each person until they had greeted everyone. They would then find a space against the wall, between other community members, and start preparing for danza. I was greeted at every practice and freely conversed while we put on our danza armor or garments or stretched our bodies. I began building relationships with the *danzantes*; my queerness was not an issue. They called me "two-spirit."

The two-spirit members led me to discover new possibilities of my true self. Our queer bodies moved effortlessly during the practice, embodying each danza. We did not fear our bodies moving flamboyantly, exaggeratedly. We interpreted the danzas beautifully, with no one to judge us. Through my two-spirit *familia*, I learned to decolonize the policing of my body. Robotic mannerisms and self-control fell off my body piece by piece as I danced. The tensions on my stiff body disappeared. I no longer felt restrained, but light, like *ehecatl* (wind), *mazatl* (deer), or *atl* (water). Through these danzas, my queer body reconnected to my spirit, feeling liberated, ephemeral, and blissfully spiritual.

The first ceremony I attended I was dressed in my regalia, with my *chachayotes* on my shins and my feathered *copilli*. I made my regalia of white manta and beads I had bought at the downtown fabric district. At that time, I did not understand Mexica philosophy and spirituality or that many danzantes created their regalia with symbols that connected to the deities, nature, animals, or saints. Still, I was proud of my two-piece *traje*. Although a simple garment, it fit nicely, and it meant a lot to me. This was my first time sewing and creating a traje. There was no symbol on the manta, except for a border design in a multicolored yarn to reflect my identity. I earned the *chachayotes* through my commitment and hard work in continuing on this Red Road of life. These animal skins with thevetia tree pods attached that wrap around our ankles and sometimes wrists were a gift. As a community, we cleaned the pods carefully, leaving only the shell. We then punctured holes in the animal skin and cut and knotted strings to loosely tie the chachayotes to the skin, letting them hang and clatter with each other. Everyone's regalia was different in style, structure, and colors. This is how we shared our inner selves with one another and how we connected to our ancestors during the sacred time of danza. I was a warrior, but not by heart; I still had much to learn.

Once, during a ceremony, I got tired and left the circle before the ceremony ended. *Mi maestro* scolded me for leaving the circle too early. I had taken my energy, my presence, and as a result, created an imbalance. At the ceremony of the summer solstice, I danced from 10:00 a.m. to 2:00 p.m. without a break. I woke up at 5:00 a.m. for the sunrise ceremony. I stood alongside other *compañerxs*, with our rattles and drums facing the sunrise, hearing the early birds sing and fly to the newly bright sun. By the early afternoon, I was exhausted. The ceremony was almost over, but I could not yet stop. I still had it in me to keep going; I just had to keep a steady pace. I could not move too fast or too slow. There were elders dancing who were just fine. I remember my teacher saying to dance at the pace of the heart and I would be able to dance until the end of the ceremony.

When a danzante finished their palabra, their dance, the *capitán* asked for more palabra and came to me to lead my prayer, my danza. I did not want to at first, but to deny palabra is disrespectful to the ceremony and the energy of the ancestors. I walked to the center and stood in front of the smoking *ombligo*, where our prayers go to our ancestors. It was my turn to lead. I chose La Danza Paloma. I danced as if I were a paloma, a queer paloma. Everyone followed my moves without judgment. I led my queer palabra.

Prayer in Motion

ISSA LINDA ARROYO

My life as a *danzante* started in the city of San Francisco. It was my reward for choosing to live the life I had always dreamed of, where I dared to be myself. In San Francisco, I learned there ARE NO COINCIDENCES and that a spiritual existence means following your heart and believing your inner voice when it tells you YOU CAN. "*La danza abre muchas puertas pero cada quien lo vive de diferente manera,*" said a danzante I met the first night I arrived in the city. I didn't know it at the time, but danza had embraced me and chosen me to walk through its doors, patiently showing me the steps and allowing me to discover its many facets through its drumbeat, pounding *ayoyotes*, smell of copal, movements in unison, unspoken energy, warrior cries, ancestral presence, sacred smoke, cantos, *alabanzas, sonajas, atuendos, fuego, plumas, toque de caracol,* four directions, *mandolinas y con el permiso del rostro de tu corazón.* It showed me a world I didn't know existed.

There is nothing that you can be good at without practicing constantly. The same is true for danza. The first night I arrived at the Mission Cultural Center, I was overwhelmed with the sound of the drums, *los huehuetls,* which represent the heart of the group and the ancestors. I had to fight with myself not to get caught up in my emotions. The smell of copal and the sound of the danzantes' ayoyotes changed my mood instantly. I had to pay attention, I had to take it seriously. Something inside me, THAT VOICE, told me that here there would be no words, no explanation no theories—just FEELING. Feel it, feel it, feel it, and then came THAT SOUND. Dear God, that sound. It took everything I had not to cry. The hair on my arms stood straight up as I heard the drum, el huehuetl, the heart of danza. "*Sigue a quien quieras, allí te van a echar la mano*," yelled Guerro. I knelt to the sound of the concha, opening each direction as the circle formed. I stood there and tried to follow the person in the middle leading the danza. I soon knew without a doubt in my mind that danza had opened its doors to me lovingly. I only needed an open heart. Lucky for me, this was something I possessed perhaps in abundance.

My time as a danzante in Mixcoatl Anahuak was a discovery of prayer in motion, *el Guerro* called it "*un rezo corporal.*" Pray using every breath, carefully marking every step and utilizing every drop of will and *ganas* I could muster. I found myself looking deep into the smoke placed in the middle of the circle, the drumbeat keeping me strong. For me, the louder and stronger the drum, the deeper I could go into myself. This experience was empowering, the closest I'd ever come to feeling magic, for lack of a better description. The longer I danced, the stronger I felt. I was jumping high in the air, clicking my ankles because I was a *venado*. I was shooting arrows from a crouching position into the sky because I was Apache. I could SEE the arrows—sometimes they were lights, like shooting stars. Sometimes I would pray so hard, with clear intentions, that sometimes my thoughts were interrupted by THAT VOICE.

I nervously tried to follow whomever I could, and I reminded myself that these movements, the circle formation, and the drumbeat are all part of a tradition that dates back thousands of years. There was SOMETHING there for me that I had to be open to receiving. During my two years in San Francisco I began to feel a connection to an intense energy that I believe was brought on when the group was in sync with one another. We would dance together, giving all of our strength and breath to the movements. I would sometimes open my eyes during an intense danza and see some of the other men and women so concentrated in their prayer that I'd close my eyes again and try to reach the same level of intensity and oneness with the group. I learned that I was able to speak to Creator directly and unequivocally. The harder and stronger I danced, the more I felt I could connect with Creator.

In search of that SOMETHING, I moved to Mexico City, where danza showed me to embrace my element, *el fuego, tletl*. I learned that fire speaks loudly and needs to be seen and heard. It can be volatile, and it attracts light and dark. El fuego protects the danzante and the energy of the group. As a *zauhmadora*, being impeccable feminine warrior energy meant greeting each danzante humbly and gratefully. The rules of when and how to hold your *popxcomitl*, what direction you start with, how many times the *atecocoli* is blown, when you're supposed to stand, turn, raise, kneel (always to your left), the names of the directions, how to open and close, what colors for each direction, how much water, who does what (can't step over the *ombligo*, only the zauhmadora is allowed to pass that way), how to find the east without a compass, where and when you shouldn't take your *popxcomitl*, what to do when visiting other groups, keeping an eye on *la puerta*, the *permiso*, and most importantly, keeping my fire lit—all of these rules and ways overwhelmed me. It was like a new language that I couldn't remember grammatically, kind of like speaking Spanish in pocha. It made me uncomfortable to think that people thought I was capable in terms of this aspect of my duties as a zauhmadora. The other side though, the FEELING side of this invisible magic, and the inner dialogue was an undeniable connection to my Mother Earth and to el Creador. I FELT the fire. It spoke to me little by little.

When a person enters a danza circle, in some groups they are welcomed with copal by the zauhmadora. The person who carries the sacred fire can also be referred to as a *malinche*, the *popxcomitl*, a *copalero*. The zauhmadora greets the danzante or visitor with the smoke and guides this person to feel welcomed and protected in the group. The zauhmadora is also the keeper of the energy in the circle. We try to make sure that the energy flows so that everyone in the group can FEEL. My responsibility as a zauhmadora was a privilege and an honor. I would get there early, wearing my long skirt, always grateful to be of service. As a zauhmadora, I could do what always comes so naturally to me, keep people together. I could remember the names of each danzante, their children's names and even the names of their pets if they came along. I was the first to arrive and the last to leave as a general rule. I greeted and said goodbye to everyone with a kiss on the cheek, as is the custom in Mexico.

One of the greatest honors as a zauhmadora and danzante has always been meeting *abuelos* who are still standing tall as danzantes. The white *canas* in the group are like an instant reminder of those who've endured, those who pass on these sacred traditions. Each person and the energy they bring to the circle is valuable, be it heavy from a week of toil or bright from personal accomplishments; in the circle it intertwines. There the sacred smoke silently cleanses the spirit of each danzante, elegantly and unobtrusively. In Mexico City, a girl named Yei taught me a song that has become an anthem for me about living life as a danzante. As a final thought I leave you with this prayer:

> *Danzan los años, danzan y los caminos nos ponen pruebas, pruebas de fuego, pruebas duras batallas y decisiones. Espíritus protectores y mis ancestros van de la mano. Cuiden de mi energía mis emociones mis relaciones.*

Wearable Prayers

Danza Ceremonial Trajes

PATRICIA JUÁREZ / CHICUEYI COATL

"That's a very beautiful *traje!*" Many people have told me this, referring to my ceremonial dresses. Cheerfully curious, some ask, "Where do you get all these ideas?" I just shyly smile.

How can I convey that it is not me who is trying to "get ideas" from somewhere? Instead, torrents of feelings come to me in many forms without my asking. These feelings come to me through dreams, while in ceremony, while practicing *teomania* (Anahuacan meditation), while working with my beloved obsidian mirror, while offering water in a sweat lodge, while working with the sacred fire, while performing a *limpia*, while sharing sacred Anahuacan knowledge, while praying through danza with my whole body.

It is not me at all; it is the sacred cosmic energies that come and flow through me and push me, literally, to start working on a new design, a new dress, a new *maxtlatl*, a new skirt, a new huipil . . . a new skin, a new wearable prayer.

Nimitzamaka campeka tlen noixayol, te ofrendo mis lágrimas, I offer my tears to you, beloved sacred energies. It is then, when those energies talk to me, not in English, not in Spanish, sometimes in Nahuatl, most of the time in feelings, sensations, sounds, *titzahuitl* (omens). Sometimes, my Westernized mind takes over and wants me to find a "logical" reason for this. Luckily for me, a dream comes to the rescue and commands me to "not give in to 'logical reasoning,' to not waste my time. You should now speak through your *maitl* (hands), through your *yollotl* (heart), through the *ayatl* (fabric), through the *nextiyol* (design), through the symbols." I then pour all of me into feeling as deeply as I can.

What is it you want me to say? Do you want me to talk about the old energy of love and danza? Ah! A Huehuecoyotl dress it is then! Wait, somehow, the sensations I'm feeling point me to the Obsidian Butterfly, ah!!! An Itzpapalotl maxtlatl then! Soon, the Mixtec mom Matlactli-ihuan-Ce-Atl (11-Water), born in 1100, demands me to pray for her and her son, Chicueyi-Mazatl (8-Deer), Jaguar's Claw. A new ceremonial traje with their symbols is in order. Tlahuiz-calpantecuhtli (known as Venus) has spoken to me, too, with such intensity and clarity that I'm hopelessly in love with it to the point that I wear its symbol on my chest on at least two ceremonial trajes.

Being the recipient of all these feelings makes me pray every day at my *momoxtli* (altar), through my dreams, through the obsidian mirror, may the energies put me on the path of healing.

Sacred energies, dreams, torrents of passion and love for the sacred cosmos; Mixtec moms whispering in my ears; Huehuecoyotl, the Old Coyote, inviting me to dance with him; Itzpapalotl, the Obsidian Butterfly, demanding me to connect with her through her symbol while praying for us all. Tlahuizcalpante-cuhtli, the Morning Star, seducing me in the early hours while facing the east.

Is this easy to understand? No! All this is meant to be felt, not to be under-stood. So, as long as I allow myself to feel what Ipalnemohuani Tloke Nahuake, the Sacred Cosmic Energy for whom we all live, gives to someone like me, a simple *cihuatl*, a *mujer*, a simple *macehualli*, a simple human being, I just accept all this and kneel down. And as I cry and pray, I move as quickly as I can to try to find the perfect *ayatl* (fabric) for the specific prayer that has been requested of me. OMETEOTL.

8

COMMUNING WITH OUR DYING AND OUR BELOVED DECEASED

INTRODUCTION

Assisting and being present for the dying, or transitioning, process offers a profound opportunity to experience Death as a teacher, healer, and loving receiver-spirit. Likewise, remaining in communication with our beloved deceased provides us with the nurturance, guidance, protection, and knowledge that we need to sustain ourselves in our experience of living, "as death brings another kind of wisdom that they [our dead] want to share with us" (Iféwarinw 2018). Mesoamerican and African Indigenous ancestral wisdoms teach us that the veil between the lands of the living and the lands of the dead is permeable, that the veil can be lifted or penetrated so that the dead may visit to assist the living (Garciagodo 1998; Somé 1999). Likewise, the restless dead may return to receive assurance, recognition, and possibly forgiveness so that they may continue peacefully on their spirit journey. In contrast, modern Western thought and practice have created a disconnection between the living, the dying, and the dead. We are taught to conveniently distance ourselves from the dying and, ultimately, to fear death. Many of us feel awkward around those who are facing the imminent possibility of death. We often lack words to express our sadness and discomfort. And once no longer visible, the dead become powerless in our lives. We often do not teach children about the reality of death. Decolonizing our relationship with death is central to living life fully. Our Indigenous ancestors knew that sustaining our relationships with our dead is central to our well-being and is a responsibility based on reciprocity. We remember our dead, and, in return, they renew the living.

In this section, we hear from the voices of those who have experienced deep healing through the process of assisting the dying and from those who have learned the healing power of annually honoring their dead through the tradition of Días de los Muertos. We also gain from the insights of those who have opened their hearts to the various ways in which their dead remain in contact during times of need or simply to offer "the Embrace of the infinite," as Gloria Enedina Alvarez writes in her poem "Ofrenda." Sybil Venegas eloquently shares the "healing sessions" she offered to her mother during the final stages of dementia, when her mother was in her late nineties. The spirit and healing knowledge of Sybil's already deceased grandmother, a *curandera*, along with Sybil's own shamanic energy training, assisted her in helping her mother peacefully release her hold on life. Sybil's integration of Catholic prayers with Eastern energy healing and Mesoamerican ritual practice reflects the inclusivity of *nepantla* spirituality. Likewise, Alan Hicks shares his journey with his elderly mother, a journey he experienced as "the most profound blessing." His prior fear of death was transformed as he witnessed death as "the loving receiver of spirit." His honoring of the Mexican and Central American caregivers as *parteras de la muerte*, who tended to his mother and taught him what physical changes to expect, shines light on the oftentimes unrecognized, grace-filled work these womxn perform in eldercare homes.

Recognizing the signs, symbols, and messages our dead intentionally send us requires awareness that the invisible realm is as real, or even more real, than the visible (Goizueta 2002). When my own sister passed over to the spirit world, I learned and experienced that it is common for our dead to send us messages through material objects and/or in signs of nature, in our dreams, and even through people we meet at opportune times (Van Praagh 1997). It is their way of giving us the ongoing support and love we might need. Maritza Alvarez's request to her dying grandmother to appear as a bird in times of need was realized when Alvarez called out for her grandmother's help. Likewise, Patricia Rodriguez recognizes when her deceased brother helps her with difficult art constructions, just as he always did. Mystical ways intervene in our lives when our bodymindspirit acknowledges the power of the ancestors. Omar Gonzalez also experiences the power of his deceased grandmother, who, throughout his life, stood by his side, healing and guiding and now still reminding him "to take your meds, *mi'jo*." Omar's integration of his *abuela's* devotion to Guadalupe into his practice of Santería teaches us that we can choose what we want to hold on to from the faith of our elders, also a reflection of nepantla spirituality.

The passing of our elders offers us the opportunity to deeply reflect on who we really are. Norma Elia Cantú writes here of the many teachings her mother passed on to her and her ten siblings. Reflecting on the lessons she learned for survival strategies, for what the responsibility of being human means, and for the power of prayer integrated into daily life allows all of us to remember what Norma states as "the intangible cultural legacy that our elders bring us." Likewise, Theresa Torres recalls what her abuela's actions taught about the power of prayer and her grandmother's presence accessed through memory. Rossy Evelin Lima also summons the memory of how her grandmother taught her the feminine powers of the universe and how they stood in contrast to the harsh prayers of her father to the Father God. Honoring all the womxn in her family for their teachings and sacrifices moves Evelin to "bow to the indelible imprint my ancestors have in me."

The profound healing power of constructing an *ofrenda*, or altar, for the dead is described by Jocelyn Vargas and Aida Salazar. Jocelyn captures the intimacy of building the annual altar with her mother, "a bonding moment" for them both and for their ancestors. Her step-by-step description of their process illustrates how much our younger generations have embraced the authenticity of Días de los Muertos. Aida Salazar also graciously shares how the annual altar ritual of welcoming the spirit of her infant daughter on November 1, Día de Todos los Santos, helps to heal the devastating wound of losing a child. As Aida states, "Building an altar provides a space for the grieving parents to place their grief. . . . The sense of peace is palpable and all-embracing."

We conclude this section with Yreina D. Cervántez's poetry honoring the spirits of the young womxn of Juárez, victims of femicide. Yreina calls forth the Mesoamerican belief of transformation at the time of death, from body to spirit to winged creatures, and our life-force energy returning to the universe. In honoring the womxn of Juárez and their mothers, we cry with those who mourn, yet we refuse to forget. In remembering the lost ones, they and we are made whole.

Lara Medina

Ofrenda

GLORIA ENEDINA ALVAREZ

An offering
of starbursts
releases us
to receive each other
for ourselves
to know
it is the spirit
which draws us near
the Embrace of the infinite
that pulls and pulses
in each of us
The Flame
an endless flight

Una ofrenda
de nebula
nos libera
a recibirnos
para nosotros
saber

el espíritu
acercandonos
el Abrazo del infinito
tira y pulsa
en cada quien
La Llama
un vuelo sin fin

Nana's Hands

SYBIL VENEGAS

Just say, "*Padre Celestial, bendiga a . . . mi hija, Angelina; curala de su dolor y permite de que viva sin dolor.*" Or, "*Te damos gracias por tu amor y esperamos una curación rapida,*" and finish with, "*Te pedimos esto en el nombre de tu Hijo, El Sagrado Corazón de Jesús.*" God doesn't need to listen to a big oratory, okay? Be brief, like, "*Ayúdanos Padre, cúrala de este enfermedad.*"

I'm writing this from notes I took when my mother, who though suffering inter-mittently from the effects of dementia in her late nineties, recalled the teachings and healings of her mother. My grandmother, Maria de los Angeles Aguirre de Ortiz, otherwise known as Angelita, was a *curandera*. She was born in Rancho Charco Blanco, Villa de Cos, and grew up in Calera, a small town outside the city of Zacatecas, in northern Mexico. She practiced healing with her hands and prayer, and sometimes used an egg for cleansing. During the Mexican Revolu-tion, she emigrated to the United States with her husband and children and, over time, ceased to practice outside her home as a healer. By the time I, my sisters, and my cousins were born in Southern California, Angelita was elderly and blind, and when we visited with her, she would recognize us by touch, plac-ing her soft, wrinkled hands on our faces while speaking our names. Even as a child, I always knew those hands were healing hands. When we were children, my mother would sometimes offer brief reminiscences of her mother's healings, but I never heard the stories in detail until the end of my mother's life, when in her dementia she gave herself permission to remember and share the amazing details of my grandmother, the curandera.

During the time of my mother's advancing age and dementia, I was involved with studies of shamanic energy healing, which involved different modalities, including Reiki, the use of a pendulum, and purification principles and cleans-ings, including egg cleansings. It was an amazing synchronistic moment in my relationship with my mom, as I was able to not only learn from her stories about her mother's healing experiences but to also share my teachings with and practice on my mother, who guided me not only with her words but also with the spirit of my grandmother's hands, which was undoubtedly with us during these encounters.

My healing sessions with my mother would begin by clearing the space and calling on my spirit guides to help and assist me. Among those whom I called on were Our Lady of Guadalupe, Santa María de Jesús Sacramentado Venegas (also known as Madre Nati), the four directions, the spirit guides of the land, and, of course, my grandmother. I used copal incense to cleanse, which my mother responded to with familiarity, and the pendulum over her crown chakra, which produced a calming effect on my mother and put her into a trancelike state. During these sessions, my mother would speak about her past, about Mexico, where she lived as a child, and about her sisters and her mother. These were stories that revealed who she was as a child and the things that happened to her that apparently she had never shared with anyone before. The stories she shared while in this state were profoundly healing to my sister and me, as we were processing not only our own family and childhood issues but also the imminent passing of our mother.

Then, I would do the egg cleansing. I would have my mother select an egg from a carton and have her hold it in her hand while we began our healing ceremony. The egg is a symbol of the beginning of life and can be used as a cleansing tool to remove negative or dense energy. It represents our body and how we are able to be in our body and the problems we have in our body. The liquid inside the egg can cool the body by removing heat and can remove what Mexican *curanderismo* refers to as *aires*, negative emotions that can manifest into illness.

The cleansing included passing the egg on her body as well as prayer. I would take the egg and begin to rub her body, starting at the top of her head. I would make a cross with the egg and then rub the egg down the front and back of her head, continuing along her body, focusing on the chakra points and joints, all the way to her feet. As I cleansed, I recited prayers, including some of the ones my mother shared with me. Then, I would crack the egg into a clear glass of water. How the egg enters the water is meaningful. The yolk may or may not break. How the egg looks in the water is how we can read the emotional and spiritual state of the person we are healing. There can be strings of egg white around the yolk, indicating connections to past emotions that are not being let go of, or bubbles in the water, representing the people in our lives, or lines of egg white that can be shaped like organs or the spinal column, or lines rising up in the water, representing higher strivings and spiritual guides in one's life. After reading the egg, it is important to discard both the egg and the water by flushing them down a toilet or sink or by burying them in the earth and to wash your hands immediately afterward. After the cleansing, it is also important to check in with your recipient. In my mother's case, she was often very calm afterward, and due to her advanced age and the depth of processing she was experiencing, she often simply went to sleep.

My mother passed in February 2014. She was four months shy of her hundredth birthday. While I performed egg cleansings on other members of my family, my mother was my continuous *client*, and our healing ceremonies together at the end of her life were some of the most important and intimate times I shared with her. My grandmother was there as well, guiding my hands as I helped my mom, her daughter, as she transitioned from this world.

Death as a Peaceful, Loving Teacher

ALAN HICKS

Fear has become the prevailing emotion in our relationship with death in modern cultures. We want to deny death's inevitability. We fear letting go of the things we have become attached to: our own lives, families, friends, accomplishments, homes, and whatever material things we have accumulated. It seems fear of death breeds fear into life itself.

Witnessing the last months of my mother's life, including her last breath, was likely the most profound blessing of my life. She was ninety-three and had lived a full life. Described as such by all who knew her, my mother was a sweet and graceful woman. And she was as graceful in death as she was in life.

She lived in the full-care facility of the assisted-living residence where my father also had an apartment. Although he visited her regularly three times a day, my father had difficulty witnessing my mother's declining health. In her last years, family came to visit on Mother's Day, her birthday, and the usual holidays—Christmas, Easter, Thanksgiving. We would have a special dinner down the hall from her room. She had difficulty verbalizing very much, although she was quite aware of everything happening around her. We might say something to her, but she struggled to respond. So, we conversed among ourselves. She ate what she could, and we would help her back to her room. Everyone felt awkward and helpless.

My mother was blessed to be in a nursing home with a staff that truly cared for her. The nurse's aides had the most intimate relationship with my mother, sharing with her stories of their lives, even taking her down the street to the Baja Cantina, where they held their celebrations when one of the staff had a birthday or when they had other occasions to get together. The nurse's aides had been including my mother in these little celebrations for years, even though none of my family, even my father, had known about these events. None of us had even noticed the pictures on my mother's wall of her sitting with them at the cantina!

The aides were the ones who dressed her when she no longer could dress herself. They bathed her; helped her to the bathroom; fed her, noting how much she ate and drank; and took her to the hairdresser, to physical therapy, and for massages, which she loved. And my mother would share one of her jackets or a piece of jewelry with them when they went out on some special occasion.

When I felt my mother had only months to live, I began to visit her weekly for what turned out to be six months. I decided to stay by her bedside in the afternoon, after eating lunch. If she could not speak, that was okay. I might share a story. Or just watch one of the old movies from the 1940s that she liked. Massaging her shoulder, I would notice my mother's breathing change from labored breaths to ones of relaxed relief.

Spending time each week with her, I began to know the women who spent the most intimate and caring time with my mother. Women who before had seemed practically invisible. These women told me things about my mother I had never known, insights into her life that had been hidden from me.

I got to know how they cared for her in her last years and during the process of dying. They were all from Mexico and Central America. I came to see them as midwives, but in this case, midwives who work with the dying and who support a personal, loving process to cross the bridge to death—*parteras de la muerte.*

They taught me what to expect and how to give both physical and emotional comfort through each step of the process. In the final hours of life, my mother's circulation would slowly constrict. Her feet would become cold, even as her hands felt like they were on fire as they turned purple. Her knees would turn blue. Her breathing would become dry. Her pulse would continue to increase in her final days, running at 120 beats per minute, the rate of strenuous exercise. Even accelerating to 140 as her heart struggled to bring oxygen to her body in an effort to hold on to life.

On the morning of my mother's final day, one of the nurse's aides texted me a song she said my mother liked and suggested that I play it for her. I didn't play it right away. We had been sitting on her bed, watching her struggle to breathe.

She had not been conscious for more than a day, having been given morphine and Ativan.

As I noticed her breathing become more difficult, I decided I should play the song. It was Psalm 23, "The Lord Is My Shepherd." I hit play and put the phone up to her ear. I could tell she was having a reaction to the song. As soon as the song finished, she passed. Her mouth opened and closed a couple of times, as if she wanted to speak but no longer had the breath to do so. And then a look of peace came over my mother's face, the peace of letting go. It was like the song opened a door for her that she could pass through without fear. Her spirit had been delivered into the arms of Death, which I saw as the loving receiver of spirit.

The parteras then asked us to leave as they washed her body, after which we said our final goodbyes to my mother. Someone from the mortuary came to pick up her body later that evening. The family then gathered for dinner in the dining room, and we told stories of my mother. At first, my father and my brother did not want to stay to eat, but as we told more stories, everyone's appetite began to come back. We had to get a larger table to accommodate all of us.

Sitting at the table, I felt both that a birth had taken place and also a shift in myself. Death seemed to be a paradox. I knew she was physically gone, but it did not feel like she would ever really be gone. When death finally came, it seemed peaceful. Being in witness so intimately to her passing allowed me to feel comfortable with death.

In reflecting on how I experienced my mother's death, I offer this thought: that modern civilization has disconnected us from death as a human experience. I felt the absence of the wisdom of traditions to guide me in really appreciating all the things that death can teach us about life. Death reminds us that we are human, rooted in nature and in the earth. Rites of passage, if observed at all, no longer give the deep sense of what a major life transition means for all of us within a family or community. So, we just move on, disconnected.

While modern Western medicine can help us live longer and can cure many things, it cannot overcome the inevitability of death. Morphine helped my mother be free of pain on her final day. Modern medicine prolonged her life, but it did not prepare her for death.

The parteras de la muerte know death intimately, and they provided the care that during my mother's last years no pharmaceutical protocol, medical technology, or surgical procedure could have done in preparing my mother for her transition to death. These women did not have degrees. Their knowledge did not come from any school or textbook. Their training as nurse's aides was influenced by their own life experiences, received from their families and communities of Mexico and Central America, and was still connected to traditions of their cultures. Through their words and actions, I was able to see Death as the loving receiver of spirit. Yet the wisdom carried by these women is the least recognized, and they are the lowest paid workers in the medical system.

As death reminds us that we are human, how has the wisdom inherent in nature-based spiritual traditions developed over thousands of years of human experience become diminished? Looking back through the history of Western civilization, I can't help but think of the terror of the Inquisition, exalting doctrine above all, and the following "Age of Reason" that buried the wisdom of our humanity under new structures of science and reason. A consequence was losing our connection with the natural cycles of life.

These developments began roughly eight hundred years ago, so for those of European descent, this represents some forty generations. Colonization spread the suppression of ancient spiritual traditions in the Americas. Valuing these traditions can help us reconnect, not as something to be copied but rather to be remembered in our collective experience. We were all deeply connected to the natural world at one time—every race and every culture. We are all kin in our journeys toward the inevitability of death.

The hospice movement, which has been growing in popularity over the last thirty years, is an example of the growing desire to become more humanly connected to the process of dying. As we evolve as a species, will we recognize and remember that we are first human beings? Can we bring our rational minds into balance with our intuitive, empathic, compassionate, and feeling natures?

Thank you, parteras de la muerte, for preparing my mother for her graceful death and for delivering her to the loving receiver of spirit-Death. And for showing me that Death is a teacher of life.

Ancestral Ties

MARITZA ALVAREZ

My prayers are about asking my ancestors for guidance. My ancestors speak to me in my dreams and through symbolism in this material world. When I went to honor my grandmother, who passed four years ago, she had asked that her ashes be given to the ocean near the town where she was born. So I went to honor her and have a closing ceremony. It meant getting up at five o'clock in the morning to go out into the middle of the ocean. I was out there on a lancha driven by a townsman, and at one point I realized we were out there alone in the middle of the ocean, and I began to feel uneasy. So I immediately prayed to my grandmother to protect me. And before she died, I had asked her to please come to me in the form of a bird when I need her. Soon after I asked for her help, a bird landed on the tip of the lancha, and it stayed there the entire time we were out on the ocean. This is part of what we have, spirit comes in many forms, and it reminds us of the power of our ancestors.

The Rose in My Heart

PATRICIA RODRIGUEZ

My painting (plate 9) was inspired by my brother, Willie Montgomery. Willie passed on November 19, 2014, from liver cancer. He had served as a soldier and medic in the Vietnam War, handling all types of injuries and death. The rose represents his kindness and generous heart for those who suffered.

Willie had a kind heart as a young boy, always thinking of others first. His friends were lifelong friends, and they told me stories of how he continued saving lives from burning cars or motorcycle accidents long after he came home from Vietnam.

He was a fine carpenter at the San Francisco Veterans Hospital, where he was known for his special skills in solving difficult construction problems. He received many awards for his creativity and problem-solving. And for me, he was my inspiration and my adviser on helping me solve difficult art projects and artistic designs for large art installations for museums, galleries, and street-art projects.

He continues to be a spiritual guide to his friends and me. Today, I still ask Willie for assistance. Before going to bed, I tell him about my giant structure made out of recycled materials and ask him how to hold it together so it can stand six feet tall on a truck; in the next few days I figure it out. I know then that Willie has intervened and has not forgotten to assist me, just like before.

Showing Me the Path Home

A Poz, Third-Gender Xicanx Constructs a Triad of the Divine Feminine

OMAR GONZALEZ

[*1999 . . . Austin, Texas, the outskirts of Aztlan . . . Occupying the* nepantla *space between life and death, I feel La Muerte's breath on my neck. As I begin my journey to Mictlan, my grandmother intercedes. Having just transitioned to the other side, she is not ready for me to join her. For the second time in my life, she does not allow La Muerte to claim my soul. I recover from the pneumocystis pneumonia and have not developed another AIDS-related illness since, yet La Muerte hovers in my shadow and in my dreams.*]

At midday and midnight, the triptych of Oschún / Guadalupe-Tonantzin / Santa Muerte prod my psyche, *take your meds, mi'jo.*

One Isentress, one Prezista, one Norvir, one Escoby—a variation of the host for people living with AIDS, keeping the disease at bay.

In each pill I ingest, I invoke the lives lost to the epidemic and the lives who fought for these medications.

Growing up in the pueblo of Ysleta, Texas, an Indigenous community annexed forcibly by the city of El Paso in the 1950s, I never strayed from my maternal grandmother's protection. Hearing stories involving her practices of *curanderismo* was not foreign to me. A devotee to Guadalupe, yet never entering a Catholic church except for funerals, my grandmother's practice of curanderismo was as normal to me as her *costillas de puerco en chile colorado* were famous in our neighborhood.

One blustery day, when I was an infant, I became ill. Through tears, my mother informed my grandmother that I had only days to live. Remaining calm, my grandmother insisted that my mother leave me with her. Knowing not to defy my grandmother, she acquiesced. What my grandmother did to cure me she took to the grave. At her funeral twenty-six years later, several people commented to me that had I not come along when I did, she would have died of a broken heart because of my grandfather's death two years prior to my birth.

Just as she taught me her secret combination of spices to add to the dried New Mexico red chile to make a perfect plate of chile colorado, she passed her devotion to the Virgen de Guadalupe to me. Even though I was the only cisgender male in a household of cisgender women, I was never considered *el rey*, but my mother constantly policed my gender as my *jotería* became more visible. (Was it my lip-synching to Donna Summer, my pretending to be Wonder Woman, or my infatuation with the lead singer of Duran Duran, Simon Le Bon, that did it?)

As I came out in my teens, and after attempting suicide because of my confirmation teacher's pronouncement that gay people are destined for hell, my distance from the Catholic Church grew, as did my fascination with the supernatural with my discovery in the 1990s of Santería, especially because of a dear friend's stories of his family's practices. Subconsciously, I knew I was destined to be part of the Lucumi tradition.

Over a decade later, I meet my future *padrino* at a National Association for Chicana and Chicano Studies conference. He informs me he is starting a "house" (a Santería clan) and is eager for me to begin my journey into the mysteries of this belief system that is a syncretism of the ancient religion of Ifá and Catholicism—a symbol of the many survival strategies practiced by African slaves taken to Cuba. Each ceremony (of which I cannot divulge too many details) brings me closer to *ashé*, a divine state of grace apportioned by the orishas (saints). I learn my father is Obatalá, the ruler of the head, wisdom, and learning. My mother is Oschún, the river orisha who represents love, beauty, and sexuality. I receive my elekes (beaded necklaces that represent the major

orishas: Eleguá, Obatalá, Oschún, Yemayá, Changó, and Oyá) in my first initiation. I receive the warriors next—Eshu Eleguá, Osún, Ochosi, and Ogún—who
will further protect me. Finally, I "crown" or "make saint"—a weeklong ceremony signifying my rebirth. Over seven days, my *madrina* and *padrino* treated
me like an infant, an experience simultaneously traumatizing and liberating.

During my *Itá*—a reading toward the end of the seven days—Oschún informs
the elder via Eleguá (the messenger between the orishas and Oludumare, the
supreme being, and humanity, and who is analogous to Hermes and Mercury)
that my grandmother has been working through her energy as my guardian.
Thus, I propitiate Oschún daily with a constant supply of sunflowers, raw honey,
sweet potatoes, pumpkins (when they are in season), and trinkets of gold (or
that *look* like gold—she knows I'm on a grad-student budget!), five yellow candles, and anything in the colors of gold and orange.

One of the most consoling aspects of the Santería tradition is that it does
not demand the devotee to renounce other belief systems. Before I undertook
any of the ceremonies of Santería, I asked my future padrino if I would have to
stop my devotion to Guadalupe-Tonantzin. He chuckled and responded that
the belief system known simply as "the religion" *no es celosa*, it is not a jealous
lover. Many devotees syncretize multiple belief systems, but they never neglect
the eggun and the orishas, particularly Eleguá, who must always be offered his
candies and toys. You do not want Eleguá to be angry—he can stop all magic and
can open the path to Ikú, Death. Guadalupe-Tonantzin remains a focal point in
my spirituality, as the original signifier of Indigenous feminine strength.

To complete my triad of the Divine Feminine is a figure I had earlier feared—
Santa Muerte. Believing the stereotypes that she only assisted those involved in
sinister or nefarious activities, I gazed upon my own crooked obsidian reflection. As a third-gender person engaging in high-risk sexual activities in the margins, *I* was one of those sinister creatures Santa Muerte embraces and protects.
I realize that Santa Muerte does not judge those who exist in the margins; she
engages her magic when I make late-night trips to the bathhouse, when I cruise
darkened parks and alleys, and when I visit the adult bookstore in search of what
John Rechy calls my own "substitute for salvation."[1] Homeless as a teenager after
I came out, I survived as a sex worker, and although I contracted HIV from one

---

1. A recurring theme in the corpus of John Rechy, a "substitute for salvation" is the
myriad of carnal replacements for the paradise from which we are forever lost.

of my many erstwhile lovers, I acknowledge that I could have been arrested, beaten, or murdered on any one of those dark nights. Over twenty years later, Santa Muerte still protects me on those nights when my carnal desires overcome my body.

Don't forget the poppers, mi'jo . . . Take your meds, mi'jo . . . Siempre te cuidamos . . .

The hunt begins . . . never ends. Ashé.

Teachings from Mami

NORMA ELIA CANTÚ

El luto. I am still wearing black six months after my mother left us to proceed along her soul's journey. El luto comes with rituals of mourning and of putting our loved one's memory and legacy into our daily practices. El luto, a practice all but forgotten. A way of marking a period of mourning through dress that existed in our cultural practices much more so when I was a child; my mother wore it for an entire year when her mother died. I don't know if I will do the same, but for now, it feels right that I shun bright colors and even prints. Black it will be. El luto was always more than just wearing black: no television, no dancing, mirrors covered with sheets, and, most of all, a time of mourning, a time when a sadness shadow covered everything. El luto is part of our intangible cultural legacy.

When I walked into her hospital room on New Year 's Eve, Mami hugged me as tight as her frail, thin body could and whispered in my ear, "*Ya me quiero morir.*" It was a difficult lesson, to let go and allow her to proceed along her soul's path. But it is one she had prepared me for with her *consejos, su sabiduría*. The lessons continue even today, passed from one generation to the next; my mother, Virginia, learned them at her mother's knee in Texas, and my grandmother, Celia, had learned them from her grandmother, who raised her in Monterrey. So, my sisters and I inherit and learn the way of being in the world through a long line of resourceful, strong women from South Texas and Northern Mexico.

Through my own devices, mostly reading, talking, and listening to elders, I have added to this repertoire of sabiduría that my mother taught me. I have acquired much through an eclectic process of gathering information. In this brief essay, I share some of the lessons my mother taught me. I have divided them loosely into three major areas: survival strategies, learning to be a human being, and things to do to secure a desired outcome.

SURVIVAL STRATEGIES

Like others who have survived the harsh and unrelenting violence of poverty and want, my mother developed strategies for survival that she then taught to her eleven children, more by example than through specific lessons. She taught us to strive to do our best no matter what it was. She was a perfectionist. Making tortillas, crocheting or embroidering *toallitas* (doilies), sewing a dress, it didn't matter, we had to strive for perfection yet realistically know we were not perfect. After all, only God is perfect. If my embroidery or crochet or knitting project was not up to par, she would undo it and have me do it again. She would exclaim, "*Esta hecho como tus patas*," meaning that it looked as if I had made it with my feet. She didn't get angry, she didn't shout, she didn't make a fuss, she would just calmly instruct and rip the seam so I could sew it better. "*Si está bien hecho, nadie te lo puede negar*," she would admonish, in some way teaching me that my strongest tool was to do things right. "*Si otros pueden, porque tú no?*" She would ask when I had doubts about anything. She gave us confidence and believed we could do anything. Survival meant doing our best, struggling and managing to *superar* whatever adversity we faced. I have many anecdotes about this strategy—doing your best and surviving—but one that seems to have started me on my path happened on my first day of first grade. As she left me in the hands of Ms. Rogelia García, at Tomás Sánchez Elementary School, she said, "*Aprende todo lo que te enseñen*." Being the obedient daughter that I was, I did just that.

She also taught me to have a sense of confidence. When we siblings were squabbling or arguing, she would wisely answer to our griping, "*Mejor que haya un loco y no dos*." We would immediately stop being locos and behave, knowing we were not the one who was wrong!

Survival often meant battling odds that would force others to succumb, but she would have none of it and would, in a loving and firm manner, communicate that we were always to finish what we started, that we would do it as close to perfect as possible, and that we were geniuses who could do anything we wanted. The survival strategy that worked best was one of optimism and commitment.

LEARNING TO BE A HUMAN BEING

Manners mattered to my mother. "*Ser bien educada*" was paramount. When we had guests, we had to greet them with a kiss; likewise when they said their goodbyes. *Teníamos que "saludar"* and not come in *como burro sin mecate*, like a burro without a leash. Such an expression was said mostly when we had company, which was often. The key to being a good person included saying "hello," "goodbye," "please," and "thank you," and being *acomedida*—thoughtful, anticipating others' needs and doing something about it.

My mother modeled a strong sense of responsibility and attention to the needs and suffering of others—our house was always a hub for our friends and family. I was often surprised to arrive home from school to find strangers—in some cases, long-lost relatives—who had arrived to spend time with us and share our meager resources. So many times we housed relatives who were having problems. My mother made sure she did what she could to help a neighbor in need, or a relative or a *conocido* who had fallen on hard times. When, in the throes of Alzheimer's disease, she would agonize over the lack of money and ask over and over if we had paid the bills, I realized how she must've worried and suffered want as a mother of eleven with a husband who worked at the smelter and at odd jobs to make sure we had a roof over our heads and at least beans and flour tortillas.

Among her *dichos y consejos* are the following: *el mundo se acaba pa'l que se muere; vive la biblia—no hay que leerla sino vivirla; de tal palo tal astilla; no lo hurta lo hereda; dime con quién andas y te diré quién eres.*

My mother's respect for animals was legendary. She believed *los animalitos* are sentient beings who know and care; sometimes they are more obedient than children, she often told her *comadres*. In her view of the world, to be human was to care for others, be it human or animal; we are supposed to care and support one another. That was all there was to it. Our family harbored many a stray animal. We cared for strangers as well as for family and friends.

SPECIAL THINGS TO DO TO EFFECT DESIRED OUTCOMES

She would cure a baby's hiccups by placing a piece of red string on the baby's forehead with saliva. I had believed this to be an Indigenous practice until I found out that it is really Arabic. To stop gossip, or to quiet a loudmouth, she would quietly say a prayer to San Ramón: "*San Ramón, ponle un tapón*" and pray a few Our Fathers. She would counsel young women who came to talk to her about their woes to pray to San Antonio to request help in finding a life partner. Also, she trusted an age-old ritual for finding things that were lost: pray thirteen Our Fathers, and before you are done, you will find the lost object. She was a firm believer in the power of prayer to effect change. Pray to San Pancracio to find a job. When I was in Spain, in 1980, I bought her a beautifully carved San Pancracio that she would then pray to, pointing the figure in the direction of the desired job site.

The saints were her friends, and she often talked to Our Lady of Guadalupe as if she were a comadre who had stopped by for a cup of coffee. She didn't have much time to be involved with church groups as a young wife and mother, but when her children had moved out, she and my father became even more active at San Luis Rey Church. She joined the Guadalupanas, a sodality that honors Our Lady of Guadalupe. Her prayer life was strong and extended throughout the day. When my mother, like her mother before her, would sweep the front yard early in the morning, she would pray a few Hail Marys; at dusk she would sweep the backyard, and this task, too, involved prayer. My mother's commitment to the Guadalupanas was sustained throughout the remainder of her life. As a young single woman, she had belonged to the Hijas de María; as an older woman she, like many others, was active in the Guadalupanas. Such women remain the backbone of many Catholic parishes, as they are involved in the day-to-day upkeep and care of the altar, often sewing the altar cloths and then washing, ironing, and setting them on the altar. On a recent trip to a parish in Mexico, I noticed that it was the women who were in charge of preparing the space for the liturgical celebration, and I remembered my mother's comadres who performed such tasks at our church.

I am convinced that my mother had a gift for healing, although she never formally acknowledged it. She no doubt inherited her mother's insight and way of being in this world. I cannot say she was a *curandera*, a healer, but many in our community believed she could heal. They would bring a colicky baby for her to *sobar* with olive oil and *espauda* to relieve the child's discomfort. She tended to her children with home remedies and healed whatever ailed us: mumps with onion poultices, upset stomach with *te de estafiate* or *yerbabuena*, earache with a cone of newspaper that my father would light with a match, cuts with cobwebs applied to the cleaned wound, the itch of ant bites with mud. The list could go on and on. She had a *remedio* for anything but always also relied on medical doctors, especially the female doctor who delivered all but the first four of her eleven children. Mom had a special relationship with Dr. Margaret Cigarroa, and they shared crochet stitches as well as remedies. Often mom would've diagnosed the ailment correctly before resorting to an office visit. Once there, she would inform the doctor what was wrong and would suggest a cure.

The traditional knowledge my mother possessed is gone, and so are the special relationships between a doctor and her patient. Perhaps it is time to resurrect both. Writing these *recuerdos* of my mother's consejos and spiritual practice brought tears to my eyes but more importantly reminded me to honor the intangible cultural legacy that our elders bring us. With each elder who continues along the path beyond death, we lose some of that knowledge, some of that wisdom. Forever lost to subsequent generations is the cultural knowledge that they embody. Thus, it is part of my work in folklore and as a creative writer to remind us of such losses and to recuperate, or at least try to maintain alive, these expressions—many of them spiritually based and focused on the life of the spirit.

What My Abuelita Taught Me About Prayer and Memory . . .

THERESA TORRES

As I reflected on the various types of prayer I rely on to give me strength and support on a daily basis and to carry me through the dark times, I had to return to my childhood. It was my *abuelita*. I am a third-generation Mexican American, and it was my grandmother who taught me so much about *nuestra cultura* and spirituality. I keep these nuggets of wisdom, knowledge, and strength close to my heart and soul. Because what she taught me was that prayer is about life—there is no division between daily life and daily prayer, they are one and the same. She taught me that the great Good that we call God is present all around us and we are one in the great Good.

Some of my fondest memories of childhood are of getting up early in the cool, damp summer mornings and finding my grandmother working in her garden and blessing the earth with her hands and her gentle spirit of reverence and awe. In the silence of the morning, as she worked, I found her at prayer—in silence and the presence of love for all of us and the earth. She was at one with the Spirit of Good, God.

She was the ground—the foundation and the presence of spirituality for me and for our entire family. Yet, her death was even more revelatory, as she grounded her spirit in the transformation of life through dying. I was twelve at the time of her death, and she died after a short illness. Because she was so strong for most of my life, I could not envision she could be so ill or even could die. I was in denial, and while my mother tried to prepare me and console me, it was abuelita herself who showed me that her goodbye was not an end. In her death, she came to me and said her goodbye through the shared memories of our many experiences, and I felt her love and spirit go through me. She knew that her dying would be hard, but her presence was not gone—we are united in the grounding of the great spirit of Good. She also showed me the unity among those who have gone before us. Her presence and wisdom continue in my life— she has returned in dreams at important points in my life, and she continues to bless me. It is in living and even in dying that we are united in the Spirit of Great Good, so long as we love and we listen deep within. In the grounding of our lives, in the silence, we come to KNOW the wisdom and the transformative Good that exist in us and around us and in the lives of the abuelitas who have gone before us.

Conjuros

ROSSY EVELIN LIMA
TRANSLATED BY DON CHELLINI

As I lie down at night, I put my hands together and start to pray. I always forgot to pray when I was a little girl. I elevate a prayer to God, a figure of an old man, a fatherly figure; the thought of him scares me and I stop praying immediately. A chant comes to my mind in a healing voice, a woman's voice, "*Ompa Ompa A babuea Amba Amba.*" My grandmother taught me about Omecíhuatl, the creator of the universe, a curious woman who touched the monsters in the deafening night and transformed them into stars. Unfortunately, my grandmother didn't teach me how to pray. My father did—he showed me how to make a cross to cover my sinful body. After my grandmother passed away, I felt guilty praying to Omecíhuatl, raising my thoughts to reach her and turn my monsters into stars. When I realized I had nothing in common with my father's God, I closed the eyes of my imposed conscience and began to write this prayer to my grandmother, a goddess I have needed and have believed in.

My *conjuro*, or incantation, Serpiente (the Serpent) is for my grandmother's gift of knowledge. The image of the serpent is also a reference to the DNA structure, which according to behavioral epigenetics carries information about my ancestors' experiences, resilience, and strong emotions. I honor many other women in my family. My mother, who would sing to my grandfather over the phone to make him feel that she was next to him, even though they were 469 miles apart. Her voice resonated as the promise that everything would be fine, "*todo va a estar bien.*" I honor my great-grandmother Tranquilina, whose name means tranquility and symbolizes the strength many traditional Mexican women carry, an apparent docility that reigns in our communities yet builds civilizations. I honor my aunt Evelia, the oldest sister, whose visits fill our kitchen with her flavor, as my mother and my aunt Silvia sit near the table and wait for Evelia to finish preparing the food they used to eat when they still had a mother. I honor my aunt Veroila, whose voice is a decree for the protection of our personal dreams and desires, the right to defend one's hopes. I honor my aunt Silvia, who has reluctantly moved to our homeland and to survive the desolation of a new land has constructed a new home, yet for whom the past must be left untouched.

I embrace my spirituality by recognizing the sacred bond in the womanhood of me and my ancestors. I recognize the gift in each of their sacrifices, enabling my right to worship in their temples, the sanctuaries in their stories and struggles. By releasing this conjuro to my grandmother, I bow to the indelible imprint my ancestors have on me; I bow to respect and honor their struggles and the impact they've made on my own path.

SERPIENTE
INOCENCIA CRUZ

Navegadora de tierras ancestrales
conexión prístina entre el suelo y el universo.
Mujer Serpiente, lengua bifurcada
que pronuncia profecías resguardadas,
cascabeles de armonía que anuncian
nuestro derecho de cruzar fronteras
sin ser percibidas.
Mujer Serpiente, cambias de piel
como cambias de patrias
y renaces lozana
para crear futuros sigilosos
en la comunión de tu cuerpo
    invertebrado
        inquebrantable,
            indivisible
aunque dejes en el camino pedazos vivos
de tu historia.

SERPENT

INOCENCIA CRUZ

Traveler of ancestral lands
pristine connection between earth and universe.
Serpent Woman, forked tongue
pronouncing protected prophecies,
harmonious little bells that announce
our right to cross borders
without being observed.
Serpent Woman, you change skin
like you change homelands
and you are reborn self-assured
to create stealthy futures
in the communion of your body:
    invertebrate
        unbreakable
            indivisible
though you leave living pieces of your story
on this path.

Life Embracing Death

JOCELYN VARGAS

Every year, for as long as I can possibly remember, my mother and I have built an altar in late October, to be ready for Days of the Dead. I look forward to this bonding moment with my mother, a time in which we honor and remember our ancestors and loved ones. Almost every person added to our altar has been deceased since before my birth. Although there is a lack of personal encounters, I hear their amazing life stories from my living family members. Upon building the altar, I also feel a deeper connection to them, as if their presence is with me during these times. However, before facilitating this deep connection, there are some necessities involved.

Before my mother and I can build our altar, we bring out our small box with all the pictures and decorations we will be using. Typically, we have at least half the things we need to build the altar, and we purchase the other half. Some of the things we purchase include the favorite fruits or snacks of the deceased, candles, *pan de muerto* (bread of the dead), and marigold flowers. Some of the objects we already have include sugar skulls, crosses, and pictures. Upon obtaining all these objects, we begin to build our altar.

We begin by creating a base that will hold the three layers of our altar. The lower layer represents the underworld, the middle layer represents the earth, and the upper layer represents heaven. After we have created our three layers, we use tissue paper to decorate each one, or any type of cloth in any type of color. Once that has been settled, we begin to decorate each layer with its meaning.

The bottom layer is often decorated with marigold flowers, which we form into a path, and candles. According to my grandmother, the path and the candles guide the deceased to our altar. The pungent smell of the marigold flowers and the light of the candles help them find their way home. Next comes the middle layer, the earth. It is filled with all the favorite foods, fruits, snacks, and drinks of the deceased. Typically, in Mexico, many families who practice this tradition cook the deceased's favorite dishes, but my family sticks to the basics, like fruit and candy. We decorate the middle layer with all these goodies, but we leave the center empty, because that space is reserved for the bread of the dead. This bread, also referred to as pan de muerto, is a sweet bread that can be sprinkled with either sugar or sesame seeds. The interesting part of the bread of the dead is the top, which is shaped like a fragment of bones, representing the bones of the deceased. This bread is a key part of the *ofrenda* because of this deeper meaning.

The top and final layer is the one that contains the images of the deceased. The images are on the top layer because we believe their souls are in heaven, and that is exactly what the last layer represents: heaven. Though this layer, unlike the others, is reserved for photographs, we can also place candles and marigolds. In my family, we like to add glasses of water, as my grandma believes it purifies the souls of the deceased as well as quenches their thirst from their long journey to our altar. Each family creates these sacred spaces differently, with various types of objects.

Days of the Dead is celebrated every November 1 and 2, right after Halloween, but it is not a "Mexican Halloween." Although both days are in remembrance of the dead, each day is dedicated to different groups of people. November 1 is dedicated to those who passed away as babies, children, or young adults, and November 2 is dedicated to those who passed away as adults. Though the spirits of the dead return on these days, people begin prepping for the celebration a week or even months in advance. This is when the altar building begins with great excitement. Even though people in both the United States and Mexico build altars, the celebration is slightly different throughout the many different regions of Mexico. In Mexico, many families go to cemeteries and place their altars or offerings on the grave. They also clean the graves and supply them with fresh marigolds and spend time with their deceased loved ones, sometimes spending the night. In the United States, oftentimes families do not make the time to go to the cemeteries, and they are not allowed to spend the night. For many, loved ones are not buried close by. The things we have in common are creating the altar and remembering our loved ones. Families also enjoy the foods remaining on the altar after our dead have enjoyed its aroma and *sabor*.

Days of the Dead helps us to feel closer to our loved ones, both living and deceased. It is a powerful tradition of life embracing death, in which we deeply reflect on our own lives. We come to the realization that we must live life to the fullest, with utmost compassion and love for one another. We realize that it is not death we should fear but rather the unlived life.

Día de todos los santos

Xicanx Healing Ritual After the Death of a Child

AIDA SALAZAR

There is no greater heartache for a parent than losing a child. Their death defies nature in its most basic sense—parents are not meant to outlive their young. We are charged not only with ushering them into life but also with providing the care and nurturing necessary for a thriving adult life. Their early death destroys us and makes us question our faith, our sense of belonging and purpose, our sense of self-worth. We carry a tremendous amount of guilt, and that can have a devastating toll on our spirits. We are forever changed by our loss.

After the death of my infant daughter, Amaly Celeste, I whirled with grief. I could not see where I might begin to heal. I was given a copy of the *Tibetan Book of the Living and Dying* by Sogyal Rinpoche. This gorgeous book provided a landscape for helping me to understand her death from a Buddhist perspective. I was new to Buddhism, and the rituals and ceremonies the book provided were an opening, but they did not truly resonate with my heart because of the cultural distance. In the thirteen years since her passing, I have created and adapted my own heartfelt and culturally relevant rituals to find spiritual and emotional healing. I first turned to our Días de los Muertos tradition to remember the dual nature of our living, life and death. Then I looked at our other histories as inspiration to imagine what rituals we, as Xicanx, might create and perform to heal after a child's passing. Performing these rituals has been a critical and beautiful way to endure and process my daughter's death. Below is my ritual on Día de Todos los Santos, to be done specifically on November 1. My Chalchiuhtlicue ritual for the anniversary of my child's death or birthday is in part 14, "Mother-Child Bonding."

DÍA DE TODOS LOS SANTOS

It is well known that one of the most robust of our preconquest rituals is the yearly Días de los Muertos. While many erect beautiful altars for our deceased loved ones on November 2, an equally long-standing tradition exists to honor children who have passed, on November 1—Día de Todos los Santos. On this day, grieving parents and caretakers build an altar for deceased children (who are also referred to as "saints" because of their unblemished souls) that can include almost every element found in an altar for an adult. However, a child's altar must be erected and its food ready and candles lit by noon. It is said that the spirits of the children arrive at exactly that hour, and they expect to find their altar waiting.

Each altar will be different, depending on each person's experience, available resources, and ability to create a space for it. The altar can be big enough to occupy a significant part of a home or small enough to fit on a nightstand, and each is valid. The intention is to provide a sacred space to honor a deceased child during a time when their spirits are looking to visit. But, building an altar also provides a space for grieving parents to place their grief, acknowledge it openly, and move through it with an open heart.

For my daughter's altar, I take great care to assemble in small portions the following elements: a picture of her in her happiest state; a little *calavera* with her name on it; nonspicy food that I loved while pregnant with her; *pan de muerto*; a glass of water; instead of a *petate*, I make a crib or small bed for her to rest on; a pacifier; her umbilical cord clip; photos of my *panza* while pregnant and other intimate *recuerditos*; a rattle, or small dishes or toys (traditionally a figure of the *izcuintle* dog is used to represent a child at play); I don't use zempoalxochitl flowers like in adult altars but fragrant white flowers whose petals I sprinkle, sometimes in intentional designs; candles or *veladoras*; and statuettes of saints and/or deities (Coatlicue, the Aztec mother of life and death, La Virgen de Guadalupe, and angels, for instance). Most everything on the altar is white to symbolize her purity of spirit and the light that she is in my memory.

On November 1, minutes before noon, I light the candles and begin to burn sage or copal and douse myself, those with me, and the entire altar with its cleansing smoke. I speak my child's name and welcome her (loudly or softly, depending on how I feel) while dousing. At noon, I sit with the altar and know her visiting spirit in meditation. I talk to my child about my grief and my joys and I pray, recite or read a poem, sing a song or play recorded music in the room, eat the food that I have prepared, and remember to leave a little on a plate for her. I spend as much time as I wish with the altar. Upon leaving, I reignite the sage or copal and douse the altar and those gathered once more and thank the spirit child for her visit. The sense of peace is palpable and all-embracing.

Lamento Cihuateteo / Llanto de Juárez

(The Lament of the Cihuateteo / The Cry of Juárez)

YREINA D. CERVÁNTEZ

This poem is dedicated to the many hundreds of women in Juárez, Mexico, who have been brutally murdered at the border. Many of these women are *maquila-doras*, women working in factories, many of them U.S.-owned businesses that relocated to Juárez as a result of NAFTA and in search of cheap labor. In ancient Mesoamerica it was believed that the heart was the seat of the soul, and at the time of death, the spirit was transformed into winged creatures, butterflies or hummingbirds, and the energy returned to the universe, a form of reciprocity. The title of this poem refers to the lament of the Cihuateteo, the Mexica or Aztec Goddesses who reside at the crossroads. These were women transformed into goddesses after dying in childbirth, also considered warriors in their own battle to give birth. They reside at the crossroads between the living and the dead and are witnesses to the tragic deaths of these women in Juárez. In some Native American beliefs it is said that a people are not defeated until the hearts of the women lie on the ground.

Our mothers' hearts lie on the ground,
Our sisters' hearts lie on the ground,
Diosa de la vida y la muerte,
The Goddess weeps, sheds turquoise tears
Wails *por sus hijas* at the crossroads
Women Warriors all

Gathered at the wound between worlds
Broken dreams, shattered bodies
"Remembered and made whole"
Shake the earth, raise their spirits, lift your voices
JUSTICIA PARA LAS MUJERES DE JUÁREZ!

9

DREAMING

INTRODUCTION

Dreaming, and dreams, is of paramount importance to humans. "Initial and unexpected contact with the Great Mysterious power must have come prior to the development of ceremonies and rituals for seeking a relationship with the spirits" (Deloria 2006). The sacred plane of dreaming and dreams is the initial and unexpected contact Deloria is speaking of here. Among the many life practices of the Indigenous societies of the Americas that were disrupted by colonization are the ancient and rich practices of dreaming, wherein dreaming and dreams are viewed as a sacred plane, the dream body is acknowledged and cared for, and the interpretation of dreams and their meaningful application in observations of the physical world are valid means by which to acquire knowledge (Deloria 2006; Gonzales 2012b). Dreams can also be prophetic—they can offer warnings and bring one's attention to an action that is yet to occur. Sometimes our ancestors, known or unknown, and our loved deceased will visit and communicate with us via dreams.

We are honored to have in this collection the work of Atava Garcia Swiecicki. Her contribution "Cultivating a Healing Dream Practice" is situated within acquired teachings based on the tradition of dreaming in the ancient Mexican world, where it was understood "that we have different energetic bodies that operate when we are awake or when we are asleep: the tonal and the nahual."

The examples of her own experience, offered here, of plants teaching her the know-how of their uses marks the importance of building a relationship with the dream world, as the knowledges shared with us through the cosmos during dreaming can strengthen us (Deloria 2006). Atava's beautiful contribution offers us a path to deepening our relationship with our dreams by cultivating a practice around dreaming!

Two out of eight hours of sleep are spent dreaming, making our dream life important enough to give thanks for. Additionally, recent studies undertaken in sleep labs affirm that dreams "help us take the sting out of our painful emotional experiences during the hours we are asleep, so that we can learn from them and carry on with our lives" (Walker 2017).

Acknowledging our dream life by developing a deeper relationship with it is an acknowledgment of how to more fully embrace a holistic human experience. Maritza Alvarez, in conversation with Lara Medina, relates her relationship with dreaming and the importance of meditation or prayer in developing her relationship with her dreams, and in the dreaming process itself. Through the dream world, Alvarez has come to realize the importance of a holistic vision of ourselves, as she relates how a dream empowered her coming out as a queer womxn.

The power of dreams is to keep us alert; if not for anything else than to assure us that we are on the right path, or a designated path. In this way, dreams can affirm growth. As part of this growth, we may encounter cleansing dreams along the way, dreams of transformative spiritual growth. Sara H. Salazar's "After the Limpia . . ." speaks powerfully to the intensity of dreams that can follow after a deep *limpia* (cleansing) of the spiritual body, suggesting that dreams themselves are part of the healing. Salazar ends her poem by situating herself and her healing in connection with the dream she experienced back within her community. Coming to have a deeper relationship with our dreams is important to us as peoples whose base is here in the Americas, for, as Patrisia Gonzales reminds us, "it is in the uncontainable dream that living Indigenous knowledge also resides, waiting to be called forth" (Gonzales 2012, 187).

Martha R. Gonzales

Cultivating a Healing Dream Practice

ATAVA GARCIA SWIECICKI

Throughout my life, my dreams have been my healing allies and guides. First and foremost, they have helped me to understand myself. In my dreams, I have explored and become acquainted with my internal landscape, the world of my unconscious. Here I have encountered my shadow and faced the *aires* I am carrying, the old winds of anger, jealousy, fear, or resentment. However, hidden in the darkness of the dream world are also many spiritual and healing gifts.

Plant allies have appeared in my dreams, sometimes as a prescription for what is ailing in my body. Other times a plant will appear to teach me something about how to work with its medicine. Sometimes my dreams have directly healed me. For example, once I became lucid in a dream and was able to focus healing energy toward my injured shoulder.

My dreams have carried me to the future and to the past. I have dreamed of my ancestors long dead. I have dreamed of events happening before they occur. I have been listening to my dreams for my entire life. This was a practice that came to me intuitively. I can still recall a strong dream I had when I was about eight years old, which sent me to the library to do research on dreams.

Nobody in my family taught me explicitly about dreams; yet over decades of observing my dreams, my dreams have become my teachers. Moreover, when I was in graduate school in 2001, I met my first mentor of dreaming, Apela Colorado, founder of the Worldwide Indigenous Science Network. She taught me that dreams were messages from the ancestors and the spiritual world. At that time, I began working with dream counselor Karen Jaenke.

More recently, through the work of Mexican *maestro* Sergio Magaña, I discovered that Mexico has a rich and ancient tradition of dreaming. The ancient Mexicans understood that we have different energetic bodies that operate when we are awake or when we are asleep: the tonal and the nahual.

I have been studying *curanderismo* for seventeen years with Doña Enriqueta Contreras of Oaxaca and Estela Román of Temixco, Mexico. Magaña's teachings helped me to expand the practices I have learned from these two *maestras* in regard to dreaming.

I offer these guidelines from my own dreamer's medicine kit. They are some of the practices that have helped me develop as a dreamer. They come from my years of experience working with dreams and are influenced by all my teachers and the wisdom they shared with me.

Each dreamer's path is unique, and I recommend that you find what works best for you. Most importantly, I encourage you to build a relationship with your dreams and allow them to guide your path as a dreamer.

1. PAY ATTENTION TO YOUR DREAMS

Dreams can be an extraordinary resource for healing, if we pay attention. Your dreams can be your friends, your guides, your teachers, your healers, your therapist, or your spiritual counselor. Our dreams are constantly sending us messages, but we need to listen. Take time in the morning to reflect on the messages that come in your dream state. Incorporate it into your daily spiritual practice. Make reflecting on your dreams a priority.

2. RECORD YOUR DREAMS

Keep a dream journal, pen, and small flashlight next to your bed. If you feel too sleepy to write the entire dream, try jotting down a small fragment of the dream. In the morning, this fragment will jog your memory and you most likely will recall the entire dream. It is helpful to write down your dreams as soon as possible after waking up. Dreams can fade away quickly when we move into our morning routine.

Be creative. Some people prefer audio recordings of their dreams. If you're a visual person, try drawing your dream. Write a dream poem. Compose a song based on your dream.

3. LEARN THE SYMBOLIC LANGUAGE OF DREAMS

The language of dreams is very different from spoken language. Dream language is hard to grasp with the rational mind. It is symbolic and energetic. When you dream of an image or a symbol, reflect on what personal meaning that image or symbol has for you. For example, if a dog appears in your dream, it might have a very different meaning if you love dogs or if you fear dogs.

Research the different meanings of the symbol in your ancestral cultures, and in other cultures as well. Many symbols have a universal meaning. Beware of any dogmatic interpretations of dream symbols. All dreams have multiple layers and multiple meanings.

Get to know your dream landscape. Pay attention to what symbols or themes repeat over time. This is your personal imagery library.

Notice how the dream makes you feel emotionally and physically. Did you wake up afraid, angry, or happy? Did you feel drained or energized? Your entire body records the dream, so observing your body helps you to better understand your dream.

4. TUNE INTO YOUR NAHUAL

According to the Mexica-Toltec traditions, we have different energetic bodies that relate to dreaming. Our nahual is the energetic body we use when we dream, and it is located around the navel when we are awake. The tonal is the energetic body that rules our waking state, and it is located around the head, like a halo.

When we are asleep, our nahual moves up and switches places with our tonal. When the nahual rules the head, we are dreaming. Lucid dreams occur when the tonal and nahual are both present while dreaming. This means we are asleep and dreaming (in our nahual) but our conscious mind (tonal) is "awake" in the dream. In other words, we are dreaming and we are aware that we are dreaming. In this tradition, we seek lucid dreaming, which in Nahuatl is called *temixoch*, or flowering dreams.

Our nahual has great power. When we dream, our nahual is not limited to space and time, and it has the ability to travel outside of the body. When we are awake, our nahual relates to our intuition, our gut instinct. Put your hands on your naval. Breathe into your belly. Feel your nahual. How does it communicate with you when you are awake?

5. PRACTICE DREAM INCUBATION

To incubate a dream is to consciously call forth a dream. The ideas for dream incubation are limitless, but here are some examples:

- heal a physical illness or ask for guidance about treatment
- heal an emotional problem or see clearly your path toward healing
- heal a relationship
- ask for guidance about an important decision
- connect with ancestors
- manifest love in your life
- learn more about your ancestral medicine
- understand things in your life that your conscious mind doesn't see

The first step to dream incubation is to set your intention. What do you want to ask of the dream state? For example, "I will receive healing for my back pain in my dreams." Or, "I ask my dreams to reveal what is blocking me from receiving love."

Write down your intention and place it under your pillow.

The night you incubate your dream, unplug from electronics and media of all kinds several hours before bed. It is important to make space in your psyche for dreaming and to clear out unwanted influences.

Next, take time before bed to create your own ritual to help activate your dream incubation. Light a candle. Smudge. Pray. Make an offering. Talk to your ancestors and spirit guides. Ask for the dream to come.

Certain herbal teas can support your dreaming. Mugwort, or estafiate, is well known to enhance dreams and to improve dream recall. Take a little mugwort tea before bed or place some mugwort under your pillow. Mugwort is unsafe to use during pregnancy, so avoid using it if you're pregnant.

Another good herbal tea that is safe for everyone is chamomile, or manzanilla. Chamomile helps to bring healing dreams and can also stop nightmares
for both adults and children.

When you fall asleep, repeat your dream-incubation intention like a mantra.
Keep repeating it through the night.

Dream incubations can take time to ripen. Sometimes it will be days, weeks,
or months before the dreams appear. Be patient. Repeat your incubation regularly. Give thanks when your dream manifests.

6. DREAM WITH THE MOON

The moon has a powerful influence on our dream state. New moons and full
moons are powerful times for dream incubations. Notice how the moon cycles
influence your own dreams. Soak in the moonlight before going to sleep. Sleep
outside under the moon and stars. Observe how these cosmic energies affect the
quality and content of your dreams.

For a more advanced practice, keep track of the astrological sign that the
moon is in and how this influences your dreams. You will need a lunar calendar.
For example, I realized that often when I had a vividly sexual dream, the moon
was in Scorpio.

7. HONOR YOUR DREAMS

Dreams offer healing, but you must listen and take action in the waking world
to fully manifest their healing potential. To do this, your dreams may require
action, reflection, prayer, meditation, or ritual.

For example, once I dreamed of being in a field of chamomile. This dream
came at a time when I had a lot of stress in my life that was affecting my
digestion. As an herbalist, I knew that chamomile could help ease the stress
I was carrying in my stomach. I interpreted this dream to be a prescription, and the way I honored the dream was to start drinking chamomile tea
daily.

A woman in my dream group had a powerful dream in which she was burying an egg in a ceremonial setting. In her waking life, she surrounded herself

with egg imagery and eventually made a ceramic art piece representing the egg exactly as it had appeared in the dream.

There are many ways to honor your dreams. Some suggestions are to:

- incorporate the dream imagery or symbols into your waking life,
- make art inspired by your dream,
- create a ritual based on the dream,
- follow the advice the dream gave you, and
- reenter the dream in a meditation.

Above all, enjoy the process! The dream world is magical, mysterious, and wise. When we take the time to listen to our dreams, our waking lives are enriched by the gifts they share.

May your dreams be good medicine for you!

On Dreaming

MARITZA ALVAREZ IN CONVERSATION
WITH LARA MEDINA

JUNE 17, 2016

We must be open to dreaming and to the unfamiliar, to what might be scary, and to what we are not prepared for. For example, from my own experience while dreaming, I was flying as a macaw in Chichén Itzá, and I was about to enter an underground tunnel. If I had more grounding in this material world or knowledge about how that can happen, I would not have stopped myself. So I believe there are guides for every spiritual path, *maestras* in this world for our spiritual journeys. So that when we dream, we know how to navigate that world with *confianza* and how to make the best decisions in the dream world. Since that dream, I have prayed for teachers, and two have come to me.

I keep myself open to dreaming through meditation and prayer. When I am deep in my prayers in front of my altar, I feel like the portal is open. This is one form of nourishing dreams. It is also when I am around certain people, due to their energies, that dreams will come. You have to be open to seeing and to trusting. The macaw dream helped me, as I knew afterward that I should have gone into the tunnel. So in subsequent dreams, I am reminded not to be afraid.

Dreaming has taught me that living is a phase, and we must strive to learn as much as we can about spirit, as that is what we are. We are spirit beings. As much as we can learn about ourselves as spirit beings will help us in the next phase, the next dimension, or where we will be next. The dreams help me tremendously with that—to shed the fears, the layers of fears that occur, perhaps that I was not born with, but that were instilled in me as a child. Dreams are healing opportunities through the beings that come. Dreams are medicine for me. They have appeared at pivotal points in my life. They are healing ceremonies for me. If you can walk through fearful situations in dreams, you can walk through fearful situations in life. An example is when I had not come out of the closet due to several reasons. A big one was the church, as I was raised Catholic. There was a part of me that was devoted to La Virgen de Guadalupe, and how could I betray her?! The dream that helped me cross over, figuratively, took place in the desert, and it was a night with a full moon: I am walking barefoot and I have this white gown down to my ankles and my hair is loose. The only light is the full moon. I see an elderly woman sitting on a chair, with her long gray hair in a bun. She is skinning a serpent! Beyond her is a mound of black serpents! Immediately I am scared. As soon as I feel my fear, there is a deep voice of a woman who says, "*Camina, no tengas miedo.*" As soon as I hear her voice, I do it. I walk barefoot over the mound of serpents! I feel like I am floating across them. When I woke up I knew that was it, that was what I needed—that power, that reminder. That is my coming out story. I was in tears. Again, it goes back to me and perhaps many others, the dreams are about my medicine, to help me navigate my place here. After that dream, I had this energy. My fear was gone. My ancestors had told me I would be fine. When I came out publicly, I was twenty-six years old.

I am really, really grateful to have the gift of dreaming. And if there are other things that I need to be doing, I hope and pray that I will be guided. This gift is here to help. Birds are very constant in my dreams, and the serpent. One dream I had, it was daylight and I was walking up a hill and I had a *bastón*. The handle of the bastón was carved in the shape of an eagle head. On the top of the ridge was a tree without any leaves. There were three eagles sitting, white bald eagles. When I saw them, I felt this strong energy. It was too strong for me and I did not know what to do. I woke up. I asked myself what I was doing at that time in my life. I remembered I was trying to find a place to sweat as I had come out, and it was challenging to find a safe space to sweat. In one instance I worked with two males who were on the Red Road and who were very protective against including two-spirit relatives into their sweat lodge circles. I think the eagles were a representation of these guards, or gatekeepers. Yet, I was holding a bastón with an eagle head! So I think that what is going on here will appear through symbols in our dreams. They are visual reminders, rather than verbal, as often there is not a lot of dialogue going on in the dreams.

After the Limpia . . .

SARA H. SALAZAR

After the *limpia*, the warrior womxn hops in her car and goes to work.
That evening, exhausted from work and the ritual far from her mind,
she falls to sleep and dreams of strangely familiar lands, peoples, and images
with immense beauty, vibrancy, and warmth.
She wakes the next morning feeling refreshed and whole.

The once-wounded womxn begins to experience the waking world and the
dream world with new eyes and new perspectives. She sees mysterious yet
deeply rooted images and symbols as comforting and familiar and listens to
stories and music with a different ear.

She realizes that the healing she undertook that morning
continues to ripple out into her life.
She understands that the healing was not just for her, but for her whole
community, seven generations forward and seven generations back.

10

HOLISTIC HEALTH CARE

INTRODUCTION

Caring for our spirit requires honoring our emotions, our intellect, and our embodied knowledge, or how we know through our bodies.[1] As *curandera* Elena Avila states in *Woman Who Glows in the Dark*, "The spirit is the sum total of our nutritional habits . . . the energy generated from our feelings . . . and the energy generated by our thoughts . . . the part of our being that connects us to the 'Great Spirit.' A strong spirit buffers negative outside influences much as the skin of a fruit protects the fruit from decay" (Avila and Parker 2000, 172–73). Our bodymindspirit is so interconnected that physical ailments oftentimes stem from emotional distress. If we do not respect our emotions, we can easily be ruled by negative energies that fragment our original wholeness. Yet if we embrace our difficult feelings with compassion, we can diffuse negativity and replenish our holistic selves with the positive—that which is nourishing to our lives and to all our relations.

Releasing difficult emotions caused by microaggressions, as well as deep traumas we personally experience or carry through our ancestral lineages, is an essential aspect of our decolonization process. The desire to heal is the desire

1. For visual reflection, see plate 10, *Coyolxauhqui Last Seen in East Oakland* by Irene Perez; plate 8, *Invocation* by Yadira L. Cazares; and plate 6, *Mayahuel* by Margaret "Quica" Alarcón.

to know who we truly are, before the wounds, before the shaming. The desire to heal is the desire to live in our creative authenticity, to live in the fullness of the sacred creativity we are born with. The work of Chicanx writers and artists initiated in the 1980s to heal and reclaim Coyolxauhqui, the dismembered Mexica goddess, provided womxn with an icon and feminist mythology to support our intentions to heal our wounds suffered under heteronormative racist patriarchy. As Cherríe Moraga wrote, "She [Coyolxauhqui] is la fuerza femenina, our attempt to pick up the fragments of our dismembered womanhood and reconstitute ourselves. She is the Chicana writer's words, the Chicana painter's canvas, the Chicana dancer's step. She is motherhood reclaimed and sisterhood honored. She is the female god we seek in our work" (Moraga 1993, 74). Contributing artist Irene Perez witnessed the unearthing of the original sculptural disk of the dismembered Coyolxauhqui in Mexico City in 1978. After deep reflection on the mutilated goddess, Irene began working on "putting her back together, to heal her."[2] Irene's painting of Coyolxauhqui (see plate 10) gives us a reconfigured icon, reflecting our process of healing our wounds and flourishing into our sacred creativity.

Our healing processes also involved a turn, or return, to *curanderismo* as practiced by many of our elders. A foundational theory of curanderismo, a complex holistic health-care system based primarily on Mexican Indigenous medicinal knowledge, is that the toxic emotions and experiences that enter into our bodies can also be released through our bodies (Buenflor 2018; Trotter and Chavira 1997). Our flesh is porous, with openings that can receive negativity but can also release negativity. Estela Román, an Indigenous healer from Temixco, Mexico, teaches that *aires cósmicos*, or thirteen difficult emotions, can unnecessarily accumulate in our bodies. Regular emotional cleansings and sweat ceremonies ensure a more balanced state of being. Also, *aires de la tierra* are winds, or energies, that carry the wisdom of the earth, the elements, and the cosmic forces. We must allow ourselves to experience the elements and the natural world so that the wisdom we need in order to live in a balanced manner can be received (Román 2012). Aires de la tierra remind us to pay attention to our environment, to the elements (air, earth, fire, water), and to the ancestors. The winds also remind us to honor our relationship with the seven sacred directions.[3]

---

2. Personal conversation between author and Irene Perez, 2018.

3. See part 2, "Honoring the Sacred Directions," for information on the elements and the directions.

Regularly cleaning ourselves emotionally is crucial in supporting our intention to live holistically, with strong spirits, strong minds, and strong bodies. Performing ritual for ourselves and with others is key for our healing. We are offered medicine through reclaiming and reinventing the rituals of our ancestors before colonization. *El temazkal,* or the sweat ceremony, is regarded by many Indigenous cultures as the best remedy for almost every ill. At the time of the European invasion of Mesoamerica, the custom of purifying and healing oneself through ritual sweating in the *temazkalli,* or sweathouse, was an integral part of daily life that was prohibited by sixteenth-century Catholic missionaries, who believed bathing was sinful (Bruchac 1993). The devastation of the spiritual and physical well-being of our Indigenous ancestors continued with the banning of the sweat ceremony in 1873 by the U.S. government. During the Chicano and American Indian movements for civil rights of the late 1960s and 1970s, the sweat ceremony, having been secretly protected by elders over previous generations, returned to our people.

Ritual opens the doors to healing. Learning to invoke our Sacred Source, known by many different names, and the spirits of our ancestors, "known and unknown," is the starting point. Learning the medicinal power of plants will aid us in healing during our rituals. Authors in this section speak to practices such as the cleansing, or *limpia*; el temazkal; spiritual bathing for self-care; the use of stones for energetic protection; and the creation of a "self-care tool kit." The poetry of Sara H. Salazar highlights the beauty and power of a healer's hands and complements the guidance that Maestra Grace Alvarez Sesma offers on spiritual bathing, or *baño de matitas,* for the release and transformation of negative emotions and unhealthy connections. Grace tells us, "Women caring for other women is ceremony, and profoundly moving." This baño can be done privately for oneself or offered to another womxn in need of rest and support. There are various forms of baños and limpias, depending on the region of origin and the skill set of the healer. Sandra M. Pacheco prescribes here a method to simulate el temazkal, or sweat ceremony, in the privacy of our homes. Her grandmother's teachings, and those of her Zapotec teachers, and her own inspirations, instruct us in releasing what is not needed through a *baño de limpia espiritual*. Atava Garcia Swiecicki offers us teachings learned from Estela Román on the thirteen aires cósmicos, along with a powerful self-limpia practice to release them. As Atava keenly advises, we must "establish a regular practice of self-limpias . . . learn to engage with the medicine, to live the medicine, to be the medicine." Estela reminds us that the traditional adobe temazkalli is the representation of the womb of mother earth and that the ceremony offers us the opportunity of rebirth and growth in relationship with the cosmic forces and ourselves. Estela instructs on the use of specific herbs for during and after the sweat ritual and the role of the *temazkalera*, the one who facilitates the ritual cleansing for others.

Felicia "Fe" Montes advises the use of sacred stones to provide protection when doing very public work, such as community organizing or participating in marches and activist actions. Felicia also describes the contents of her portable "self-care tool kit," intended for personal and community care. In closing this section on body care and limpias, Jessica Lozano Rodriguez shares the creation of a poppet, a handmade effigy of the self that carries healing energies when made with intention and placed on one's altar. Drawn from her training with her *bisabuela* and from her own intuition, Jessica creates a ritual that greatly assisted her in managing post-traumatic stress disorder and other imbalances. And Pedro Alvarado offers a final prayer for our healing work. As a whole, these prolific writings of cleansing rituals[4] remind us to turn to our ancestral practices for integrating bodymindspirit and to always express gratitude and to trust where we are on our path!

Lara Medina

---

4. These various limpias can produce strong emotions that might require or motivate one to seek advice from a professional counselor or therapist.

The Curandera Begins . . .

SARA H. SALAZAR

The curandera *begins the* limpia *by gently activating the thirteen joints,*
portals of the body,
through touch.
She sweeps the wounded womxn's body with the bundles of herbs and wafts copal
while quietly offering prayers for protection and guidance.
The healer's hands deftly glide over her body, paying close attention to the energy
centers and come to rest on the womxn's heart.
She begins to sing in Nahuatl, the language of the ancestors,
softly calling back the soul, calling the names of loved ones, calling the names of the
goddesses and gods, calling the names of those still to come.
Through her song the healer tightly weaves a web of
trust and love which allows the medicine of her words
to sink deeper and deeper into the warrior womxn.

Womxn Caring for Womxn Is Ceremony

GRACE ALVAREZ SESMA

Mira mijita, that *pesar* that weighs you down, that dampens your spirit and saps your strength, and that *sombra* that keeps your light from shining have all been seen before, been felt before . . . been healed before. Our *abuelitas* knew the ways, the *costumbres*, of using blessed *ramitas de ruda y romero* to brush away *susto* and shame. Of using *un huevito* to cut *cuerdas de envidias y mal ojo*. Of sinking deep into a *tina* filled with prayed-over water and petals of carnations drifting on the currents created by too-tired-to-carry-this-anymore shoulders and limbs to release the tendrils of energy tying our wombs to ghost-partners from our *pasado*.

As passionate womxn who are lovers and sacred wonders, nurturing mothers and daughters, activists and healers, we continually send forth our personal energy into the world in the form of sinuous vines made of light that reach out from our auric body to connect to the bodies of men, womxn, and children with whom we exchange words, both loving and harmful, to friends whom we love, to partners with whom we have sex, to people who have *envidias* toward us or us toward them. Depending on the depth of the investment we have in the reasons for the emotions felt, these energetic vines can, over time, either contribute to a healthy exchange of mutually supportive feelings, or they can drain us of our *ganas*, of our willpower and motivation. For some, the profound trauma of childhood abuse has left a younger aspect of themselves still hiding in a closet, shielding themselves, in a place from which they have long since escaped but that has left them with a gnawing sense of not being altogether present in the here and now. They may feel like the images we see of the moon, Coyolxauhqui, dismembered and fragmented.

The abuelitas are calling you: leaders, activists, homemakers, community makers, and *chingonas*. You must be as dedicated to your spiritual self-care as you are to your families and community. Just like our beautiful Coyolxauhqui moon calls back her energy to become whole again, you can call back to yourself any energy you have given away or that has been taken away from you, whether done consciously or unconsciously, so that all aspects of you are called forth from hiding and you can become integrated and present in your daily life.

CORTANDO LAS CUERDAS (SEVERING THE TIES)

Two decades ago while helping one of my elders "doctor" people at his home in Tecate, Baja California, Josefina, his wife, chided me gently for not taking better care of myself. She said, "*Si no te cuidas, como vas a cuidar a otros?*" A reminder that I had to take care of myself to be able to take care of others without taking on their illnesses and *malestares*.

After another very long day of having cared for many persons with a variety of illnesses, both physical and spiritual, with prayers, *barridas, sobadas*, and *baños*, I was surprised by Josefina and her two daughters firmly saying it was time for them to take care of me. They then guided me into a small shack outside their home, where Josefina lovingly insisted on helping me undress while her daughters brought two large white buckets. Looking in, I saw that they had filled it to the very top with clean, clear water on which floated *romero* (rosemary), sage, and fragrant petals of roses and carnations. They proudly yet humbly told me that they had gathered the sage and romero themselves in the traditional way and had infused the herb and flower water with their prayers for my protection and well-being. As I stood inside the humble little bathing shack, I felt their love and the medicine of the earth cleanse away the needs of the sick and take away the pain from my back and legs, from having lugged buckets of water to and from their well for the spiritual baths I gave our patients.

Womxn caring for other womxn is ceremony, and profoundly moving. So I share this *baño de matitas* now with you in support of your healing. Know that my love and prayers join with you as you honor yourself with this bath. This bath is our beautiful ceremony of loving self-care in the service to others. While ideally it is taken during the full moon, you may also take this cleansing bath during the waning phase. If you feel especially *cargada*, or heavy, with unwanted energy, taking this bath on three consecutive days or nights is best: one bath on the day/night before the full moon, one bath on the day/night of the full moon, and one on the day/night after the full moon. You can also simply take one bath on the day/night of the full moon.

As with most rituals, one's body should be clean before beginning. While not required, I also recommend abstaining from sex one day before the bath, on the day of the bath, and the day after the bath. If you do not have a tub, you can take a clean bucket filled with the herbal infusion into the shower with you. Your intention for a good outcome is clarified by setting aside plenty of uninterrupted time for preparation, reflection, meditation, and the actual ceremonial bath.

Once you are ready to begin, bless yourself with the smoke of white copal, sage, or cedar (or all three), and clarify the intention for your *limpia* by reflecting on what it is you wish to experience. For example, it could be transforming the root cause of illness, anxiety, fear, chronic negative self-talk, or envidia directed toward you or that you feel toward another into healthy boundary setting, supportive self-talk, confidence, and self-assurance. It could also be removing obstacles to harmonious relationships in your personal and professional life, releasing unforgiveness toward another person and/or toward yourself, or severing energetic connections to sexual partners who may be preventing you from having a healthy, loving, supportive relationship. Most importantly, be willing, or be willing to be willing, to release the physical, emotional, mental, and spiritual effects of trauma, fear, hurtful words, spiteful actions, and wrong thinking in the form of envidias directed toward you and from you toward others. Be willing to forgive others and be willing to forgive yourself.

1. Light a glass-encased white seven-day candle, also known as a deity candle. As you do so, remember to offer prayers of gratitude to Creator/God/Goddess for the healing virtues of the plants you are using that Creator has given us for our good health and well-being. Ask for protection and blessings from Creator, good healing spirits, holy ancestors, Grandmother Moon, and your guardians/angels.

2. Bring to a gentle boil in a very large pot a generous handful of either fresh or dried rue, white sage, rosemary, and basil. These plants are known for their purifying and spiritual cleansing qualities, so it is best not to substitute them with other plants or flowers. It is a good idea to place the plants inside a large

cheesecloth or old clean pillowcase so that the leaves and stems do not clog your drain. You may also bundle them together so that you can use them to gently brush your body while you bathe. While you are boiling the plants, you can begin to fill your tub halfway with very warm water; you will be adding the infusion of herbs to it.

3. Once the water and plants have come to a gentle boil, let the infusion sit for a few minutes, then carefully remove the pot from your stove and add the herbal infusion to the already warm bathwater. Soak in it for at least fifteen minutes, while pouring the water over your entire body from head to toe and all places in between. If you have experienced sexual abuse or have been in unhealthy intimate relationships, it is especially important that the herbal infusion makes contact with your genital area as well as buttocks.

4. Allow your body to relax into the water and give yourself permission to receive and accept the blessing of healing from the sacred medicine of our abuelas, our Mother Earth, and the spirit of water. As you do so, say out loud three times, with feeling and awareness: "I now return any energy that I may have taken from someone, knowingly or unknowingly, to its source, with blessings of love and peace." Pause and feel the energy that doesn't belong to you leave.

    Remain in the bath quietly, and receptively say the following phrase out loud three times: "I call back any of my own personal power or energy that I have given away, knowingly or unknowingly. I call it back to myself that I may be restored to wholeness and balance."

5. Bring your ceremony to an end by thanking Creator, Mother Earth, the spirit of water, and all the good healing spirits for the blessings received and those yet to come.

    "Tlazocahmati Tatita Sol for this day now ending, knowing that for others another day is just beginning. I greet your sacred duality, Grand-mother Moon, with offerings of smoke and prayers that all obstacles, inner and outer, may be removed for the healing and well-being of all those with whom I share my medicine, in person and in spirit. As you set, please take with you all that no longer serves the highest vision of myself so that I may be of service and a blessing to all creation. I say these words with a good heart and for the benefit of All Our Relations."

    Allow your body to air dry so that the medicine of the plants remains on your skin and continues its healing work. Nourish yourself by drinking a *tecito de manzanilla* or damiana. Eat lightly and rest and relax with a book of poetry or a good beach read or write in your journal. Be aware of any dreams or guidance you may receive. For three days after the bath, limit your interactions to friends and family members who love and support you and your goals and dreams.

May this ceremony root you, empower you, and bring you clarity and good health and healthy and joyful relationships, and may your path be filled with flowers and your inner light shine brightly!

Important note: Please refrain from this bath if you are pregnant or have health issues such as high blood pressure or if you are menstruating. Griselda (Grace) Alvarez Sesma (www.curanderismo.org) is not a physician, therapist, nurse, or psychiatrist. The information provided is for educational purposes and is not meant to replace medical or psychological diagnosis and treatment. It is recommended that you see a licensed physician or licensed health-care professional for any physical or psychological ailment you may have. ***For legal purposes we must state that this traditional folk remedy is offered as a cultural and educational item only and that we cannot guarantee its effectiveness.***

Baños de limpia espiritual

SANDRA M. PACHECO

I honor the Ohlone and their land.
I honor my ancestors.
I honor your ancestors.

I write this just days before departing for Standing Rock to join the Sioux Nation in protecting the water for all people. In preparation, I have begun to isolate and remain in prayer for longer periods of time. This is necessary, as the energy at Standing Rock will be intense and draining in the best-case scenario, trauma-tizing in the worst-case scenario. In my preparations, I have also begun to think about what I will need to do while there to care for my spirit, and the healing I will need to do upon returning from an Indigenous land where the trauma experienced by the ancestors continues today.

In the past, when faced with the most intense traumas, traumas that affected my spirit, I have known that what I needed for healing could not be found in a therapist's office. While I honor and respect the role of therapy in a modern world, I find that the practice of analyzing traumatic experiences is more an ameliorative than a transformative process, which privileges the mind over body and spirit. Spirit and body are rarely addressed, and if addressed, not in the manner taught by my grandmother, Doña Mague, a Guamares woman born in 1910 who practiced *curanderismo*. From my grandmother's teachings and from those of two of my current teachers, Doña Pastora and Doña Queta, I know that when addressing trauma, spirit needs to be tended to, and one's soul needs to be called back to the body. Body, mind, and spirit need to be reintegrated. Whether the result of a particular explicit trauma or the accumulation of microtraumas from living in a white-supremacist, capitalist, heteropatriarchal society, there comes a time when more intense work must be done. That is when I am called to sweat, and to do so with plants.

While the ideal way to sweat is in a *temazkal* (sweat ceremony), it can be hard to find one readily available, and if you are able to find one, it might be challenging to arrange to do your personal healing work in it. There are rituals and rules associated with each one, depending on the Indigenous lineage of the person who tends to the space or *temazkalli*. In Mexico, el temazkalli varies in use, from ritual healing work to social space where families gather. In addition to a scarcity of spaces to sweat, the amount of time required to prepare a sweat is great. However, it is possible to have a comparable healing sweat at home, with a bathtub or large basin. In curanderismo, we refer to this as a "baño de limpieza espiritual."

There are various forms of *baños* that are done. One of the most common is a ceremonial baño that is done with the full moon to work with stuck or negative energy and to set intentions. Another kind of baño is for working with more intense trauma that requires more intense healing and that simulates the experience of a temazkal, or a sweat. It is this second one that I will share with you.

BAÑO DE LIMPIA ESPIRITUAL

Typically, this kind of baño is prepared for you by a *curandera*, a *tía*, an *abuelita*, or a good friend who can assist you and hold space for you, who can *apapacharte* (indulge you lovingly). Given that we live in a modern world where the ability to share extended time together is not always easy, I will share with you the process for tending to your own baño. This particular baño is a combination of my grandmother's teachings and those of my Zapotec teachers in Oaxaca, with my own contributions to address the modern context in which we live. What I share with you is with permission from my teachers and with respect to my grandmother. In preparation for this baño, avoid alcohol for twenty-four hours.

Antes que nada, do you have a home altar? Within Zapotec curanderismo, everything begins with the home altar. It does not have to be elaborate, but it does have to include a candle, preferably white. The flame must be tended to and never go out, even if this means using electric candles, as my grandmother did, for fear of fire. While you may select different items for your altar, such as pictures of ancestors, deities, flowers, and incense, the candle is a must.

The candle is our way home. The flame of the candle is the light that speaks to something greater. It is the light that connects us to the Creator, the cosmos, to a deep sense of our own divinity. Gazing into the flame reminds us of this. The altar is also where you will set your intentions for healing as your prepare for your baño. What are you holding on to that needs to be released? What do you need to mourn? What pain is your body holding? What do you need to cry out of your body?

Once you have tended to your altar, tend to your space and spirit. You will need uninterrupted and private space for your ritual, at least two hours right before your usual bedtime. You will need time to prepare the herbs, prepare the bath, prepare a tea, and prepare your bed and bedroom. During all this, keep copal, sage, palo santo, cedar, or sweet grass burning and available to smudge yourself with as you feel called to do. Throughout the preparation phase, stay inward, and start prayers, meditations, or centering.

The first step is to prepare the plants. It will take at least one hour to prepare the plants into a murky tea. You will need an extra-large pot, like for tamales, and about one paper grocery bag loosely filled with plants. *Las plantitas* you use are very important. Common plants we use for baños are basil, sage, rosemary, rue, *pericón* (Mexican tarragon), roses, *manzanilla* (chamomile), and calendula. Select what you are drawn to, but with respect. We are taught that the plantitas are our ancestors; they give so much and have the medicine we need. If harvesting your own plants, first ask permission from them. Hold them and thank them for the work they will help you with during this evening. Thank them for their medicine and wisdom. Set the large pot with plants and water to boil and then simmer for at least an hour. We do not measure; we do it *al tanteo.* That is, we sense the proportions. You want the water to be very dark and murky when it is done simmering. If you have a large-enough bathroom and portable cooking plate, prepare the plants in the bathroom to avoid having to carry the large pot from the kitchen.

Once the plants are starting to simmer in the water and are releasing their medicine, it is time to tend to your bedroom. On top of your fitted sheet you will need six flat sheets spread out in layers. On top of all the sheets, you will need a heavy blanket or two. Prepare your bed in such a way that the three top flat sheets are folded over the blanket, so you know where to enter into the layers once you come out of the bath. Once you enter the bed, you will not be getting out until morning. It is helpful to have a heating pad that can warm the sheets to ease the transition from tub to bed. Be sure to keep the bedroom warm. Tend to any of your usual bedtime rituals, such as brushing your teeth and using the bathroom to empty your bladder.

> *Return to the simmering plantitas and check on them.*
> *Experience them through the steam that is rising.*

Make yourself a soothing tea. Something like manzanilla, *pasiflora* (passionflower), or *melissa* (lemon balm) is calming. Pour the prepared tea into an insulated travel mug and place it on your nightstand, within reach from your bed. You will sip the tea for nourishment and for additional relaxation of the body. Place a small white votive candle next to your bed.

> *Return to the simmering plantitas and check on them.*
> *Experience them through the steam that is rising.*

With care, fill your bathtub. You want the water as hot as you can tolerate, perhaps a little hotter than tolerable to account for any time it may be left waiting. Fill the tub only about half way with water. While the tub is filling, remove all your clothes and change into the robe you will put on after you get out of the tub. Have two extra-large towels available, such as a bath sheet or beach towel. One towel will be for placing over your head and body (*cuevita*) while you are in the tub. The other will be for drying yourself before you put on your robe.

> *Return to the simmering plantitas and check on them.*
> *Experience them through the steam that is rising.*

Once the plantitas have released their medicine and the water is dark and murky, remove the pot from the stove and carry it carefully to the bathroom. If the pot is too heavy, use a pitcher or small pot to transfer the medicinal water. Gently stir the medicinal water into tub water. It is now time to enter the baño.

Slowly step into the tub. It should be hot enough that you have to ease into it because of the discomfort, but not so hot as to scald. Once seated, cover yourself with a large towel to create a little cave over your body. (The towel will get wet and you can worry about cleanup the next day.) If there are sliding glass doors or shower curtains, keep them closed to keep the heat and steam from escaping. The slight discomfort from the heat is an *assist*. It helps with surfacing the trauma/pain that needs to be released.

Sit under the towel for at least fifteen minutes, or as long as you are able. Allow emotions to surface. Allow tears to flow. Allow guttural sounds to release. Take in the aroma of the plants working to support you, breathe in the steam. Thank the plantitas for their support. If you have a healing mantra, recite it, sing it. When you come to a point where you are feeling "done," and feeling close to getting out of the tub, remove the towel or place it just on your head and wash yourself with the plant water using a loofah or a sprig of rosemary, something with texture. Do not stay in the tub with water cooling down. It is important to keep your body temperature elevated.

When you are ready to get out of the bathtub, quickly dry yourself, place your robe on, and head to your bed. Slide into the bed naked, with three layers of sheets beneath you and three layers and a blanket on top of you. Keep sheets and covers snuggly around body and head. Continue to sweat. It's time to *reposar*, to relax into the sweat. As you feel the sheets fill with moisture, remove them so the next layer continues to pull the sweat away. You want to do this without getting out of bed or exposing yourself to cold air in the room. After removing the third set of top and bottom sheets, prepare for relaxing into sleep.

Sip the tea you have prepared for yourself and gaze into the candle flame, the reminder that you are precious and deeply connected to Creator, the Ancestors, and the Cosmos. Lie back, close your eyes, allow yourself to drift off to sleep, and whisper to yourself:

I am light.
I am love.
I am healing.

Que descanses . . .

The Thirteen Aires and Self-Limpias

ATAVA GARCIA SWIECICKI

A central practice of *curanderismo* is the *limpia*, a ceremony in which the *curandera* uses her prayers and her sacred tools, like herbs and copal, to bless and help release *aires cósmicos*. Los aires cósmicos are the emotions we carry that can cause us to be imbalanced.

My understanding of los aires is based on the teachings of Mexican curandera Estela Román. These aires are a natural part of the universe and are ruled by Ehecatl, the wind. They move around us and through us, and sometimes they decide to take up residence in us. When we hold on to our aires, they can block our happiness or they can make us sick. They can act like children or tricksters. But they are also our teachers, as we learn so much about ourselves by working with our aires. In addition to our own personal aires, we also carry the old winds of our ancestors.

When the aires are in our bodies, we can feel strong emotions and we can also experience physical symptoms like pain. Most of us recognize the aires we carry; we even take ownership of our aires when we say "my fear" or "my anger." The aires can move like a gentle breeze, or they can blow like a hurricane. When the aires are released in the limpia, they can make us cry, shake, scream, vomit, or feel paralyzed. The aires are no joke! But when we can finally let them go, we feel lighter, happier, and healthier.

A good way to learn about los aires is to observe the wind and yourself. How does the wind blow? What effect does a strong wind have on the environment? What aires do you carry? What strong and difficult emotion(s) do you feel?

Where do they live in your body? What effect do they have on your physical, mental, and emotional health?

Below is a list of the thirteen aires. Thirteen is a special number in the cosmology of ancient Mexico. Thirteen relates to the completion of a cycle, and the Mexica calendar is divided into thirteen-day weeks called "trecenas." In this cosmology, there are also thirteen heavens and thirteen major *puertas* (doorways/joints) in our physical body (neck, shoulders, elbows, wrists, hips, knees, and ankles). The first three aires all relate to different types of fear, so I am giving more explanation for these.

1. *Susto* (Trauma): Susto is a sudden shock, big or small. For example, witnessing a car accident can give us a small susto or being in a car accident can give us a big susto. Chronic susto is related to what psychology calls post-traumatic stress disorder. For example, survivors of violence or war can suffer from chronic susto.
2. *Espanto* (Supernatural fear): Espanto is a state of being spooked; a fear that comes from encountering supernatural forces like ghosts or spirits of nature. Animals and children can be prone to espanto.
3. *Miedo* (Fear): Miedo is related to worry and can also be like a phobia.
4. *Tristeza* (Sadness)
5. *Corage* (Anger)
6. *Celos* (Jealousy)
7. *Resentimiento* (Resentment)
8. *Pena* (Sorrow)
9. *Egoism* (Egotism)
10. *Envidia* (Envy)
11. *Vergüenza* (Shame)
12. *Culpa* (Guilt)
13. *Angustia* (Anguish)

SELF-LIMPIA PRACTICE

A good way to work with our aires is to establish a regular practice of self-limpias.

The path of a curandera is not a technique, it is a lifestyle that requires hard work, discipline, focus, practice, and commitment. We must learn to engage with the medicine, to live the medicine, and to **be the medicine.**

Self-limpias are a necessary first step to take before giving limpias to others. It is important to learn how energy moves in a limpia and how your different healing tools work. In addition, doing self-limpias regularly is an essential part of self-care. As healers, we must learn how to clean and maintain our own energies every day.

There are many different kinds and levels of limpias. Some are short and gentle; others are long and intense. Try experimenting with a variety of tools for your limpias, such as different herbs, instruments, or crystals. Practice your limpias in different settings and locations. For example, a limpia in your house will feel very different from a limpia at the ocean or a limpia at a waterfall in the mountains.

BASIC STEPS FOR A SELF-LIMPIA WITH HERBS

1. Create time and space for yourself.

    Build an altar and include something to represent each of the four elements: earth, air, fire, and water. Add special objects that represent your healing intention. Your altar can be simple or elaborate, but most importantly it should create a space that feels sacred to you.

    Make sure you schedule enough time for your limpia. It's best to pick a day and time when you don't have other plans immediately afterward. Allow yourself time for rest and transition.

    Sometimes we only have enough time for a short limpia, which is fine. If you take a few minutes to cleanse yourself with some fresh herbs, it can make a big difference in your day.

2. Gather your herbs.

    Many curanderas grow their own herbs and flowers that they use for their limpias. Others gather them from public spaces or buy them at the market. Fresh aromatic herbs are best. Some of the most common herbs used in limpias are rosemary, pirul, rue, basil, sage, and *pericón*, but many other plants will work as well. It is good to use what grows around you.

    When you gather your herbs, talk to the plants and share your intention with them. Make an offering to the plants and ask permission to harvest them.

    When you have your fresh herbs and flowers, first wash them off with water. Next, assemble them into a bundle and tie the bundle together. Smudge your bundle of herbs with some sage or copal.

You may also choose to utilize a *huevo* (egg). The egg is a powerful tool for drawing out negative energy. It can act like a psychic vacuum cleaner. The egg contains all four elements (earth, air, fire, and water) and therefore is a perfect tool for balancing the elements in our own bodies. The egg also represents life, rebirth, and unmanifested potential.

3. Ground and center yourself.

Grounding is especially important when we work with others, because the energy released in the limpia can be strong. Get in the habit of grounding yourself every time before doing your self-limpia. Make a conscious connection to earth. Imagine you have roots going down into the ground. Breathe into your belly.

4. Connect to your divine source.

Most curanderas work with a divine source of energy to guide their work. This may be God/Goddess, Universe, Creator, Ancestors, Great Spirit, or whatever you call the Divine. Most important is that you resonate with this energy and can draw on it for strength and guidance during your limpia.

5. Set your intention for your limpia.

Energy always follows intention. Therefore, the intention you set will guide the direction of your limpia. Here are some examples of intentions:

- releasing emotions and aires, like anger, sadness, or fear
- cleansing yourself of toxic energy
- healing pain or physical illness
- letting go of people or situations
- honoring life transitions, such as birthdays or graduations

6. Cleanse yourself with the herbs.

Sweep your body with your bundle of herbs. Move the herbs over every part of your body, from your head to your feet. Use your intuition to guide the herbs to the places on your body where they are needed the most. Take your time. Breathe. Feel how the herbs are helping to absorb the energy you are releasing. Know that the herbs are also infusing you with their healing properties.

Maestra Estela Román advises that we use the herbs to focus on each of the thirteen puertas on the body. By giving special attention to these thirteen major joints (neck, shoulders, elbows, wrists, hips, knees, and ankles), we can help to move and release the aires that tend to accumulate in these areas.

I like to start my self-limpias by holding the herbs to my face so that I can inhale their aroma. I imagine the healing scent of the herbs going deep into my body and helping to move the aires.

There is no right way or wrong way to cleanse yourself with the herbs. Each limpia will be different. Each curandera develops her own style to work with the herbs and her other sacred tools.

If you use a huevo, rub the egg over your body as you do with the herbs. Then you may crack the egg into a glass of water and dispose of it back to the earth or down the drain. If you are not trained to "read" the egg in the glass of water, you may simply bury the egg uncracked, as it has absorbed the negative energy.

7. Completion and closure.

How do you know when your limpia is complete? The length of a self-limpia will vary. Observe your energy and listen to your intuition. Do you feel finished? Does it feel like something still needs to be released?

The final part of the limpia is proper closure. The limpia ceremony can open you up emotionally and energetically, and afterward you must seal in your energy. Tightly wrap yourself with a rebozo or blanket and lie down and allow yourself to rest. Another method for closing is to squeeze each joint of your body. Imagine that your joints are like energetic doors that were opened and now must be closed.

Give thanks to the divine energies that supported your limpia and to the herbs that assisted you. Find a place to offer the used herbs to the earth, so that the earth may compost the energy they gathered.

Make yourself a cup of hot tea or chocolate. Eat lightly. Rest.

SELF-LIMPIA JOURNAL

Creating a self-limpia journal can help you keep track of what you learn in your practice. Suggested information to keep in your journal includes:

- The date you perform the limpia.
- Astrological aspects of the date (for example, the phase of the moon or astrological moon sign). In this way you can track the cosmic patterns and how they affect your limpia.
- The date from any other cultural calendar you follow as well, such as the Maya or Mexica calendars.
- The time of day (morning, noon, evening). Each time of the day has a special energy that we can harness for our limpias. Some curanderas have special

ceremonies that occur only at sunrise or sunset. Experiment and see how this makes a difference for you.

- The location (at your home, outside, in the mountains, near the ocean, etc.).
- The direction you are facing for the limpia (north, south, east, west). The four directions have different qualities and meanings. For example, north is often associated with the ancestors. If the focus of your limpia is on ancestral healing, try facing north.
- Elements you are working with. Some examples include:
  - Herbs and flowers (rosemary, rue, pirul, sage, roses, etc.). Which herbs did you pick, and how do they work? Are they calming, stimulating, heating, cooling? Do you notice that certain herbs work better for certain emotions? How do they work differently alone or in combination?
  - Huevo
  - Rattle (sonaja): drum, crystals, water, earth, salt, copal, feathers, etc.
  - Tools (herbs, egg, stones, etc.) that were most helpful in your limpia.
- The intention for the limpia.
- The aires you are working with.
- How you feel before the limpia. Are you in your body? Check in with how you feel in your physical body (tired, stressed, pained, sick, etc.), your mental body (anxious, worried, obsessive thoughts, etc.), and your emotional body (angry, sad, afraid, etc.). How would you describe your spiritual state?
- How you feel afterward. What changed in how you feel physically, mentally, emotionally, or spiritually?
- Whether you were able to shift or let go. Where did you feel stuck or blocked?
- What you learned from this limpia.

El Temazkal, a Place for Rest and Purification

ESTELA ROMÁN

Temazkal—a heat ceremony or sweat ceremony
Temazkalli—a small house of heat

The temazkalli is a small space, a little house, a small cave where the body can accommodate and rest. In the Mexican Indigenous cosmogony, the temazkalli is the representation of the womb of the Great Mother, our mother Tonantzin Tlalli. It is also a reproduction of the cosmos, where we can see specifically how cosmic energies move and lead our life; what is here on earth is there in the heavens. It offers the opportunity to see our conception and the possibility of rebirth and growth within the cosmos. Our ancient people knew that it would be very difficult for us to connect to the universe, with the infinite, after having gestated in the womb of our birth mother, where it is so small, so comfortable. Our people then developed ways and specific techniques that allow individuals to reconnect with themselves, and thus develop a stronger connection with the universe and all its elements, especially our mother, Tonantzin, the earth. From the connections and understanding of ourselves in relationship with the elements and the cosmos, we can receive the mystery of the infinite, the indecipherable in our lives.

LA CEREMONIA EN EL TEMAZKALLI

While in some cultures a line of communication with the infinite is attempted through the use of psychotropic sacred plants, other cultures develop this ceremonial work in the temazkal, where the body can achieve the same effects as that produced by a psychotropic plant. The warmth or heat, the aromas, and the ways in which the temazkal is treated as an ancestral bath; the sensation of being held, loved, advised, connected allows the body to enter a state of ecstasy. This aids the person to release that which gets in the way of seeing clearly. Only in this way can a solution be provided to that which seems unresolvable in day-to-day living, where it is very cold, where the person has been disconnected from themselves and from their fellow inhabitants of this planet.

The temazkal is an opportunity to lift *el alma*, which has been in hiding. The ceremony has the sole purpose of unifying bodymindspirit. Without this purpose, the ceremony does not have much reason for being. Only in this way will the ceremony be able to simulate the effect of the psychotropic plant; only in this way will the heat produced in the womb of the earth be able to help the body produce its own heat, its own light, and free itself and liberate the alma.

Fear is the first mystery in the universe. It is the first feeling that a newborn on earth must face, struggling to grow, but it is also an ally of the infant to strive for life. Then, with the warmth of the temazkalli, where love brews, clarity is increased, confidence is reinstated, and sensations of pleasure are experienced and fear fades away. In the temazkalli, we prepare to restart the cosmic birth and journey. It is from here that light emerges and we recognize the infinite that tells us why we are here and how we are to face our destiny.

THE TEMAZKAL UNDER THE PRINCIPLES OF TLAZOLTEOTL, THE CLEANSING MOTHER

The work of preparing a temazkal and having it ready to serve entails a series of abilities and responsibilities. The *temazkalerx* is conscious that temazkalli is a sacred space and is always making adjustments, ensuring that all the necessary materials are at hand and that their energy is fluid and harmonious. In general, the temazkal is built in a corner of the house or yard where there is sufficient privacy. The ancients built sophisticated adobe structures, always ensuring art and beauty as well as accessibility and privacy to give those receiving the temazkal a joyous experience, a purification and strengthening of the bodymindspirit. The temazkalerx is an artist and should have the ability to connect, reconcile, and hold the space. It is through the temazkalerx that the elements involved in the temazkal can be synchronized to produce the warmth, the light that will guide us toward removing what weighs on us and limits us in life.

The preparation of the temezkal includes a series of elements that make it an art, and it is important to ensure that each one of the details is attended to. It is important that both the ones receiving the sweat bath and the one attending to the bath observe the details to produce the most pleasing and effective experience. Comfortable cotton clothing is worn in the temazkal, but it is also recommended not to wear anything if possible. It is important that participants feel comfortable in all forms.

Knowledge of medicinal plants is important, as the sweat will be more restorative if the herbs hold the properties necessary to cleanse the skin, to detox and relax the whole body, to open the respiratory pathways, and to strengthen the bones and muscles. The most commonly used herbs in the temazkal are *el muicle*, rosemary, estafiate, *toronjil*, *albahacar*, mint, chamomile, lemon tea, *poleo*, catnip, eucalyptus, peppermint, fennel, *ciprez*, lemongrass, pennyroyal, and peppermint. They can be mixed or blended together or used individually.

Palm leaves or any other leaves from a fresh tree—mango, *pirul*, guayaba, avocado, *chapuliste*, capulín—will serve to move the steam coming forth from the stones and can be distributed and used by each participant. These leaves can also be utilized to tap or rub the body in places where energy may be stuck—on the back, shoulders, stomach, thighs, or legs—to improve circulation. Natural elements like aloe vera, yogurt, honey, and natural soaps can be used for deep cleansing. Exfoliating stones can be used. The temazkalerx guides the ceremony with prayer and song.

At the end of the ceremony and upon leaving the temazkalli, a pail of cold water for each participant is necessary to close the pores. Towels, sheets, or warm blankets to cover the body and the head and *petates*, or blankets, to lie down on are necessary. Fresh and comfortable clothing to wear after the temazkal can include a shawl or a sweater. The person may continue to sweat, the body may continue to be cleansed, and it is important to lie back and rest until falling asleep. The time for rest allows the body to recuperate from the work. A tea made of *muicle* permits the body to restore the minerals lost when sweating; a mint tea with honey will pick one up if feeling faint.

After the temazkal, we should eat warm, nourishing foods and drink beverages with no ice. Vegetables like green beans, squash, corn, carrot, spinach, and chard, steamed or slightly minced with a little garlic, are good; aguacate, a light sauce, garbanzos, lentils, and black beans are best.

Wellness Ways for Beginning Self and Community Care

FELICIA "FE" MONTES

As an activist and womxn who identifies as a spiritual ARTivist, I have always believed in the good in people and that we all have a good heart. *Tías*, mentors, and spiritual guides have reminded me that as I am often in the public eye as an activist and an artist, feelings and energy can sometimes be transported to me without intention. Energies like *mal de ojo*, jealousy, or just negative energies picked up on at performances, activist actions, and marches.

As a result, some of my mentors and friends have shared ways to take care and protect myself. These practices are especially supportive to me on my path to share knowledge in the community. Such teachings and my own research have brought me to utilize and wear items that I consider to be self- and community care items for body, mind, and spirit.

Some of these items include grandfather and grandmother stones, jade, turquoise, and obsidian—all seen as sacred in our Mesoamerican ancestral cultures and traditions. Each has varied uses and understandings across the Americas, but most are for protection and deeper connections. I have been gifted and have learned more about other stones and crystals that are known to protect, take care of, or give support to us in different ways. For example, rose quartz, which as a Xicana working to smash the system, has had a calming and light effect on me to remember to be led by my heart. Another is red coral, for clarity and my throat when singing and wanting to share truth via my voice.

Now, when I head out daily or for specific political marches, artivist performances, and the like, I prepare myself with these stones and other light-invoking rituals to take care of myself before and after going out. I carry obsidian or a tourmaline stone in my pocket or on a bracelet or ring, or I wear jade earrings or a necklace. I have also taken to using mirrors in jewelry as a protective measure. Whatever comes to me via the other person—they will see it also or it will reflect back to them. Every culture and tradition has its own ways and items, and I am thankful to know some of my own.

In addition, white candles, copal incense, and smudging of my body, my home, and my sacred items keep them cleansed and has kept me grateful and balanced. Participating in sacred community circles and spaces also keeps me strong and centered. Wearing powerful and sacred stones, along with lighting candles and smudging, grounds me as I pass through various circles and spaces and meet many people. I am thankful for these ways, for the stone medicine and for ways of self- and community care.

Placing one's self- and community care items together in a container is a way to make a self-care tool kit. As I share about wellness and herbalism with different communities and circles through Mujeres de Maiz and La Botanica del Barrio, both projects I founded, I take a toolbox full of items to share. The toolbox is useful to carry the items in and is also a symbol to me of the tools we can use to take care of self and community. My tool kit usually includes incense, aromatherapy sprays, stones, herbal tinctures, glycerites, essential oils, salves, ointments, teas, and loose-leaf herbs. I encourage all to build their own self-care tool kit and to get to know what works best for them. These kits can also be made in small/mini versions for on the go or in your car and can include inspirational quotes, photos, and special symbols or small objects.

Many of us, as womxn of color, are often doing our best just to survive. But I trust that by practicing self and community care and connecting with our cultural traditions and ways, we can not only survive, but we can also live and thrive as we engage to transform ourselves and the world.

A Poppet for Mental Health

JESSICA LOZANO RODRIGUEZ

My practice originates from the Los Altos Norte region of Jalisco, Mexico. This is a place where magic exists in everyday life, and the supernatural is embraced as natural. I work as my great-grandmother, a *curandera/bruja*, worked: using herbs and stones, boiling things together, touching, cleansing, praying, and engaging in magical rituals (spells). But, as an anthropologist and a curious individual, my practice deviates a little from hers due to its eclecticism. I am undoubtedly blessed to have been exposed to and trained in various family members' and elders' practices—from learning basic *remedios* and acquiring the skills to make plant extracts to banishing spirits and learning to trust my clairsentience.

The spell I have decided to share is the first one I created without any help or encouragement. As a survivor of sexual violence, I had been managing clinical depression, post-traumatic stress disorder, panic disorder, and agoraphobia for quite some time. I developed the following spell during my last bout of depression two years ago. I realized that I needed something besides pills and therapy—I needed to heal from within, on a spiritual level, where the most profound part of my being resides. Wielding power and energy is itself therapeutic, and I have found that when it is done for the sake of self-care and empowerment, the changes that result are truly amazing.

A POPPET FOR MENTAL HEALTH

It may take a few days to gather materials and get them ready for making the poppet, and that is to be expected.[1] Once everything is set, it is important to construct the poppet all at once, since its creation is part of the spell process. Something else that is important to note is that certain things can be modified to fit your specific needs, geography, beliefs, and preferences.

This spell is best done during a waning moon on a Saturday. The waning moon and Saturday are both associated with endings, changing, dwindling, transforming, and renewing. It is not necessary to perform it at such a time, but it will give the spell some extra help.

Ingredients and tools:
- cloth (from your own clothing is best since it carries your energy and essence)
- scissors
- white sewing string (white is the color of protection, peace, and purification)
- sewing needle
- black gemstone (obsidian and onyx both work great since they absorb negative energy)
- optional gemstones (crystal quartz to boost the energy of the black gemstone and/or a piece of turquoise, which is a protective stone and keeps away negative energy)
- herbs associated with protection and cleansing (fresh or dried—rue, rosemary, basil, and sage are my favorites)
- herbs associated with calm and good mental health (fresh or dried—I use lavender, mint, and chamomile)
- white taper candle and candleholder

Preparation:
- Purify your gemstone(s) by putting it in a bowl of salt for a day and a night. After, wash the gemstone(s) under running water for seven seconds. As an option, you can charge your gemstone(s) with sun energy by putting it in the

---

1. A poppet is a doll or effigy representing a human being for ritual use and/or to aid a person in energy work and spells. For this spell in particular it is for both purposes. The poppet will represent the self and will aid in directing energy for improving mental health. The word "poppet" is of European origin but is used in various cultures around the world.

sun for a day and moon energy by putting it in the light of a full moon for an entire night.

- Gather all the materials you will use in one place.
- Prepare for the ritual by taking a shower right before—it helps me to feel cleansed, focused, and ready.
- Fold the cloth in half and cut a hand-sized shape of a human body. It should have a head, two arms and two legs, and a torso. When you finish, you should have two symmetrical pieces of cloth roughly resembling a human figure.

Spell:
- If you have an altar, put all your materials on your altar.
- Begin with a simple thank-you to the deity of your choosing.
- Sit somewhere comfortable, with the materials ready at hand.
- Breathe in through your nose and out through your mouth. Focus on your breathing for a few seconds. Then, visualize that you are taking in positive energy as you breathe in. Visualize getting rid of negative energy as you breathe out.
- Feel the positive energy course through your body with each intake of breath—a nice warm sensation in your chest, your shoulders, your neck. Next, you will feel it in your face, your head, your hair. The warm energy fills your arms and hands. Keep breathing steadily. Feel the energy fill your torso, pubic area, legs, and feet. Once you are filled with energy and your body and mind are calm, proceed to the next step.
- Put the white taper candle in its holder (preferably on your altar), and right before lighting it, use the match/lighter to bless it with the sign of the cross or the four directions.
- Imagine that the candle's flame is your companion. The light of the flame will accompany you during the ritual process and fill everything with purifying, protective, and peaceful energy.
- Thread your needle with the white sewing string. Pick up the two pieces of cloth and start sewing them together, leaving an opening to insert the gemstone(s) and herbs into the poppet.
- Remember the qualities of each gemstone and herb as you insert it into the poppet and visualize each one doing its job and making you feel better. There is no need to rush; mindfully and lovingly put each stone and herb into the poppet. The poppet represents you, and as you fill it with the energies of each item, you are filling yourself with healing energy. (I recommend putting

the gemstone(s) in one of the legs of the poppet, since it will be the heaviest component and you want the poppet to sit upright.)
- Sew the poppet closed once you are finished putting everything into it.
- Stand up in front of the white candle, with your poppet in hand.
- Visualize some of that warm energy you filled yourself with earlier exiting your hands and going into the poppet. Once the poppet is filled with positive energy, cup it in both hands and say these, or similar, words:

> Into the black stone, my pain goes
> The herbs protect me from my woes.
> The herbs and candlelight fill me with hope.
> This poppet will heal me, my mind, and my soul.
> In the name of the Creator and all good beings,
> It will be as I say, and will remain so.

- Extinguish the candle flame with your fingers so that the energy of the spell remains within the candle.
- Put your hands on the floor and push any magical energy you have left into the earth to ground yourself.
- Sit your poppet on your altar or somewhere where you can see it every day to remind yourself of the healing that is taking place.
- The spell is done!

HOW TO USE YOUR POPPET AFTER THE SPELL

If you are having a particularly difficult day, you can do a couple of things: (1) light the candle you used for this spell, pick up your poppet, smell it, take some of the positive energy that fills it within yourself, and repeat the words above, or (2) light the candle you used for this spell, pick up your poppet and pour all of your negative energy into it, saying the words above. You will have to purify it (put it in salt, pass it around a candle flame seven times, smudge it with sage, etc.) afterward.

Once you no longer feel like you need the poppet, burn it in a safe place after taking the gemstone(s) out, and thank the deity of your choosing for the healing work you were able to do with the poppet.

Happy spell work and blessings!

La oración

PEDRO ALVARADO

I pray that you heal.
I invoke the name *de la virgen.*
De la divina femenina.
I pray that your heart can rest.
You work so hard
For yourself and others.
I offer you my home
Take what you need
Take what you want
I ask that Coyolxauhqui keeps you safe
In everything that you do
I pray you find peace
I pray that you heal.

PLATE 1 Liliana Wilson, *La hija del maíz*, 2018. Acrylic and pencil on paper. Courtesy of artist

"Corn, the corn plant was the first totem: before the eagle, the jaguar, the serpent, the fish,"
Andrés Henestrosa

PLATE 2 Yreina D. Cervántez, *Maíz, el primer nagual*, 2008. Watercolor on arches paper. © Yreina D. Cervántez

PLATE 3 © Yreina D. Cervántez, *Canción y Cura*, 2016–2017. Acrylic on wood. Courtesy of artist

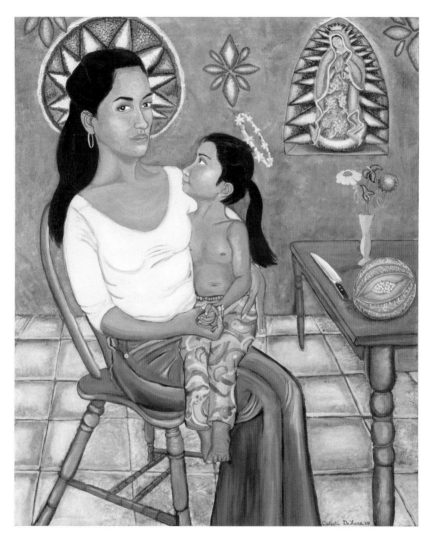

PLATE 4 Celeste De Luna, *Corazón de melón*. Acrylic on canvas. Courtesy of artist

PLATE 5 Ofelia Esparza, *Mujeres poderosas*, 2016. *Ofrenda* constructed at Museum of Latin American Art, Long Beach, California. Courtesy of artist, photo by Rosanna Esparza Ahrens

PLATE 6 Margaret "Quica" Alarcón, *Mayahuel*, 2008. Oil on canvas. Private Collection of Monica Menendez

PLATE 7 Jessica L. Rocha, *De maguey*, 2015. Digital illustration. Courtesy of artist

PLATE 8 Yadira L. Cazares, *Invocation*, 2018. Mixed media on plexiglass. Courtesy of artist

PLATE 9   Patricia Rodriguez, *A Rose in My Heart*. Painting, mixed media on canvas board. Courtesy of artist

11

LIFE CHANGES

INTRODUCTION

Life's many changes, both expected and unexpected, fill our lives with joys and sorrows, with times for celebration and periods for grieving.[1] The aging process that begins at birth offers us multiple opportunities to grow into our personhood with a strong face and heart. Modern Western societies dismiss traditional ways that honor stages in our physical growth and developing leadership potential, other than birthdays and graduations that usually do not involve spiritual ritual. Reclaiming our Indigenous practices that honor the stages of the life cycle serves to recognize the spiritual power in bodily changes and the various levels of leadership and distinct skills we bring to our communities at different points in our development. Childhood is a time when the values and traditions of a culture are transmitted and we learn to recognize the sacred in the environment and our responsibility to care for it, as well as the sacredness in all our relationships. Adolescence is the time to learn one's interdependency with the community and one's responsibility to give to the family and community by offering one's emerging talents and practicing one's leadership skills and acting as a role model for the younger ones. Adulthood is the time to fully integrate and adapt into one's life the traditions and values learned and to step into the role

---

1. For visual reflection, see plate 1, *La hija del maíz* by Liliana Wilson.

of nurturer and advisor. It is a time to heal any emotional wounds previously experienced. Elderhood is a time to share one's accumulated wisdom and to be honored by one's family and community. Each stage of life is strengthened by ceremony that reinforces one's sacred relationship to self, to others, and to the planet. As Inés Talamantez writes in reflecting on her Apache Mescalero initiation ceremony, "The society and family that surrounds and sustains these girls and women they become must take seriously the nurturance that an emphasis on ritual and ceremony requires. . . . It must recognize them as serious focal points for the entire culture" (1993, 132). Rites of initiation acknowledging our young ones of all genders or rituals honoring the accumulated wisdom of our elders are important aspects in our process of decolonizing beliefs that shame the menstrual cycle, gender fluidity, and the aging process.

This chapter opens with "A Rite of Passage for a Young Woman" by Linda Villanueva, who offers her deep reflections on the ritual she designed for her daughter. "Our community would reprogram an old paradigm of self-worth, reinforcing the cultural and social understanding that to bleed as a woman is something of joyous wonderment, a living miracle that we each own, an empowering experience." Villanueva participated for many years in Fiesta de Maíz in Los Angeles, sponsored by Calmecac, an organization of Chicanx mental health professionals, social workers, and teachers. Fiesta de Maíz, a communal ritual, integrated and adapted aspects of Nahua and Maya teachings honoring the growth cycle of *maíz* as synonymous with "the season of youth within the cycle of life. The time of growing, learning, stretching out to the road in becoming Xilonen and Centéotl," the protectors of the young corn (Fiesta de Maíz 1993). Fiesta de Maíz constituted an important part of the decolonizing work begun by Chicanx activists in the 1970s and is a ceremonial model very applicable to and needed today. An excerpt of the ceremony held in 1993 is included in this chapter.

In "Transceñera: A Transformative Ceremony," Jacqueline Garza Lawrence shares with us the need she felt for acknowledging her gender transformation with a communal ritual, a vision of a transceñera ceremony marking the passage of one identity to another. Such a communal recognition of a person's transition is highly effective for transforming heteronormative consciousness. We need even more examples of rituals honoring gender fluidity.

"Luna Mia: A Xicanx Guide for a First-Moon Ceremony" by Aida Salazar offers a puberty ritual "to celebrate the magic of the first moon for a young girl/menstruator as the beginning of a major transformation from childhood to womxnhood." Aida's extensive research and intuitive knowledge are integrated in this communal ritual and also reflected in her 2018 publication *The Moon Within,* a groundbreaking novel for adolescent readers that closes with a translated fifteenth-century Yucatec Maya poem read during a precontact moon ceremony.

"Leaving Home" by Lara Medina creates a ritual space for blessing one's young-adult child as they transition out of the parent's home to begin their adult journey. For a young person, the prospect of leaving home can be both exciting and frightening, especially if it involves leaving home for college, where one is now the adult making one's own decisions in the new world opening up. Receiving the blessings and advice from one's elders for this new phase and then being asked to share one's young wisdom are empowering moments not easily forgotten.

Grieving for the child that was dreamed of but never conceived requires healing that will come with deep self-reflection and prayer. María Elena Fernández pens a prayer to Madre Tierra and the elements as offering of her profound grief and gratitude for the healing she has received full of "compassion and understanding."

In "Mynopause," beloved Elisa Facio suggests a transformative method for reconceptualizing the stage of life when Western society begins to discard womxn. Compounded by a life-threatening illness that Elisa had little control over, she "situated [her] understanding and negotiation of a traumatic two-year men-o-pausal journey in Gloria Anzaldúa's concept of *conocimiento* and accompanying stages of transformation." Elisa prompts us to an understanding of mynopause as part of our human dynamic growth, our evolution or journey through life, a conocimiento and learning to live and appreciate the knowledge gained from the bodies we live in. We honor Elisa, who passed into the spirit world in August 2018. We are grateful to have her most personal experience with her illness recorded here.

Martha R. Gonzales and Lara Medina

A Rite of Passage for a Young Woman

LINDA VILLANUEVA

In the moment when my eleven-year-old daughter came to me letting me know her womanhood had arrived, I embraced her with so much joy and many congratulations. I shared with her the teaching of understanding that her monthly moon cycle of shedding and renewal was her ability to give birth to a new life and was a positive life-maturation process. The development of a Rite of Passage ceremony required creating a structure for it and thinking about what significant lessons to teach. The process transformed us both. It became a great healing, a living prayer. Her decision-making strengths took form at a new level, requiring her to think differently about herself and those she would find support from throughout her life. In essence, honoring my daughter in a Rite of Passage ceremony would be an acknowledgement of a death, a marker of time ended and of rebirth.

Sacred ceremony and initiation rituals are powerful. They allow us to hold the balance of life on to Light. They are a living and breathing aspect of a mindful process meant to catapult the Initiate and those present to arrive at a new level of understanding and wisdom, deepening one's connection to the Divine Goddess within. All those present, the collective, would be Initiates. Our community would reprogram an old paradigm of self-worth, reinforcing the cultural and social understanding that to bleed as a woman is something of joyous wonderment, a living miracle that we each own, an empowering experience.

As a mother, I thought of all the complexities, the dualities, we all face within this human lifespan, those forces of life that give rise to joy and grief, happiness and suffering. I wanted to integrate all those ideas metaphorically into her honoring ceremony. I thought of how to present the polarities of life's sweetness, of life's bitterness, of the successes and the seemingly insurmountable obstacles. My daughter would be faced with making choices in the moment when difficulties presented themselves. At a much deeper level, she would acknowledge that her life choices are made with free will and that there would be those around her to support her journey. She would experience the love of community.

I thought of the beauty of a goddess, a queen, a leader in beauty, and how she would present herself, wearing a crown and a handmade dress with all adornments. She would wear no shoes, as her step with bare feet would be on our ancient mother, giver of life. I drew on the knowledge of Indigenous ancestral ceremony, the Xilonen, esoteric and Eastern beliefs, in order to incorporate various teachings essential in this Rite of Passage ceremony.

Our ceremony took place in the Malibu Canyon near the California coast, outside the home of our dear sister, Linda Vallejo, in a beautiful forest setting. In preparation, my daughter chose three pairs of godmothers, *tías*, who would impart a particular lesson, a *consejo* that would honor her strength and courage. They collaborated in developing teachings that would raise her self-confidence and decision-making, her integrity and honesty, her forthrightness, compassion, and love, helping her to trust her own wisdom, to make good choices, to always live in spirit.

In real north, south, and west directions, each pair of godmothers created their own altars, honoring one of the four elements, from which they would impart gifts and words of wisdom. The eastern door was left open for entering the sacred circle and from the center would be the space from which all would evolve. Our central fire would be limited to candles to protect the surrounding nature and forest.

On the earth, we created a sacred mandala made of hundreds of colorful flower petals and filled in with large dried *maíz* seeds, blue and white maíz. As if guided by a divine source, the women gathered and we intuitively gave form to the shape of the robe worn by Our Lady of Guadalupe. There was no conscious awareness that we were intentionally forming her sacred robe. It was our collective feminine inner wisdom, and perhaps guidance by ancestral knowledge, that led us to form this absolutely magnificent and beautiful mandala on which my daughter would walk from this moment forward. The trees, the forest, the water flowing in a nearby creek, the wind and the fire, all the elements conspired to join us in perfect harmony.

We adorned our daughter with a crown made of sage and a white huipil dress, symbolizing purity and virginity. Two of her godmothers made both these gifts. Accompanied by her primary *madrina*, she was led barefoot from the eastern door, moving clockwise, to receive teachings. Each direction had a specific symbol and life lesson. For example, at the western altar she was given a taste of vinegar then a taste of honey. She would meet times of bitterness, perhaps difficulty, as well as times of sweet success and joyfulness. All that in between would offer her the gifts of living a full life.

Our ceremony included a trickster, a *heyoka*, personified by a close friend, whose role was the physical and outward representation that life's daily distractions must not deter us from our goal or path. The lessons and symbolisms were many. After receiving counsel from the ancient mothers' wisdom and the four directions, the entire community shared in offering prayer, dance, poetry, music and song, *palabra y consejo*. Many honoring gifts were shared, from the community circle as well as from the Initiate to the community. She herself made a special prayer candle to give to each participant and attendee. She shared thoughts about what the ceremony meant to her and addressed the community with a closing prayer and well wishes. Lastly, everyone brought foods to share and we ended in the breaking of bread and celebration. It was a very profound experience, one that would leave the deepest imprint to be passed on to the next generation.

I continue in complete gratitude. I contemplate the profoundness of a timeless wisdom, which presents itself when one participates in sacred ritual and initiation. I acknowledge its own intent, its own power and force meant to open the hearts of those present. It opens us to shift our consciousness, moving us to greater heights of living, of being, deepening our connectedness to one another at a cellular level. It is an invitation to reside inside that unspoken space wherein the unseen, the holy, presides, magnifying love for self and others. It is a quiet space in each of us that when we reflect on its symbolic representations of life gives us new hope and vision to transform our soul in this vast universe. We each are gifted to being witness, to seeing life's magic unfold, in that moment becoming unified breath, ONE.

I wish to thank all relatives who participated and gave of themselves. Your contribution is written into the ancient sands of the earth. I give blessings to you and your families and bless all the goddess's born unto you. I thank you, my daughter, for having received the highest grace as a mother. You have been a greatest blessing in my life.

Fiesta de maíz

A Ceremony for Our Young Adults

LARA MEDINA

CALMECAC–LOS ANGELES, 1993

Maíz, society, culture, and history are inseparable. Our past and present have their foundations in the maíz. Our life is based on the maíz. . . . We are the People of the Corn.

Today's youth, both female and male, are in need of acknowledgement and spiritual integration into the fabric of our community. They need our individual and collective nurturance, teaching, comfort, guidance, protection, and example of living in balance and harmony.

Traditionally, we have recognized the value of the forces of nature on which our lives depend. The Giver of Life has blessed us with the vision of the universe, the power of Father Sun, the love and strength of Mother Earth, and the counsel of Time. We humble ourselves and gain strength through the fiesta. Throughout the year, we experience the enactment of birth, growth, maturity, and death. We see this cycle in the four seasons. We see it in the cycle of el maíz and all living things. Humans also belong to this sacred cycle of life. Each season of our life is a passageway unto the next. Each period of our life is important and needs to be honored and recognized.

The youths chosen for this year's ceremony symbolize the spirit of Xilonen and Centéotl, who represent the balance between the female and male elements, the energy of youth and the wisdom of the aged, and outward action and inward reflection.

The steps associated with the cultivation of maíz can help us to understand with greater clarity the task we hold before us that gives meaning to our lives and how best those tasks can be accomplished.

- Planting: We exchange ideas and teach cultural values and lessons to the younger ones. For this the soil must be prepared and made fertile.
- Sprouting: We take the lessons and begin to integrate them as part of our being—reaching out and breaking ground.
- Clearing/weeding: We eliminate aspects, behaviors, or characteristics that threaten our healthy existence. We provide adequate room for growth.
- Pollinating: We are limited when alone. Through sharing and balanced cooperation of males and females, life is enriched.
- Harvesting: We gather the fruit, the enjoyment now of our previous efforts, and prepare to begin another cycle of planting.
- Drying: We come to a balanced ending in our lives, passing on the best part of ourselves to others for continued germination, for future generations.

Ritual Protocol

- Preparation of a large circle with an altar placed in each of the cardinal directions. Symbols on the altars represent the significance of that direction.
- Procession of *danzantes* and youth of the community into the circle.
- Honoring of the directions and prayer for permission to hold ceremony by elder.
- Dressing in ritual attire of Xilonen and Centéotl by adult helpers.
- Walk of the Xilonen and Centéotl to each cardinal direction, beginning in the east, then south, west, and north, with teachings offered about the directions and the life cycle from the elders sitting in front of each altar. This represents the journey from childhood to adulthood.
- Sharing of *consejos* (words of wisdom) from the youth (Xilonen and Centéotl) to the community.
- Giving of symbolic handcrafted gifts to the Xilonen and Centéotl by adult helpers.
- Invitation to join the Community Round Dance—to dance in the circle following drumbeats.

- Recitation of the closing prayer of gratitude by an elder—"La Palabra."
- Giveaway of handcrafted symbols of maíz to all present.
- Sharing of food among community—*la convivencia* (potluck).

This communal ritual can also include the planting of maíz seeds in small pots to teach younger children about the steps in the life cycle of maíz and of humans.

Transceñera

A Transformative Ceremony

JACQUELINE GARZA LAWRENCE

As a child, I was raised with traditional teachings from my *abuela* about the healing customs of our Indigenous ancestors of Central Mexico. After decades of learning from my abuela, I now use this experience to help others. My grandmothers and great-grandmothers and beyond have left me with the knowledge and teachings of their mothers, grandmothers, and so on. Our spiritual existence does not begin when we are physically born, but rather through our life in the spiritual realm and in our connection to our ancestors we are allowed to be reborn in human form. My teachings start in the space of spirit and take root in the personal journey I am experiencing here and now.

The process of finding the true self has become difficult, as one gets further away from our roots. My ancestors passed down a coming-of-age ritual to me. My abuela was very clear that the teachings we share can only be sacred if done in a sacred way. This means that no other medicines or mind-altering substances can be present during this sacred ceremony.

A transceñera is a transformation ceremony to reclaim one's gender identity. One day as I was praying and focusing on the way our current social structure defines gender, I realized that as a society we had gotten way off track about gender identity. I was meditating on this thought and that night I had a dream; the dream revealed what I now call the transceñera ceremony. The ceremony is for anyone struggling to find their true gender identity in a spiritual way.

The ceremony begins with a person making an offering to an understanding elder they respect and asking to be taken through the ceremony. Next the person participates in a *temezkal*. After the purification is complete, the individual fasts for three days. Following the three days, the individual goes to their elder and is given instructions for a cleansing bath consisting of fresh medicines. Upon completing the bathing process, the person is dressed and brought out to the ceremonial space by a helper who is assigned by the elder in charge. At this time, the individual is brought to a sacred space where they will be smudged and placed on their knees on a blanket. The elder asks several questions, and the participant answers according to their heart. Once the individual has answered, the elder prays and blesses them with a mixture of several plant medicines. The individual is asked to stand and then greets their spiritual family, and the elder as well, and greets the group as they have defined themselves through this process. The ceremony is sealed with a feast to celebrate.

It is important to note that the ceremony is not set in stone. Instead, it is there to guide the fluidity of one's growth and spiritual existence, honoring the fluidities in identity. This is a starting point for a person to claim who they are with the understanding that how one defines themselves grows and changes throughout a lifetime.

Luna Mia

A Xicanx Guide for a First-Moon Ceremony

AIDA SALAZAR

While people of different cultures around the world have participated in rituals for the moon in varying degrees, the following communal ritual is inspired primarily by traditional Indigenous womxn's practices in the Americas, coupled with my own ideas of symbolism and the significance of the first menses. The term "menstruator" is used in addition to, and sometimes interchangeably with, "girl/womxn" and "her" as an act of inclusivity and acknowledgement of gender-expansive people who also menstruate. The following guidelines are the culmination and synthesis of my research and intuitive explorations, and they are offered with radical love and resistance for all young Xicanx/Latinx and their mothers.

Why a Ritual for a First Moon?

We celebrate the magic of the first moon for a girl/menstruator as the beginning of a major transformation from childhood to adulthood. The first moon is our body's way of signaling that we are now able to create life and carry a child within our bodies. And as life-bearing creatures, womxn are charged with a deep responsibility and a deep connection to the circle of life and death. Often, girls/menstruators enter into this transition without any understanding of its beauty, power, and complexity. With each ritual, we honor the moon girl/menstruator because she is now part of a lineage of life givers and menstruators. We hold her as she leaves her childhood behind and becomes a new moon, a womxn.

When we gather and sit in circle to celebrate this transformation, we do so to foster a sense of community and gather collective feminine strength. By creating and performing rituals, we take the time to focus as a group on the magical energy inherent in the transition and to hold space to offer wisdom and to answer the girl/menstruator's questions. Approaching the first moon in a ceremonial way creates a spiritual support system and an experience of kinship and bonding that the girl/menstruator can always access to help her resolve personal problems along her journey.

When to Do a First-Moon Ritual

Once the first menses arrives, the first-moon ritual can be held as soon as the following full moon and up to six months after. The wisdom, perspective, and power that the girl/menstruator receives from the ritual will serve her as she experiences each of her cycles. Because the full moon carries an energy of celebration, of harvest, and of the full blossoming of all that we have planted during the new moon (dark phase of the moon), it is important to hold the ritual at night, beneath the potent and celebratory full-moon energy.

Participants

The main participant, the moon girl/menstruator, above all others, should be consulted and included in the planning and preparation of this communal ritual. It is always best to invite womxn who have played a significant role in the moon girl's life. But also, it is equally important to bring teachers and elders who have heightened spiritual knowledge to share with the group.

Each guest is invited to bring a symbolic gift—a poem, song, or other small offering—for the moon altar that will be created in the center of the ritual circle. Also, each womxn is charged with bringing a bit of wisdom to be shared with the girl/menstruator. It is also important to invite young peers (who may or may not have yet bled) to the ritual. This opens the circle of energy, offers moral support, and also serves to teach other youth the spiritual path and power of this communal ritual.

Preparing the Space

If creating the ritual in a garden or in a living room, make a clearing that will hold the number of people you have invited. Burn sage or copal in the clearing before setting out chairs and/or mats and pillows in a circle. Creating an open, clean space is an important part of creating a sacred circle that will optimize receiving the full-moon energy.

Building a Moon Hut or Moon Lodge

The moon girl/menstruator will sit in a moon hut during the ritual. The moon hut represents the lodge to which Indigenous womxn traditionally retreated during their moon time—the sacred space reserved for fasting, dreaming, making art, and listening to our psychic and intuitive power.

To create a moon hut, tie together bamboo sticks or use an arbor or, if necessary, simply use a pop-up tent. You can drape your moon hut with rebozos, bedspreads, or large pieces of fabric and can decorate it with wind chimes or bells. You can decorate the inside with candles or lights to represent gaining new knowledge, fresh flowers to represent her blossoming, and evergreen shrubs to represent longevity and feminine endurance. You should decorate the moon hut in a way that feels personal and sacred to you.

Building an Altar

Building an altar is an essential component of the ritual. It is the heart of the circle. The altar must reside in the middle of the circle, and, if possible, it should be mindful of the four cardinal directions—east, west, north, and south—and the energies accompanied by each.

To build an altar, you can place images of female goddesses and fill the altar with symbols of transformation and fertility, such as butterflies and flowers. As with any of these offerings, please feel free to improvise and do what speaks to your heart. But be sure to cleanse each object with burning sage or copal before you place it on the altar.

Four Directional Poles

The four directions remind us that we are connected to a larger universe. Make four prayer poles by taking four long sticks and covering them with colored yarn specific to each direction. Be mindful to cover the tips of each with hanging red cloth to represent the first blood. Place each pole outside the circle in each of the cardinal directions to ground the connection.

Sacred Fire

Fire is an important element in creating a sacred space. While fire can be a destructive energy, it is also the source of life and is sustenance for our bodies and our well-being. It represents our passions, our creative energy, and our transformation.

You can make a fire pit in a hole in the earth or use a metal container or simply light a group of candles—whatever is most available to you but so as not to burn anything or anyone in the circle. Designate a participant to keep the fire lit. Place thirteen rocks around the sacred fire or around the circle or altar. These rocks represent the thirteen full moons in a year and are a reminder of our lunar processes.

Moon Water

The rays of the moon infuse and bless any water they touch with healing energy. To take advantage of this energy, you can make moon water during the ritual. It is a simple thing to do but provides an enormous blessing when drunk, as it helps heal mind, body, and soul. Fill glass jars with purified water and place them in the direct rays of the moon, near each attendant's seat. At the end of the evening, they can take home this moon water to drink during any time they need healing.

Shakers

Provide participants with small rattles, maracas, and bells. They can use these whenever they feel inspired to clap. Drums aren't used in a moon ritual because of the male energy associated with drums. In addition, Coyolxauhqui, Mexica goddess of the moon, had bells that fell on her cheeks, and so by ringing bells and rattles, we invoke her.

Food

Food is an essential part of the ritual. It is important to offer foods that are based on *maíz*, squash, bean, nopal, amaranth, chia, or cacao, "the warriors of nutrition." These foods are rooted in the Americas and were and continue to be used both daily and during celebrations and feasts.

Ritual

As guests arrive, greet them with an offering of food and drink so they feel nourished and relaxed before the ritual begins. Start the fire and/or light candles.

After eating, invite the elder womxn into the circle first. Designate one knowledgeable participant to smudge each womxn before they enter the circle to take their seat. The smoke will purify the body, mind, and heart of all negative emotions. Wait until all the older womxn are seated before the young peers and, finally, your moon girl/menstruator enter the circle. She will sit inside the special moon hut.

The ceremonial leader or facilitator welcomes everyone present—those that bleed, those who no longer bleed or do not bleed, and those who will soon bleed. Give thanks to our Creator, Ancestors, Mother Earth, Grandmother Moon, Grandfather Sun, the creative and divine feminine energy present, and, finally, give thanks to the moon girl/menstruator. Then all turn to each of the four directions to receive the blessing of each direction. Also touch Mother Earth or the ground and then look up to the sky or ceiling to thank the entire universe. A knowledgeable one can blow a conch shell to honor each direction. Shaking a rattle can replace the sound of the conch. The leader or designated person can sing a song related to the moon and can ask all to join in.[1]

The facilitator then passes a feather around and asks that each person say her name and one thing she is grateful for. This allows for a circle of gratitude and sacredness to be created by each womxn's heart energy. The facilitator can then talk about why all are gathered, the significance of the circle, and the meaning of the elements that make up the altar.

Cleansing

The moon girl is now asked to come out of her moon hut and stand in the center of the circle, next to the altar. The facilitator and/or mother takes the bowl of prepared *agua florida* (flower essence water) and washes the girl/menstruator's hands and feet and also gently sprinkles agua florida over her clothes and body. The water is a symbol of the release of all that does not serve her and it welcomes her moon with renewed and open energy.

1. See part 17, "Prayer and Song," for examples.

Flower Crowning

The moon girl/menstruator continues to stand while her mother and a few others adorn her with a crown of flowers and a flower necklace, bracelets, and anklets. As she is crowned, the mother can speak to the ways in which her child has blossomed. The flowers are the representation of this blossoming; they represent the cycle of life—the culmination of the creative act and also the genesis of creation. After her adornment, the moon girl/menstruator may return to the moon lodge.

First-Blood Giving

The moon girl/menstruator now offers her first blood to Mother Earth, Tonantzin. Traditionally, womxn dug a hole inside the moon hut and squatted and bled directly into the hole. Tonantzin receives this blood to fertilize the earth. Or the blood can be collected in a ceramic bowl over the toilet during menstruation and mixed with agua florida and preserved for the ritual. The moon girl can then dig a small hole into the earth. She can decorate the rim of the hole with flowers as she gives thanks to Tonantzin. She then pours the mixture of blood and agua florida into the earth and offers a prayer such as this one:

> Madre Tierra, Tonantzin
> please receive my first blood,
> please receive my first moon.
> Tlazocahmati Ancestors.
> Gracias, Grandmother Moon.
> Gracias, Abuela Luna.
> Tlazocahmati Ometeotl.

She can then place a healing plant inside the hole and cover it with earth. Planting represents her power to give life, like Mother Earth.

Words of Wisdom

During this ritual, we see the power of community come alive. Each womxn approaches the moon girl in her lodge and offers her a story, a poem, a song, words of wisdom, or best wishes. This is also the time when each womxn can give the moon girl/menstruator a small gift or can place something meaningful on the moon altar. The gifts and advice will vary as much as your guests vary, and it is a beautiful time to observe the magnificent group of people you have gathered in circle for your moon girl/menstruator. Perhaps most importantly, this is a time for the young menstruator to speak for herself, to thank the womxn and peers in the circle, and to reflect on the ritual or what she might be feeling.

Walking Around the Altar

Throughout the entire ritual, the girl has had with her in the moon hut a beloved doll or toy that represents her childhood. While still in her moon hut, the leader asks the girl/menstruator to say goodbye to and thank her toy for the bond they shared during her childhood. She gives her toy to the facilitator, who places it on the altar in the south, the direction of childhood. The moon girl can then leave her moon hut and walk around the altar, beginning in the east, the direction of infancy, moving to the south, and ending in the west, the direction of adulthood. This simple act represents the process of leaving childhood behind and entering into a new self.

Flower Dance

Womxn dancing in circle beneath the light of the moon is one of the most sacred and unifying of rituals. The full-moon energy is time for celebration, and with this ritual we harness the power of dance to release and lift up the spirit. You can sing and rattle or play recorded music for all to join in dancing.

Closing

The mother and moon girl/menstruator thank all those present. The moon girl/menstruator can offer *palabra* or a poem, a song, or other expression of gratitude about what she has received from the ritual. The facilitator can close by saying, "To All Our Relations, we thank you. Let the circle always protect us."

Leaving Home

LARA MEDINA

This ceremony came to me when asked what could be done to bless a young womxn leaving home for college. It can be adapted for any reason that a young person is leaving home to begin their adult journey. Thus, it is written here with gender-neutral pronouns.

Create a ritual space with many flowers on the ground in the shape of a circle that everyone will gather around. Flowers enhance and transmit the blessings. Have a smaller circle of flowers in the middle with a glass bowl of water with flower petals in it that will be used for the blessing. Also, light incense in the middle of the smaller circle: sage, copal, etc.

Mark the cardinal points on the circle (north, south, east, and west) with a symbolic object representing the stage of the life cycle at each point. East represents infancy; south, childhood; west, adulthood; and north, elderhood. Choose one person to be the guardian of each direction who will stand and offer the young person words of advice and encouragement related to the direction. These should be people who are close relations. The parent(s) can be the guardian(s) of the west.

The *madrina* of the ritual can start with prayer words of thanksgiving for the day and for the community of family and friends who have come to bless the young person. Always pray from the heart.

Invite the young person to stand in the east, where they began their life cycle. They will eventually move around the circle to receive the blessing from the guardian of each direction. Ask each guardian to offer their own words of gratitude and encouragement and a teaching related to the significance of the particular direction. They may recall memories of the young adult as an infant (the east) and then as a child (the south). When the young adult arrives in the west, the parent(s) offers their words of gratitude and wisdom. The madrina brings them the bowl of water for the blessing. They may bless the young person on the crown, forehead, throat, heart, and hands—all energy sites. When the young person arrives at the north, an elder guardian could offer their insights about living a wise life along with the final blessing. The madrina then asks what the young adult would like to tell all the guardians and everyone present. It is important that the young adult's voice be heard.

The ceremony will finish in the north, as the young adult is now prepared to go farther into the world in pursuit of knowledge. The madrina may close this communal ritual by thanking everyone present. Group singing or playing music is always good. Drumming is great! Have fun with this ceremony. Adapt it to your context, and speak from the heart!

Querida Tierra-Sol-Mar-y-Viento

Querida Tierra-Sol-Mar-y-Viento,
I offer at your feet the overflowing river of grief from my heart
that I did not bear from my body the children that I dreamed of

Desde niña me imaginaba
abotonándole a mijita un vestidito blanco y bordado
peinándola con dos colitas de caballo
and when she grew older, passing down to her the prissy peach dress
with the lace collar I wore under the black gown
as I walked across the New Haven lawn
the first in my family to receive the coveted college degree

Please give me the courage to speak of my loss with my sisters
together cry all the tears of the well within us

Please lift each anvil of shame from my shoulders
the hammering *reproches* that misshaped my body
and with your breath transform each into clouds aflight
Cloak me in your rebozo woven of only compassion and understanding
that I could not make family when I was fertile
and like an eternal full moon, remind me

I was protecting myself, fighting for survival
keeping my distance so my spirit could stay alive
May I forgive my blindness to this invisible battle
and release resentment of the teachers from whom I sought answers, but had
   none

Above all, I ask you to please give me acceptance of the landscape I stand in now
Gratitude for what I do have
that I found the teacher who explained my internal world
And now I weave my own cloak of compassion

I remember I am the mother of the mothers
la comadre pillaring my beloved girlfriend-mamas in their daily labor
and in the classroom I am mother
of ancestral knowledge for two decades to thousands of *jovenes*

I glimpse my curvy silhouette on the horizon
that again will sway and seduce on the dance floor
a horizon that can also welcome the laughter of children

Life's ferocious energy seeping in again
Sweeping into my womb seeds of *buganvilias* and *azucenas*

Amen

Mynopause

From "Change of Life" to a Nepantla State of Enlightenment

ELISA FACIO

Men-o-pause is rooted in patriarchal ideologies and epistemologies regarding women's psychological health, womanhood, identity, and sexuality.

Mynopause is a decolonial process of naming, negotiating, and moving toward a nepantla *state of enlightenment involving wisdom and continuous human evolution throughout a womyn's life journey.*

Men-o-pause for many Chicanas/Mexicanas is associated with loss of fertility, sexual identity, and womanhood. Generally, women biologically move beyond childbearing and child birthing, and consequently are considered asexual. Hence, patriarchal biological determinism is employed in how women understand their bodies and negotiate men-o-pause. In heterosexual relationships, men-o-pausal/post-men-o-pausal women are generally no longer considered physically and/or sexually desirable, regardless of how they engage their sexuality. Many women experience men-o-pausal conditions such as vaginal dryness, pain, inconsistent sexual drives, unpredictable emotional states, exhaustion, etc. And, men-o-pausal/post-men-o-pausal womanhood, or the value of women as significant and important "women," can decline among respective families and within the Chican@/Mexican@ community. Given space limitations, this message focuses on the physical challenges of men-o-pause, "a physical condition referred to as 'the change,' an illness involving uncontrollable and unpredictable emotional displays of *locura*, or 'madness,'" as my mother says!

My early onset of men-o-pausal experience resulted from a full hysterectomy, a strongly recommended procedure for fourth-stage endometrial cancer.

Men-o-pause, which I later named *mynopause*, abruptly ignited in my body within twenty-four hours following an emergency eleven-hour surgery. Generally, the men-o-pausal process can range from months to years, with women negotiating copious physical and emotional challenges, finally yielding to estrogen supplements and/or treatments or finding holistic medicines. Given that I was diagnosed with an estrogen-based cancer, I could not consume estrogen supplements, including black cohosh, as the disease could immediately return.

DECOLONIZING MEN-O-PAUSE

Desperately, I situated my understanding and negotiation of a traumatic two-year men-o-pausal journey in Gloria Anzaldua's concept of *conocimiento* and accompanying stages of transformation. The first stage, *el arrebato*, refers to a "rupture, fragmentation, an ending, a beginning" (2002, 546). The finding of endometrial cancer in a relatively young, healthy Chicana was extremely rare, leaving doctors and my family completely stunned. Feelings of anger and betrayal by universal life energies consumed me. How could my body, which I loved with all my being, betray me in such a brutal, violent manner? I was a nonsmoker, nondrinker, marathon runner, and (re)membering body, mind, and spirit via a recovered Mexican-Otomi spirituality. I ultimately had to embrace those feelings of anger and betrayal with self-compassion and acceptance, enabling me to move forward into the second stage, nepantla, an in-between place. In nepantla, I reluctantly mourned my past life, diligently but cautiously, and sought Indigenous, traditional, and holistic medicinal knowledges and practices to (re)embrace my body and passionately understand my human evolution. These knowledges served as guides in moving the most difficult energies and experiences from my body out to the loving universe for their transformation. This included moving through extreme night sweats; insomnia and exhaustion, averaging only three sleeping hours; hot flashes with severe nervousness; and emotional imbalances with unpredictable and frightening bouts of crying, frustration, uneasiness, and desperation. I continuously find myself in the stage of nepantla, as this is the stage where critical transformation of body, mind, and spirit continue to be negotiated. Transformation and full healing is a long process, and nepantla offers a safe and supportive space. Following are the *remedios* and *consejos* that have most helped me in my nepantla:

- Acupuncture—strongly recommended.
- Soy products.
- B12 supplements (injections recommended).
- Black cohosh (*if* recommended by physicians).
- Progesterone cream—Mexican yam root base.
- Yoga, walking, meditation.
- Altar-*sitio* for understanding and honoring the relationship among body, mind, and spirit. Praying daily to Tonantzin for strength and courage; burning sage to the four directions.
- Third-space sites for *gentle assessment* and creative expression of emotional/psychological challenges via music, gardening, cooking, journaling, painting, etc.
- Talking circles—use/share talking sticks blessed by mynopausal/post-mynopausal womyn.

By redeeming painful and challenging experiences, we transform them into something valuable, *algo para compartir,* and we can share what we've learned with others so they too may be empowered (Anzaldúa 2002, 540). Mynopause is not an illness but a gift for empowering oneself, friends, family, our communities, and the larger society. As we journey through the stages of conocimiento, we gain wisdom, clarity, and confidence, and we embrace our *nepantlisma* as a way of living.

12

MEDITATION

INTRODUCTION

I learned early in my spiritual journey that meditation is like free medicine that awakens our consciousness and sustains our well-being. Medicine that leads us to our "inner refuge" and to the "treasury of our natural mind" and teaches us how to simply be. Western culture has not taught the value of being still but rather emphasizes action for productivity. An important aspect of decolonizing is learning how to control the business of our minds that pushes us toward constant worry and activity. We must also learn to connect deeply with the elements in nature and in our bodies.

Up until now, my most profound lessons on meditation have come from the Tibetan Bon tradition, the Zhang Zhung lineage, as taught by Tenzin Wangyal Rinpoche, founder and spiritual director of the Ligmincha Institute. His teachings on our natural, pure state of body, mind, and speech experienced through meditation provide clear guidance for recognizing "the inherent completeness of each moment," which is the goal of meditation. Upon recognizing our completeness, we are able to transform perceived limitations, challenges, and problems into gifts of inner peace, joy, and liberation. The teachings I offer in this introduction are a brief synopsis of Tenzin Wangyal's teachings from *Awakening the Luminous Mind* (2012). I also highly recommend the audio recording *Sacred Circles: Honoring the Ancient Traditions of the Ancestors Aztec/Mayan Guided*

Healing Meditation, produced by Jerry Tello, Susana Armijo, and others, which offers culturally specific meditations.

Tenzin Wangyal writes that there are three doors leading to the gifts of openness, awareness, and joy. These doors are body, speech, and mind. Our breath carries us through the doors. We must learn to shift our attention to the stillness of the body, to the silence of our speech, to the spaciousness in our mind. As we sit still in meditation, we allow our pain body (challenges, problems, obstacles) to breathe. By focusing our attention on our breath and our stillness rather than the pain narrative, we will soon arrive at a deep place within, full of spaciousness and peace. That spaciousness is our refuge, where the power of pain dissolves. Next, focus our breath and our attention on the silence, not on the chattering voices within. If voices persist, simply allow them to be while we focus on the space and silence around them. Listen and remain open to the silence rather than to the voices. Do not give the voices energy or attention. Finally, and most importantly, feel the spaciousness of your mind. In the Bon tradition, the root nature of the mind is clear and luminous. The difficult emotions we experience, such as anger, can be brought to the spaciousness of the mind for healing. Rather than deny or rationalize anger, look at it directly, not at the story behind the anger but the anger itself. Host the anger in spaciousness. It will dissolve. "The moment you have some glimpse that you are bigger than what you are thinking or feeling is a healing moment" (Wangyal 2012, 4).

In this section, we open with the soothing words of Sara H. Salazar, as she poetically describes how in the healing process in meditation "the heart gently cracks open as the silver ribbons of grief untangle and dissolve." A meditation with the sacred elements follows, which I learned through Tibetan Buddhism and Mexican Indigenous teachings. Brenda Romero offers us her practice based on Transcendental Meditation, which she has been committed to since the early 1990s. And Linda Vallejo shares a meditation for releasing tensions around personal relationships, as taught to her by a Seneca Oneida elder. In closing this section, Heidi M. Coronado offers her practice with the Medicine Wheel, inspired by Maya and Navajo epistemologies and her own intuition.

Lara Medina

The Warrior Womxn Envisions . . .

SARA H. SALAZAR

The warrior womxn envisions herself in homespun ritual attire
kneeling at her own altar,
her life spread out like a banquet before her.
Her breathing, slow at first, becomes labored and short,
lifetimes of pain and fear move like waves through her blood and muscles
rising to the surface of her skin to be released.
With each wave of breath,
knots of wounding come undone.
Her heart gently cracks open as the silver ribbons of grief untangle and dissolve.

The curandera continues to sing until the body, mind, and spirit find balance
then she slowly closes the 13 portals with gentle touch and gives thanks.

Connecting with the Elements

LARA MEDINA

In shamanic healing practices, connecting with the elements—earth, air, fire, water—and space in the universe and in our bodies is essential for balanced well-being. Shamanic practices "call upon the essential forces of nature such as the winds, sacred plants, smoke, rocks, animals, fire and rivers for healing" (Roberts and Levy 2008, 7). Victor Sanchez (2004) writes that Indigenous shamans of Mexico work with *Poderios*, or "the forces of nature that are experienced as living, conscious, sacred entities with which they interact in the shamanic ceremonies" (14). When we deeply connect with the elements in nature and experience our "inner connection with them," we are able to enter into our own shamanic states of awareness for healing purposes (15).

We carry the elements in our bodies; they are understood as the foundational sacred energies of our existence. "In the shamanic worldview, each element has spiritual qualities . . . physical properties and energetic attributes, though all arise from the same primordial source" (Roberts and Levy 2008, 58). The fire and warmth of the sun correlates with the range of healthy human body temperature, ocean waters correlate with the water in our bodies, our flesh and bones are of the earth, and the air in our lungs matches the air we breathe. The spaciousness of the skies "is one and the same with the vast internal spaces in our bodies and cells" (59).

In urban life, it is easy to lose touch with the sacred elements. Our heaters keep us from interacting with the cold. Our faucets regulate the water. Our floors cover the earth. We end up protecting ourselves from the elements. Yet when missing any one of the elements, we yearn for it. For example, in a desert, we need water. In the cold, we require fire. If in water for a long time, we intuitively want earth to stand on. We die from lack of air. Meditating with the elements provides us with emotional, physical, and mental balance, offering spiritual well-being. I offer this meditation taught to me through Tibetan Buddhism and Mexican Indigenous knowledge to strengthen our relationships with the elements.

Sit or stand in a quiet place, preferably outside or at least facing a window where you can see the sky. Close your eyes. Focus on your breath until you begin to relax. . . . Then visualize your breath traveling from your lungs up to the crown of your head and then moving back down through your entire body, down through your feet. Do this a few times. Scan your feelings. . . . Are you feeling unstable or unsure? Or perhaps too rigid in decision-making? Do you feel cold or low on energy for your creative passions? Do you feel physically or emotionally weak? Scan your body to feel where you might be holding on to this feeling(s). Continue with your focused breathing. Next begin to visualize and connect to the first element that comes to your awareness. Use your active imagination. As examples, visualize earth as a mountain or vast desert or large tree and feel the stability that earth offers, visualize and feel the fluidity of air/ wind blowing, visualize a body of water and feel its cleansing power, visualize fire and feel its ability to transform what you do not need to carry. Stay with each visualization and feeling long enough to really breathe in the elements you are in need of. Breathe in the stability and confidence of earth, the fluidity of air, the renewing power of water, the warmth and transformative energy of fire. You may breathe in all the elements, if needed, in sequence. Continue with this meditation until you feel your body/mind/emotions arrive at a balanced state of being.

When you are ready, open your eyes slowly and gaze into the vastness of the sky. Enter the mystery of the sky and your existence. Feel the elements merging into the space around you and within you. Breathe deeply a few times. Place your hands on your heart and express gratitude.

Meditating with the elements opens a sacred path connecting the center of ourselves with the center of the universe. We embrace our existence that is full of mystery, transformative power, and potential.

To All My Relations

Following My Breath

BRENDA ROMERO

I was raised going to Mass at our village Guadalupe mission church, which included praying while hearing choirs of nuns or priests singing Gregorian chant in unison amid incense and ringing bells. This tradition came with mysterious stories of inexplicable occurrences, such as hearing footsteps when someone died. It seemed clear there is a divine presence that is ultimately unknowable but whose nearness is sometimes perceived. I started doing yoga at nineteen and taught a yoga class at age twenty, which was around the time I rejected my religious upbringing. It was another twenty-five years before I went back to Mass. I continued to pray daily, but this time they were Baha'i prayers, which I still recite.

I began meditating early on, including in a life-changing group yoga/meditation session from Yogi Bhajan, in Berkeley, California, in 1969. In the early 1990s, I started going to the El Dorado Ashram, just a few miles southwest of Boulder, Colorado. For a month I had been the only person attending a yoga class in the Tibetan Healing Room when others began joining in. One night, I was standing to the right of the shrine when I heard a man's deep voice say, "I am here." I turned to look in the direction the voice had seemed to come from, all the while thinking I was probably the only one hearing it. I took it to be the voice of one of the swamis pictured on the wall, although the voice came from the shrine. A couple years later, I took a meditation class and learned that my experience is not uncommon among the devotees who gather at the ashram.

Sometimes people see the statues get up and walk to them, and other such activations, presumably caused by the profound meditations. I began to understand I had been given a mantra: "I am here." Not here last year or yesterday or tomorrow or five years from now but right here, right now. I realized I was always living in the past or in the future, and here was my guide to mindfulness.

My meditation practice is based on Transcendental Meditation, so I follow the breath from the base of my core to the top of the lungs. At my shoulders I inhale, hold, exhale. I return to the breath when I realize I am thinking about something. The idea is to get to "no mind," a door to deeper perceptions and tranquility. I do all I can to calm myself, as some days I am anxious about something negative I experienced with a colleague, or a student, or some random someone (no doubt sometimes imagined). I sit on large cushions at my altar, which holds beloved prayer books and objects, adjusting my legs for comfort, touching thumbs to middle fingers, and resting hands on thighs. I used to meditate for twenty minutes, and sometimes still do, but a friend told me to try thirty minutes, and the extra time helps. I light a candle and ring a bell (once to begin, three times to end) as points of focus, then I recite prayers and burn a bit of sage. I always pray for healing, as there is always something or someone needing healing. Then I close my eyes and meditate on the inner image of the candle flame. In a good meditation, I can feel the gradual change in my brain and facial muscles as I release tension. I often pray for detachment from all except Divine Presence. I also consult Tarot cards, practice breathing meditation while swimming twice a week, and sometimes, I go to Mass.

A Meditation on Beauty for Releasing Pain and Trauma

LINDA VALLEJO

Taught to me by a Seneca Oneida Elder

This is a beautiful and simple meditation that will help you to release tension and stress surrounding personal situations and relationships. Begin by sitting comfortably in a quiet location with your legs folded and arms resting gently on your knees. Close your eyes gently and breathe slowly in through your nose and out through your mouth four times. Remain calm. Close your eyes and imagine a beautiful flower in your mind's eye. Continue breathing. See the flower large and fragrant. Place the object of your concern or the individual of your concern in the center of the flower. Imagine them resting quietly in the beauty of the petals. Continue to breathe and stay with this image for at least five minutes. Then count to three and blow the flower. Watch the petals fly all around you with beautiful streaming colors. In your mind's eye visualize the situation or the individual walking away to your right, eventually disappearing into the distance. See them smiling and enjoying their walk or the situation surrounded by peace. Wish them/it well and send them/it peace. Take all the lessons that you've learned from the situation or individual and place them in a beautiful box. You don't need to understand all the lessons now. Trust that you will understand them as you learn and grow. Repeat the exercise three times and end the meditation with a prayer of gratitude. I wish to thank my elders for teaching me this beautiful meditation. It has helped me to find balance and harmony in my life.

Learning to Breathe

Ancestral Healing, Spiritual Activism, and the Medicine Wheel

HEIDI M. CORONADO

When you begin to feel you are a spiritual being, which, in fact you are, you begin to activate the medicine wheel in your life.
— TONY TEN FINGERS, OGLALA LAKOTA (2014)

To connect to your inner self, to your spirit, to your wholeness is a critical act of resistance and decolonization. My Maya ancestors were forced through colonization to hide wonderful, powerful knowledge and spiritual practices. My immigrant parents were given labels based on their skin color, accent, and documentation status. Their hard work and positive contributions to this society became invisible. My first language, which was not English, was seen as a threat and a disadvantage in school rather than an asset. Connecting to nature, honoring my intuition, participating in and being inspired by talking circles, and talking about healing were seen as strange practices rather than critical and powerful acts needed for societal change.

In addition to my own traumas, I carried the historical trauma of my ancestors, and for many years I felt fragmented and incomplete. I only recognized my intellect—what I was taught in school yet, ironically, the part of me that was most often not good enough. My spirit felt a void; a voice in me insisted there was more. Many unrecognized emotions and body messages and connections to my ancestors, to the unseen, and to something bigger than myself were screaming to be heard. Connecting to my spirit and Indigenous epistemology has become an acknowledgment of my wholeness and of the resiliency of my ancestors, my culture, my community. Indigenous knowledge teaches us that every action we take in our lives affects all living things. We understand that if we act negatively, our actions affect all life negatively. When we act positively, we affect all life in a good way. When we live the Maya code of In Lak' ech Ala K'in, we know that every action we take is out of respect for all life and we are living and giving through our hearts.

SPIRITUAL ACTIVISM

Spiritual Activism is not about religion, it is not about any form of dogma, it is activism that comes from the heart, not just the head, activism that is compassionate, positive, kind, fierce and transformative.

—VELCROW RIPPER (2009)

Through honoring the practices of my Maya ancestors as well as the practices of various Native American and other wisdom traditions, I have been able to heal and reconnect with my inner wisdom. Wonderful messages from my ancestors that come through dreamtime, nature, books, and powerful, wise teachers have guided me to where I am today. The more open I am to healing, learning, and sharing, the more opportunities and resources open up. This work is more powerful than I can explain. It calls me to create spaces and share tools to reconnect with our own spirits and inner wisdom for the healing of intergenerational trauma in our communities.

Gloria Anzaldúa (2000) believed that for oppressed people, spirituality is a weapon of protection and a guiding force for understanding our place in the world. Spiritual practices such as mindfulness and ceremony help me deeply understand my authentic self in society, in my community, and in the world. Rather than just accept the roles and expectations of society, my spiritual practices allow me to be grounded in my own truths. I identify with Lara Medina's words: "For women struggling not only to survive but also to prosper spiritually, culturally and economically, the manner in which they engage in this struggle becomes key to understanding their spirituality" (2004, 124–125). Engagement in my own spiritual practices gives me strength to fulfill all my roles as a mother, womyn of color, mestiza/Maya womyn, wife, teacher, counselor, coach, scholar, activist, immigrant, amiga . . .

I have always been an activist and an advocate for social justice. For many years, this activism came from a place of anger and frustration toward societal injustices. My activism now comes from a place of love and connection.

This doesn't mean that I don't get sad, frustrated, or angry at times due to the injustices I witness. However, now I am able to create a space of mindfulness where I listen and recognize these emotions and the messages that my inner self, my ancestral wisdom, and the natural environment around me provide. Because of mindfulness and spiritual connection, I am able to tap into the wisdom that my body, mind, spirit, and emotions provide to continue creating change. Being a spiritual activist means taking part in transformation within ourselves and in the transformation of our communities. Spiritual activism facilitates and honors transformation from a holistic place of love, compassion, and interconnectedness.

CONNECTING TO MY BREATH AND THE MEDICINE WHEEL

Connecting to my breath in mindful meditation and to the teachings of the Medicine Wheel came to me via powerful teachers, and I am eternally grateful to them. The International Council of Thirteen Indigenous Grandmothers and the teachings of individuals such as Estela Román, Valerie Nunez, Don Carlos Barrios, Deepak Chopra, and Thích Nhất Hạnh provided some of the first tools that allowed me to feel whole again and to understand that connecting to my spirit is part of my activism. The Medicine Wheel is very complex and contains infinite and powerful wisdom. I respectfully share teachings that are most relevant to the Wheel while recognizing the Wheel's complexity and the vast body of knowledge beyond the limitations of this essay. It is also important to mention that there are different versions of the Medicine Wheel. The knowledge shared here represents a combination of the teachings of Navajo and Maya epistemologies.

TEACHINGS OF THE MEDICINE WHEEL

The Medicine Wheel concept from Native American culture provides a model for who we are as individuals. We have an intellectual self, a spiritual self, an emotional self, and a physical self. Strength and balance in all quadrants of the Medicine Wheel can produce a strong, positive sense of wellbeing, whereas imbalance in one or more quadrants can cause symptoms of

*illness. Addressing issues of imbalance can potentially diminish
a person's illness and enrich their quality of life.*

—MONTOUR (1996)

Wholeness represents a principal symbolism of the Medicine Wheel and is the underlying worldview present in all four quadrants. The concept of balance, harmony, and holistic health is a specific attitude toward the world and the interrelationship between humans and all the other elements in our environment (Meissler 1993). The Wheel has spiritual, cultural, social, economic, political, physical, cognitive, and psychological dimensions. It shows how each individual is part of a wider context—family, community, world—and how these different aspects are interrelated. This work reminds us to be at the center, grounded, and to reach for balance. The goal is to gain knowledge about oneself, knowing that the effect of this wisdom will not only be for the individual but also for the entire community. Laframboise and Sherbina (2008) refer to it as an outward expression of our internal dialogue with all creation and our spirit within.

The four quadrants represent balance and unity (Barrios 2015). Each of the quadrants signifies one of the four directions (east, south, west, and north) as well as one of the four elements (fire, water, earth, and air). The quadrants also exemplify one of the four seasons (summer, fall, winter, and spring) as well as the energy and attributes of a specific animal. The Medicine Wheel also has some variations among different groups.

THE FOUR QUADRANTS

East is the direction where the Wheel begins (see Sections of Medicine Wheel image below). It represents a place of new beginnings, of enlightenment, and of the awareness of the present moment, the spiritual self. It is this mindfulness and spiritual connection that makes everything possible. Being present is the necessary first step in acquiring will power (Four Worlds Development Project 1986). The color of this quadrant is yellow, representing the direction of the sun and the element of fire.

South is the place of sensitivity and relationships, the emotional self. This quadrant represents the importance of honoring and managing our feelings and relationships and of acquiring the ability to think clearly and to deal with different emotions and challenges, leading to the experience of connection between

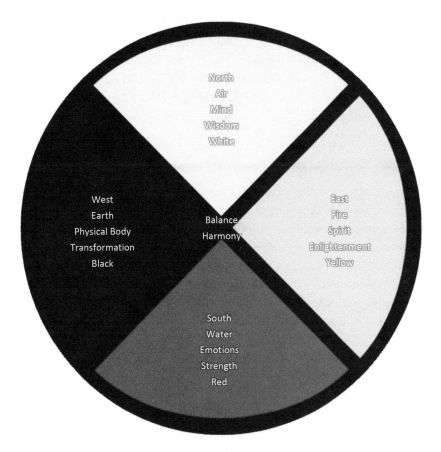

Sections of Medicine Wheel designating cardinal directions, corresponding elements, human aspects, qualities, and colors.

the human spirit and the entire universe (Four Worlds Development Project 1986). The color red and the element of water represent this quadrant.

West is the direction of dreams, prayer, meditation, and transformation, the physical self. Here is emphasized the importance of remaining committed to one's challenges, strengthened by prayers and meditation. The element is earth.

North is the place of intellectual wisdom—the ability to think, analyze, and understand, the mental self. This is also the place of completion, where the individual fulfills the goals previously set. The color of the west is white and the element is air (Four Worlds Development Project 1986).

MEDITATING WITH THE MEDICINE WHEEL: BRINGING BALANCE TO MIND, BODY, EMOTIONS, AND SPIRIT

Meditation is not to escape from society but to come back to ourselves and see what is going on. Once there is seeing, there must be acting. With mindfulness, we know what to do and what not to do to help.

—THÍCH NHẤT HẠNH (1975)

I use my breath as an anchor while I practice mindful meditation. My breath is the anchor that keeps me present in the moment to observe, without judgment, what is happening in my body, mind, spirit, and emotions. Breathing helps me connect during meditation to inner peace, so I can then reflect on the teachings of each quadrant in the Medicine Wheel. Connecting and breathing to the teachings of the Medicine Wheel strengthens me to continue my journey in creating spaces for community healing and social justice. The concept of In Lak' ech comes alive, and I see the connection to everyone and everything.

In the following section, I describe one way in which I use the wisdom of the Medicine Wheel. When I started learning about the Medicine Wheel, this meditation came to me intuitively. I have practiced this by myself and have led other people and groups in this meditation.

CREATING A SACRED CIRCLE

Most important is to first prepare a sacred circle where you can connect to your inner self and where you can truly focus and listen to all aspects of the Medicine Wheel. This sacred space can be created in different ways, depending on what I need that day. I decide if I wish to create my sacred circle outdoors or indoors. Next, I acknowledge the ancestors for the land and space. In my circle, I bring the ancestral medicine of plants, such as sage, or different flowers, such as roses, or other plants that I feel need to be there at that time. In the center, I create an altar, which includes organic objects representing the four elements: fire, water, earth, and wind. Last, I add objects that represent either things I want to let go of or things I want to bring into my life. For example, I might add a white flower, representing peace, or a picture of my family, representing connectedness. If others are present, I ask them to bring their own symbolic objects so everyone is represented in the altar.

We then create our own representation of the Wheel using colored paper. There is also a writing component to this meditation that allows for mindful reflection on balance and integration of the wisdom teachings in your life. I encourage you to allow space for your creativity when creating your Wheel. Trust yourself and give yourself the freedom to truly listen to the messages, ideas, and feelings about working with the Medicine Wheel. The creative process is also part of the healing.

In order to create a Medicine Wheel, I often use construction paper, markers, and tape. I use white, black, yellow, red, and green or blue paper. First, I draw and cut a circle with the green or blue paper to represent Mother Earth. This will be my base, on which I will glue the four quadrants. Each quadrant represents one of the parts of the self—physical, spiritual, intellectual, and emotional—and is cut in the form of a triangle in the color of its cardinal direction, as previously stated. All the pieces are now ready to start the meditation, and I place them in front of me as I sit in the circle.

I open the space with an acknowledgement to the four directions. I often use a prayer given to me by one of my teachers. Or I follow my intuition and allow the words that come directly from my heart to honor the directions, Grandmother Earth, Grandfather Sky, and the center. I then set my intention, connect to my breath, and allow my breathing to bring me to the present moment. I utilize my breath as my anchor so that when thoughts come, without judgment I refocus on my breath. After doing the initial breathing exercise for about five minutes, I start a visualization of the Medicine Wheel. I close my eyes and visualize the four quadrants and their teachings, using my breathing to ground me and to allow me to really take in this wisdom. When you do this meditation for the first time, I recommend writing or a drawing the most important aspects of each quadrant that you want to meditate on and really focus on. After you familiarize with the quadrants, your inner wisdom will connect to what you need, and you can do the meditation visualizing the Wheel with your eyes closed.

I then allocate about ten minutes to the first part of the writing aspect of the meditation. I write on the top side of each quadrant about that specific area of my life. First, I write about the positive aspects of each of the areas. For example, on the intellectual quadrant, the north, I might write something like, "I've been reading and learning more about literature on Chicanx/Latinx people in education" or, "I've been having great conversations about what my purpose in life is." For the physical section, the west, I might write, "I exercised three times this past week" or, "I have been eating foods that are nourishing for my body." I begin with everything positive or for which I am grateful. I include people, things, and experiences that have contributed to the positive development of each of those areas. The next ten minutes are spent on the second part of the writing. I turn the quadrants over and write things I want to improve on or to develop in each of the sacred directions. For example, for the section on spirit, the east, I might write something like, "My spirit needs more time for ceremony." For my emotions, the south, I might write, "I feel the need for connection with people concerned with social justice." What is important when doing this writing meditation is that you allow the different parts of yourself to speak and you truly listen. It doesn't matter how strange it looks on the paper or how bizarre you think it sounds. Sometimes it will be a drawing or a color, other times it will be names of people or a list of sentences. What each of the quadrants looks like is not as important as how much you have listened to the messages. Pay attention to the emotions, to sensations in your body, to the ideas, words, and pictures that come to mind. Listen to the different messages that are around and within you. All those are important and will help you in your search and journey into balance.

The last ten to twenty minutes of this practice are spent on mindful breathing, allowing the teachings of the writing exercise to be processed and internalized. This is the part where inner wisdom comes most powerfully. As you close your eyes and focus on your breathing, you visualize again the different quadrants of the Medicine Wheel. This time, however, you focus on what came to you during the writing exercise. It is important that you do this without judging yourself or the information. Remember to use your breath as an anchor and to have an attitude of gratitude for the messages that come. Even if you don't understand the messages or there are tears or emotions that you don't feel comfortable with, they are there for a reason. All these are forms of important information. In my experience, mindfully listening to all parts of yourself and utilizing the guidance on your path are what bring transformation, balance, and wholeness.

The final part of this practice is acknowledgment and gratitude for all the information, guidance, feelings, and ancestral connections that happened in the sacred circle. I thank the four directions: the east for enlightenment, the south for strength, the west for transformation, and the north for the wisdom that came forth. I express gratitude to Grandmother Earth for protection and Grandfather Sky for empowerment. I thank my ancestral connections and the connections to my inner wisdom and wish blessings and love to ALL on this day and all days.

13

MEDICINAL FOODS

INTRODUCTION

Awareness of the nutritional and healing value of ancestral foods native to Mexico has received tremendous momentum with the 2015 publication of *Decolonize Your Diet* by Luz Calvo and Catriona Rueda Esquibel.[1] Their personal and political journey in researching, planting, harvesting, and cooking native foods enlightens us to return to the foods of our Indigenous ancestors "to regain physical health and nurture a spiritual connection to [our]selves, each other, and Mother Earth" (17). The work of Roberto "Cintli" Rodríguez in *Our Sacred Maíz Is Our Mother* (2014) also enables us to reclaim the original knowledge that, as peoples of this continent, we are *maíz*! Nahua creation stories tell us that humans were gifted with maíz for sustenance by the Creator couple. Maya creation stories tell us that humans not only eat maíz, they are made of maíz. Maíz was and is a sacred food that remains a staple in our diets today. According to elder Julieta Villegas, the fact that we continue to eat maíz provides the foundation of our identity as Indigenous people of this land base (Rodríguez 2014). The maíz we know today, having been mutated by Mexican ancestors over several thousands of years, starting around 9,000 BCE in southern Mexico, from

---

1. For visual reflection, see plate 2, *Maíz, el primer nagual* by Yreina D. Cervántez.

a small inedible plant, teosinte, to the multiple colors of corncobs we have today, is nothing less than a scientific development of immense magnitude (Rodríguez 2014). This knowledge was shared with Indigenous peoples to the south and to the north, then spread east.

With the passage of NAFTA in 1994, genetically modified (GM) corn seeds have disrupted the livelihood of farmers throughout Mexico and forced their reliance on GM seeds sold by agribusinesses. Widespread resistance efforts have challenged the spread of GM seeds in Mexico, but the battle is not over, as GM seeds from the United States continue to find their way on to Mexican farmlands, into markets, and into our bodies. The original highly nutritious foods of Mexico, including organic maíz, beans, squash, amaranth, chia, and spirulina, are now commonplace in high-end natural food markets in the United States, while the folks whose original ancestors cultivated, harvested, cooked, and ate these foods often do not have affordable access to them. Reclaiming our medicinal foods is vital to our holistic health and fundamental to the process of decolonization.

In this section, herbalist Berenice Dimas shares her *remedios y rituales* for a nutritious *licuado* and warm tea. Neomi De Anda reflects on her family recipe for *atole* made from oats that never failed to sooth her mother's migraines, a reflection emphasizing the surprises we can find within the *mestizaje* of many of our foods. Gloria Quesada shares her grandmama's easy recipe for her favorite chile-chicken posole. And Melissa Moreno explains with humor how to organize a Decolonize Your Diet conference at a public university. Food scholar Claudia Serrato shares her practice of making spirit plates to ensure that the deceased ancestors and spirits are also fed.

Lara Medina

Remedios y rituales

BERENICE DIMAS

When I get sad or stressed or feel alone, I call on my ancestors for support. I drink water. I take deep breaths. I make time to be outside. Sometimes, it's the simple things that help the most.

Tecito para el corazón: bougainvillea, rose petals, *toronjil*, orange peel, hawthorn berries, *yolotlxochitl*, lemon balm, *zapote blanco, pasiflora, y cedron*. Sometimes I add skullcap, *cola de caballo*, or *manzanilla*. The tea helps my heart and helps me process my emotions. The herbs support my nervous system and ease, sooth, and calm.

Morning licuado: *Me hago un licuado con* 2 tablespoons of oats, ½ tablespoon of cacao powder, ½ tablespoon of *linaza*, 1 tablespoon of hemp seeds, 1 tablespoon of maca root powder, ½ teaspoon of canela powder, a handful of nuts (almonds or walnuts, or whatever I have). I add agave or honey to taste. If I need something warming, I simply add 8 ounces of hot water. If it is warm outside, I add nut milk (homemade or store-bought). Sometimes I add banana. *Le tengo mucha fe a este licuado.* It has been supporting me for several years.

When I need more grounding, I make a *tecito de canela con cuachalalate*, burdock root, and *estrella de anís*. Sometimes I add *diente de leon, ortiga*, or hibiscus flower.

I use what is around me. I use what I have.

Atole

NEOMI DE ANDA

When I was a child and my mother had a migraine, my father would take out a large bowl, pour in oatmeal, and add water. He would ask me to squeeze the oatmeal with my little hands for about half an hour. After the water was very cloudy, he would drain the oatmeal and boil the cloudy water in the pot with a little sugar. He would then take the beverage to my mother to help with her headache.

Little did I know that my father was teaching me to make atole, a drink that can be traced back to the Nahua people of Mexico. When I began doing research for my book on breast milk, I learned the basis of water for life from the perspective of the people of the Triple Alliance, the people who have for centuries spoken various forms of Nahuatl and reside in what we now call southern Mexico and Central America. The connection between water, breast milk, and life is largely attributed to the goddess Chalchiuhtlicue (Kroger and Granziera 2012). I also learned relationally, breast milk is life because many gifts of the earth can be made into milk, such as nuts, corn, and oatmeal. Yet, oats were brought by the Spanish to the lands now inhabited by my family. The Spanish most likely learned the tradition of Avena byzantina from the Moors. The Spanish probably used the oats to feed their horses (Coffman and Stanton 1977).

Because of the overt racializations and culturecide of the native people of the Americas, I was never taught any of this story as a child. I was merely given a bowl, oats, and water. Of course, I loved it as a girl, especially because I knew it would help my mother feel better. When I asked my father where he learned this *remedio*, he told me that my mom had taught him. When I asked mom, she said that her grandmother had taught her. I was then more dumbfounded. For my entire life, I had been told that my maternal grandmother was a criolla. Both of her parents were born in Spain and migrated to Mexico, where my great-grandmother and her ten siblings were born. So, the question became: how did this remedio of making milk from the oats, which seems so native to the Americas, come to be part of my great-grandmother's repertoire of recipes? Was she taught this recipe by someone whose background was native to the Americas? Or is this recipe really from Spain? Has my entire family been told a certain story so that we may be able to claim a purification of blood that still seems extremely culturally important to them?

Recipe atole de avena
1 cup oatmeal
2 cups water
Sugar to taste

Mix oatmeal and water in bowl and squeeze oatmeal to release the starches. Once water is quite murky with a milky color, drain the oatmeal. Boil milky substance and add sugar to taste. Substance will thicken as it boils. Serve warm.

Nourish Your Body and Soul

GLORIA QUESADA

Here is my favorite chile-chicken posole recipe. It is easy and delicious. I make it on cool Sunday afternoons during the fall and winter. It reminds me of my grandmama, Virginia Domingues-Valdez. I recall she woke up well before dawn in the winter to make us *caldos* or menudo to warm up our house on Kentucky Avenue in San Antonio, Texas.

My mama had seventeen children and fifty-plus grandchildren. Due to the instability of my parents' relationship, I was given to my grandmama and lived with my mama until I was five years old and spent most every summer with her or one of my tías. My grandmama was a lovely, strong, wise mestiza woman.

Chile-Chicken Posole
INGREDIENTS

    1 pound skinless, boneless chicken breasts, diced

    1 teaspoon dried thyme

    Kosher salt and freshly ground pepper

    2 tablespoons of extra virgin olive oil (Grandmama used vegetable oil)

    1 large white onion, diced

    1 jalapeno pepper, chopped (remove seeds for less heat)

    2 cloves garlic, minced

    3 (6-ounce) cans whole green chiles, drained

    1 cup fresh cilantro

4 cups low-fat, low-sodium chicken broth

2 (15-ounce) cans hominy, drained

Sliced avocado and radishes and/or baked corn chips, for garnish
   (optional)

DIRECTIONS

Season the chicken with ½ teaspoon thyme, and salt and pepper to taste; set aside. Heat the vegetable oil in a large saucepan over medium heat. Add the onion, jalapeno, and garlic and cook until soft, about 4 minutes. Transfer to a blender, then add the chiles, cilantro, and the remaining ½ teaspoon thyme, and puree until smooth. Return to the saucepan and cook over medium heat, stirring, until the sauce thickens and turns deep green, about 5 minutes. Add the broth, hominy, and chicken to the saucepan. Cover and simmer until the chicken is tender, about 10 minutes. Garnish with avocado, radishes and/or corn chips, if desired.

Cultivando semillas y culturas en la Madre Tierra

(Cultivating Seeds and Cultures on Mother Earth)

MELISSA MORENO

"Get out of the field!" As a daughter of farm workers from the heartland of the westside of the San Joaquin Valley, I heard this message many times. With structural opportunities, I became the first of my family and decedents who had lived on this land for five hundred years to earn a doctorate degree. Indeed, I "got out" of the agricultural field and "got into" the ethnic studies field, where I came to understand how the regional foods of Mesoamerica, the Southwest, and California emerged. I learned to reclaim my Native food and realized that "we are one" as Patrisia Gonzales and Roberto Rodríguez have indicated. Now as an ethnic studies professor, my passion is serving and educating the next generation of Chicano/Latino leaders across the disciplines. I introduce them to concepts of cultural "food justice" inside and outside the classroom. In the interdisciplinary field of ethnic studies, some know that ethnic culture, ecology, and politics are intertwined. I have learned from Gloria Anzaldúa and Devon Peña that to focus solely on politics of culture or politics of ecology is a dominant worldview that members of racial ethnic communities cannot afford to hold, especially given the implications of colonialism on the conditions and health of racial ethnic communities living in this homeland. Some like Luz Calvo, Catriona Rueda Esquibel, and Jennie Luna understand that the next frontier of colonization is the human body through the food consumed. What we consume is already having great effects on our current and next generations.

Recipe for Organizing Decolonize Your Diet Conferences on Campus
MAKES 225 SERVINGS

1–3 times asking campus to host the conference (or check a local community organization)

1–10 times reaching out for funding in general (e.g., USDA Organics, Nutiva, Dr. Bonners, Western SARE, MEChA National, or SLOLA)

1–2 interns for a season

10–20 student and community volunteers for the day of the event

5–10 drafts of a program

5–10 times outreaching to invite local North American Indian and Chicano community members and local schools to attend

5 times circulating a call for workshops

1 press release inviting everyone

2 inspiring keynote speakers familiar with Indigeneity sensibilities and familiarization with food justice and/or care for Madre Tierra movements (e.g., Luz Calvo, Jennie Luna, Devon Peña, David Serrena, Corrina Gould, Chief Caleen Sisk, Michael Preston, Jasmine Vargas, etc.)

6–12 workshops (e.g., food, plant, soil, seed, and art)

1 panel with 4 community speakers; half from local North American Indian and Chicana/o communities

1 amount of decolonized food (most difficult task)

1 seed library table with envelopes (homemade with newspaper)

1 resource packet with recipes, native plants, and foods, films, nurseries, and ways to follow up or participate in local efforts surrounding gardens and sustainability

1 Mexica danza and/or California Native dance group to begin the conference

X times of conference organizers engaging in drinking water, eating healthy foods, gardening, and other self-care practices to be in shape for such a historic event

1 or more times of reaching out to Profe Melissa Moreno if you need suggestions for speakers or ideas in planning and organizing

Spirit Plates

CLAUDIA SERRATO

Offering prayers up to the ancestors and to all our relations is a way of showing and giving thanks for all life's blessings and creations. In my sacRed space, *la cocina*, I offer prayers up by creating spirit plates—sacRed *platitos*. These platitos come in all sizes, directions, and seasons, and they carry unique *sazones*, energies, memories, and prayers. In this respect, as a humble ceremony of gratitude, spirit plates become *ofrendas*, food offerings, to the cosmic spirits of all our relations.

Spirit plates as food offerings, as it has been taught to me, acknowledge, respect, and center ancestral teachings from time-place-space immemorial to the present, and from the present to the future, and from the future to the past. By creating these sacRed platitos, the messages they carry are transmitted into a cosmic language that is seen, heard, touched, tasted, and smelled from sacRed realms—spirit worlds. In turn, the spirits of these sacRed realms, such as the ancestors and the spirits of the land, air, water, and fire elements, reciprocate the honor by continuing to provide sustenance for the generations to come. In being a responsible relative, creating spirit plates, as a form of prayer, maintains ecological balance within the sacRed realms. This spiritual practice is vital to the continual survival of Indigenous principles of ecology, kitchen-space ethics, and food traditions, all of which provide lessons of gratitude and healing.

How does one go about offering prayers up to the ancestors and the elements through the making of spirit plates, sacRed platitos? First off, it is important to view kitchen spaces with an ancestral mind. This means seeing the kitchen space as a sacRed and healing space where food is medicine and medicine is food. With this ancestral mind-set, the food gathering, preparation, cooking, spirit plating, and eating become a ceremonial practice of gratitude and healing. Having an ancestral mind-set in kitchen spaces also realigns the human and nonhuman spirits into a realm of connectivity. Once connection is made, spirit plates as prayer plates become food offerings to the cosmic spirits of all our relations.

In making a food offering as a spirit plate, one has several choices about how to plate. Do you wish to offer raw or cooked food, or a combination, to the ancestors? Will the ingredients be together or separate? Is there a specific relative from the spirit world who you are reaching out to? There are many other questions one can ask to determine the energies and prayers to put into spirit plating, like how the plating presentation should look. Will the plate honor a specific direction? Should other elements be included, like cedar, sage, and/or stones? Generally, spirit plating is a simple prayer task where one places a small *puño* of all foods about to be eaten on a plate. Then the spirit plater places their sacRed platito in a safe location, preferably where sun energy can penetrate and transmit those prayers into sacRed realms, keeping life in balance for the generations to come.

As an ofrenda, I share this three sisters *receta*. May your spirit-plating experience be filled with love, honor, and connectivity, and may your prayers always be seen, heard, touched, tasted, and smelled.

Ancestral Ingredients
Corn (kernels)
Beans (whole, cooked)
Squash (diced, raw)

Ce (one): Place a large puño of each ancestral ingredient into heart-size bowls.

Ome (two): Take a pinch from each bowl and place on a small flat or round plate. Before doing so, make certain to acknowledge that food relative, its history, and its journey into your kitchen space. Give thanks and place this spirit plate directly under the sun or outdoor elements.

Yeyi (three): Return and place the ancestral-ingredient bowls near a warm fire or near the stove flame. Welcome that element and place your cast-iron *comal*, or any other *abuelita*-type pan, over the flame and allow it to heat up. Listen for the sizzle. Drop some cedar if available to allow the steam to rise and to cleanse your kitchen space.

Nahui (four): Add a little avocado oil or any other Indigenous-based *aceite* to the warm pan, and once slightly heated, add the corn relative. With your wooden spoon, stir corn in *caracol* swirls. Then add your squash, and do the same. Once squash is tender, add cooked whole *frijolitos*. Carefully stir and add your favorite *sazones*. *Buen provecho!*

14

MOTHER-CHILD BONDING

INTRODUCTION

Raising our children with decolonized knowledge is extremely challenging as we navigate a society embedded in individualism and consumerism.[1] Our relationship as parent to child, whether we are mother or father, plays a central role as we seek to return to ancestral ways that understand our relationships as sacred responsibilities. The mother-child relationship holds profound importance, as the mother's womb gestated a life nourished from the mother's heartbeat, her own nutrition, and her emotional complexity. We become our own persons, yet the mothering, the parenting, shapes the journey to personhood. If a birth mother is absent, the mothering hopefully is done by loving adoptive parents, a father, or other loving caregivers. The absence of mothering, of parenting, ultimately requires deep healing. My own journey to healing required that I forgive my mother for her emotional absence. But to forgive, I needed to mature, to experience my own motherhood, to uncover the secrets that she carried, to understand the complexity of her life. Reaching the place of complete forgiveness and compassion after many years of blaming and anger liberated me to love her deeply and to be forever grateful.

---

1. For visual reflection, see plate 4, *Corazón de Melón* by Celeste De Luna.

Mothering is extremely challenging, even more so for employed mothers. We juggle so much as we seek to decolonize. We desire to offer our children empowering information about the sacred, their bodies, their nonconforming genders, their journey to own their voices. We must teach our young ones authentic respect for one another, respect for the planet, and respect for their role in our households and in our communities. We are creating ways to do this through our *palabras*, our actions, and our ritual.

In this section, we hear from the wisdom of mothers across generations. Brenda M. Sendejo collected the *consejos* of several mothers, each one offering their precious teachings passed on to their children. Brenda opens with sharing the value of knowing one's family history and of holding *familia* as sacred support. Lessons on our responsibility to care for our trees as living beings comes from Karen Mary Davalos, along with words to her daughter in preparation for resisting external oppressions. Elvira Prieto tells the hundreds of little ones she teaches to devote time to discern their TRUTH and to follow it in all endeavors, as TRUTH comes from love, not fear. Remaining mindful of the moments in our lives when our children call out to us is the wisdom of Maria Elena Cruz, wisdom so important for working mothers. Naya Armendarez Jones lovingly instructs our youth how to arrive at inner peace during times of challenge in our fast-paced society. Learning *chingona* history through public murals and visual art supports Jackie Cuevas's efforts to teach her daughter about the survival of her people. María Elena Martínez stresses the importance of teaching our young ones about their relationship with the living plants and the earth through experience. Alicia Enciso Litschi reminds our young that they are never alone. We are blessed beings walking on this blessed earth. And Modesta Barbina Trevino reflects deeply on the values she learned from her mother, who immersed herself in community, culture, and compassionate living. Martha P. Cotera reflects here on her own childhood and the profound lesson she learned to care for others, to make a difference, to commit to justice.

Birthing children is not always an easy process. Miscarriages, C-sections, and fatal complications after birth require deep, ongoing healing. The loss of a child does not sever the mother-child bond. The strong and loving spirit of Corina Benavides López shines through as she shares how she soothes the ongoing grief of miscarriages amid the beauty of raising their adopted son. Likewise, in "Welcome, Nova: Consejos for Surviving Pregnancy Loss," Patricia Marina Trujillo offers up from her place of deep loss a regenerative outlook, a heartfelt series of advice for womxn undergoing this difficult yet transformative phase in their lives. Times for cyclical grieving are addressed in "Chalchiuhtlicue—The Passing of One's Child," by Aida Salazar. Aida relates how by following the call of the ocean, her family finds a way to ritually annually honor both the Great Mother of all the Waters, Chalchiuhtlicue, and their beloved deceased child. Jennie Luna, a doula, offers us a post-cesarean ceremony to provide "the sense of closure needed for the mother and the baby who did not travel the vaginal canal to make the journey to the mother's heart."

Supporting our adolescent daughters to move into their young womxnhood is a central concern of many *mujeres*. How do we provide them the information that we so much needed but most often did not receive? Irene Lara invited *comadres*, *tías*, and friends to share their wisdom with her daughter in an inspiring ceremonial talking circle. And we close this section with Laura Pérez's poem calling our attention to the movement, the creativity, the passion that we carry as mothers in deep relation with the earth and with our daughters/our children.

Lara Medina

Radical Mami Love

Chicana Consejos del Corazón

BRENDA SENDEJO

I've long yearned to write something from the heart, something about love—the kind of love that grips you from your soul, that touches you at the depths of your being . . . the kind of love that inspires radical change within and outside us. It is love that exists beyond emotion in its capacity to transform ourselves, and then the world (hooks 1994; Anzaldúa 2002). This essay is inspired by such conceptions of radical love, which I write from my position as a Chicana feminist mami looking within and seeking out *consejos* to share with my children.

It is February 2017. Our world, nation as we know it, is experiencing a major shift. The ground below us is shaken. How do we prepare our children to respond, to exist while raising them in a way that is oriented toward justice and rooted in their Tejana/o/Chicana/o heritage? I constantly think about this, but it is ever so present in my mind now.

I reached out to many of the amazing women who inspire and sustain me. I am so grateful to have them as part of my community and my family always but particularly during these challenging times, as I search for words of wisdom to pass along to my children. This essay is a collaboration inspired by my desire to cultivate a spiritual practice and way of being in the world that I can pass on to my children, to all children. I hope to offer one small step in illustrating the power and spirit we possess in our fierce and unwavering commitment to justice. I share here *consejos del corazón* that take the form of words of wisdom, advice on how to deeply connect to the earth and trees, inspirations from our ancestors, spiritual knowledge, tools for attaining inner peace, and suggestions for moving forward in this world. Not all the contributors are mothers, but they are all creators, in the literary, artistic, justice, and spiritual senses. They are healers, and they are warriors. I am grateful beyond words to them and for the opportunity to share their consejos del corazón with you here.

ROOTS

Over the years, I have learned how important it is to know your history and to know there is power in knowing where you come from. As Yolanda Leyva once told me, "To know your history is healing." I constantly remind my children and students of this. I was raised by Tejanas and Tejanos, symbolized by the *nopales* that my grandpa Tomás would cut and de-spine, selling door-to-door from the back of his pickup truck in the 1950s and 1960s in Corpus Christi, Texas. My Tejanidad is also represented by my grandmother Victoria's experience as a pecan sheller in San Antonio during her late teens. She was part of the early Tejana labor history that was unknown to me until after she passed and I learned of the strikes and work of organizer Emma Tenayuca. Gloria, *mi mamá*, has shared many *testimonios* with me about growing up on the westside of Corpus. They didn't have much materially, but they had each other—a family of twelve that was protected by grandma Vita's deep and unwavering devotion to La Virgen de Guadalupe. My mother was taught to work hard, to care for others and for her community, and to be proud of that work. She passed along her strong work ethic and love of music to me. And I now pass along these qualities and her love of life to my babies, as does Mom as she assists in their raising. My two *hermanas* also inspire me with their fierce love for their children and for me. My sister Polly, though far away living in Australia, was by my side through the difficult journey of trying to become pregnant. Her counsel and the herbs from the naturopathic healer in Australia gave me much hope during a seemingly hopeless time. She helped me get to Australia when I did not have the funds to do so, so I could meet with that healer. He would tell me that I would one day have twins. Three and four years later, my babies were born, thirteen months apart. My sister Priscilla is an old soul whose spirit shines through in her long embraces. She is loyal to the core, and I know she will always, always have my back. She reminds me not to sweat the small stuff, and these are lessons that carry me through difficult times. These are relationships I've had since birth, and I've made many more over the years; all have greatly enriched my life, and now my children's lives.

Be Stewards of the Earth

KAREN MARY DAVALOS

I taught my children to respect trees. The trees are living beings, and we must not abuse them. I learned this lesson from my father, but it was taught in a subtle way. I made a conscious choice to overtly teach my children to respect trees, because they grew up in Southern California during a drought, and they lived in Los Angeles and we regularly witnessed kids—children to teens and young adults—pulling on small trees or peeling the bark from trees or climbing on trees whose limbs could not hold their weight. I wanted my children to know that the earth is alive and that we are her stewards. Again, this is ancient wisdom, which I learned from my Mexican grandmother and from my father, but they conveyed this knowledge in subtle ways.

The other *consejos* I have are directly connected to today (January 20, 2017). I wrote these words to my daughter, María Olivia: "Remember, there are aspects of you that have yet to blossom. They will bloom even in times of darkness. And remember to share these gifts with those you love and trust. One day, we (the world) might call on your skills to carry us forward."

I also wrote to her about fear: "Do not be afraid of oppression or suppression, for that is precisely what fascism and hate depend on."

Find Your Truth

ELVIRA PRIETO

I see myself as a mama to hundreds of little ones during an incredibly forma-tive part of their life journey. I say to them at every opportunity, and try to live the example for them, that the most important endeavor they can take on for themselves is to devote time and space to finding their TRUTH. To live in and by their truth at all times, and in every aspect of life—academic, educational, professional—because all these are, at their core, extremely personal. I tell them that I believe their TRUTH is inherently of the Spirit and much more powerful than simply of the mind, because our soulselves reside in our heartspace, not our "intellectual" mindspace. I also share that I believe everything in life is a choice and that our journey is determined by the choices we make, which come from two extremes: FEAR and LOVE. If we choose to act or live from a place of fear, we end up hurting ourselves and hurting others in the process. All that is ugly in this world is a result of humans making choices out of fear, and all that is good and beautiful in this world comes from love, which is also Spirit. If we make our choices from a place of love, we will always find joy, even in times of great challenge. Finally, I tell my young ones that they are perfect just as they are, just because they are alive and in this world, and that they don't need to live up to anyone else's standards. Rather, they must learn and explore their own values and standards for what brings them fulfillment and allows them to serve their purpose with LOVE.

Live in the Present

MARIA ELENA CRUZ

All I can say about being a mama, and doing everything, is to remember that when you are with them and spending time with your babies, be there, be ever so present because they need us to see them and know that they matter. Take that extra ten minutes to play with them, even if you're late or you have a deadline, because one day they will be big and gone and you would have lost that one moment. I live by this . . . I know I can't always be playing or going to volunteer at his school, but when he says, "Mama, let's play," I do! I love it, too, and then I go back to my work. It's hard being a mama and doing this academic juggling . . . but doable in a sane and fun way if you just take those ten minutes.

Receta for Radical Wholeness

TÍA NAYA / NAYA ARMENDAREZ JONES

Mijos queridos, el mundo de hoy es muy rápido. Usualmente es más rápido que el ritmo del alma.

When/if you feel torn between mind, body, and spirit, and if your soul pace is slower than the world around you, find a piece of *la tierra* where you can sit or lie down. Find a place where you feel quiet on the inside. And speak with Her, *la Tierra Madre*.

And listen. With your palms on your heart, breathe in. Breathe out. Breathe in. Breathe out. Feel all of you against the earth as you return to radical wholeness.

In this radical wholeness, air is your breath, earth is your body, water is your blood, fire is your spirit, and ether is the space within. In this radical wholeness, you find yourself feeling all the elements. You face the four directions all at once as your breathe into your sacred center.

In this radical wholeness, Xicanx and Latinx histories are here in their fullness. Spanish/*Español*, Indigenous/*Indígena*, African/*Africana*, and other lesser-tended roots take their place.

In this radical wholeness, breathe in. Breathe out. Breathe in like you mean it! Breathe out like you mean it! Laugh like you mean it! Do whatever you need to, like you mean it! Remember Who You Are.

To deepen your earth work, add oils to your heart space or wherever you please. Combine the essential oils of rose and orange with almond or apricot oil for sweet uplifting. Combine essential oils of patchouli or rosemary with almond *or apricot oil for grounding. Check first, though, that these are kind to your piel.*

"We Are Not a Conquered People"

JACKIE CUEVAS

There are moments when I feel a connection to a long history of womyn's survival as a form of what might be called spiritual knowledge. Lately, my daughter has wanted to know more about the histories of the various cultures she comes from, including Jewish and Chicana/o, and we've been reading lots of civil rights struggle/survival stories. I have shown her an image of Terry Ybañez's mural of Emma Tenayuca, titled "We Are Not a Conquered People." The mural, painted on the side of a San Antonio washateria, depicts Tenayuca alongside pecan shellers of the 1930s strike. Knowing about labor rights organizers like Tenayuca helps her see that we come not only from histories of colonization but also from histories of womyn's smart, organized resistance. The mural offers a good message to teach her as she struggles to understand that oppression continues in the present—and yet, "we are not a conquered people." The saying and the art, they give me hope, and they provide a way of sharing our Chingona history.

My Relations

MARÍA ELENA MARTÍNEZ

The women in my family have always had potted plants or gardens. When I was little, with asthma, my mother would go out to the garden and get sedum. She'd put it on my temples. . . . I remember my grandparents and the power of prayer, from my ancestors . . . some males, but mostly females. They are the ones who mostly led in family prayer. I remember there was a storm . . . coming from a distance. There were many cotton fields around the house. Aunts covered mirrors and took grandmother the cross for her to hold toward the storm. It was like she was standing face-to-face with the storm, telling it to not hurt anyone. You can talk to Spirit. Confront it. And that was what inspired me to do my work. Those women inspired me. That is why I think it's important to take children to the garden. Have them smell plants . . . mint, etc. Have a tea party so they establish a personal relationship with the plants. So they don't just walk past them. If we don't acknowledge our connection to plants and express appreciation to them, this knowledge will be lost to our children. Children can get their hands in the garden and work the soil to establish a sacred relationship with Mother Earth, to learn early not to deface earth, to see rocks and plants as living beings. I think what happens is that we lose a connection to earth; the human ego becomes more important. Our ego thinks we know it all—that we are special and can desecrate land or cut down a tree without reverence. . . . I hope it's shifting. Making these connections to our young children through experience is so important. Use lavender if they are sad to help them settle down and be calm again. Or acknowledge that the tea is coming from a specific plant. If plants weren't around, we could not breathe. It is all about our relationships and relations. . . . If you're taking care of something living, you have more compassion; you see differently. Experiencing plants, having a garden, tending to it, caring for it . . . you then expand that to caring for the earth and one another. You establish a closer relationship with another being, a plant being.

Consejos of Remembrance

ALICIA ENCISO LITSCHI

You are blessed beings. Your presence on this earth, at this time, was meant to be. These are complicated times to be human. As humans—the two-leggeds—we are peculiar creatures to walk the earth. We forget that every fiber of our beings is connected to Mother Earth. We think ourselves independent beings. We puff up our chests, our heads get a little too big, and we think we can do everything alone. Sometimes that can actually leave us feeling lonely and scared. We find ourselves forgetting that we are part of our Madre Tierra, just like all creation. Our Mother is the water that flows through our bodies. She is the air filling our lungs, and the spark of fire that beats our hearts. Our bones are made from the mineral and stones of our planet. We are generously fed by the plants and animals of this earth. We are never alone—even in our loneliest moments.

My prayer and *consejo* to you is to remember. When times are hard, turn your hearts to this great Mother. The trees, winds, rivers, oceans, plants, animals, birds, and community of people will come to you. All you need to remember is that no matter what, your Madre Tierra holds you. There are trees on this planet that are much older than our nation. Feel yourselves held by the wisdom of that which is ancient. She only knows love. Listen, She is there.

My mamina, my great-grandmother, used to love gardening. She would say that the best cure for an aching heart is to put your hands in the dirt, feel the soil, smell it, talk to it, listen to it. Go to the Mother with all your heart's whispers. *Con mucho amor.*

Petra's Gift

MODESTA BARBINA TREVINO

Petra, the root of my Mexican American heritage. I feel proud and privileged to have been her daughter, to have had her as my primary teacher. The world around her knew that Petra was a very giving and compassionate mother, daughter, wife, and friend. No matter what set of tragic or triumphant circumstances confronted her on a daily basis, she concerned herself with the needs of others before her own.

Never participating in trivial talk, she would always remain silent whenever she heard words of judgment. Her actions would tell us that some things weren't meant to be spoken about, like when she bought a bag of groceries for the lady and her loved ones next door. It was her way of connecting with those who were experiencing hard times. She allowed herself to be used as a pillow, a handkerchief, a sense of hope. It was through her actions that she demonstrated what some took for granted: "Practice what you preach!"

We never questioned why we had to attend as many funerals as we attended weddings or other celebrated events. As far as she was concerned, it is our God-given duty to pay respect to those who have gone before us, as those who lived among us. So be it neighbor, relative, or distant friend, we were obliged to honor them with our presence. Despite the fact that no one in the household drove, she always managed to get us to many events.

So today, in the center of my home, is a physical reflection of her spiritual presence—an altar with its lighted candle. The candle serves as an offering for some special request or as an offering of thanksgiving. Alongside the candle lies the Virgen de Guadalupe, known as *la patrona de las Americas,* and during ancient time as Tonantzin, the mother of all and everything.

It's through my mother that I acquired my grandmother's hundred-year-old metate. It is the type that I have seen only in museum displays, with the Indigenous mother kneeling on her knees, grinding her corn. Never before seen by her grandchildren, it now sits on my living room floor. I suppose I was honored as the chosen granddaughter to carry this valuable gift to the next generation. I placed this beautiful Indigenous metate on the living room floor next to a painting of an aloe vera plant, facing the eastern sunrise. I chose this special place because of what the east and the sun symbolize: rebirth, a spirit of hope, and healing warmth, elements that reflected my mother's nature.

I thank my mother for the gift of life, the kind of life that led my heart to remote places, places that revitalized and energized my ancestral spirit, from the Tulum pyramids located on the white sands of the Yucatán Peninsula to Guatemalan villages where each native woman was identified by the patterns on her woven huipil, to Machu Picchu, a timeless and contemplative paradise. These journeys not only affirmed and validated the origin of my identity, but they also explained where I am now and where I might be heading. Thanks, Mom! You will always be in my heart and in my dreams.

Why Being Truly Popular Is Hard to Do

MARTHA P. COTERA

"*Hijita, siempre esfuérzate para ser popular*" ("My daughter, always strive to be popular," or, as a bilingual child, this is the way I translated this *consejo* from my grandparents and my mother). Of all their consejos, this one puzzled me the most, since we were a very spiritual, hardworking family, deeply involved in Mexico's historic revolution and in community building and definitely not one to glorify "popularity" as understood by a four-year-old. Like most children, I was too awestruck to ask for clarification. When we were told *consejos*, we said, "yes, ma'am," and then watched closely for clues.

Being more than a bit bookish, with thick glasses, pinafores, and cotton stockings, unable to sing, and, in fourth grade, a proven failure at hootchie dancing, as done by Brazilian Carmen Miranda, my idol, I was proof positive that bookishness was no road "ser popular," in the obvious sense of the word. How about brilliant in writing, eloquent in church discourse, awesome for my memory skills? Could sustaining a conversation with anybody, anywhere, regardless of education, age, gender, and race make me "popular"? How about getting a reading certificate for reading 150 books in one semester? Or not missing a single day of school in seven years? My grandparents and mother were thrilled with my accomplishments, but privately, although I felt I was on the road to achieving something somewhere, I still worried about my "popularity" quotient.

Still, I felt the love. I wasn't "cheerleader" popular, but I felt happy and satisfied and won praise for using my talent and energies in peer tutoring, collecting books for the African American school library, helping other immigrant children learn English, volunteering in school projects, and advocating against injustice in high school. I hardly realized I was becoming "popular" as counseled, by emulating my grandparents' and my mother's lives and actions. Finally, in my midteens, through my family's approbation, pride, and love, and especially through their praise on how "popular" my actions were in school, in church, and with the community (HUH?), it dawned on me that for my family, being "popular" was not celebrity or a cover spread in *People* magazine (although I did once get a cover spread in *Parade* magazine!).

My family's admonition "ser popular" (be popular/a populist) came from the Latin *popularis*, meaning to act as a member of the public/*el pueblo*, on behalf of the public/el pueblo. It also meant to commit to populist action—movements with the people, on behalf of the people. By extension, as a young activist, I expanded its definition to include embracing great ideas that might break with convention, to generate a revolution/change (as my grandparents had done) and acting on improving what is there, unashamedly and idealistically, to elevate our people's spirit, knowledge, and well-being!

Enlightened, from my teen years on, I vowed to act on my elders' consejos and to devote my life to being "popular." Shortly before my dear mother, Altagracia, passed away in December 2016, she made me immensely happy, whispering how proud she was because I was "*tan popular*" with the staff at the nursing center, *no por las galletas ni pizza, hija* (not because of the cookies or pizzas), but because of my advocacy on their behalf.

These words are your *herencia*, from your *familia* and *comunidad*. They are gifts—*recuerdos*—to hold dear. When you feel weak or sad, alone or rejected, know that you are loved by many and deeply.

Our bonds are of the spirit; I bore you from my heart and my soul. It is from this place that these offerings to you, and to the other children, emerge. You have the gift of the language of your ancestors, and that gives me such great joy. Treasure it, and hold it close. Above all, embrace your light within, and let it shine for all to see, even if at times it must emerge through the cracks, in the hard times. You have the power to persist and prevail, and to do so for others.

Do not be afraid to state your truth, stand for justice, and be one with the earth, *la tierra*. Connect. I want you to know that, like so many parents, we do what we do for you out of love, but we must give beyond our immediate familia. That is what I want to instill in you. Yes, you are powerful, you are beautiful, you are amazing. Say it to yourself, feel it, embody it. BE it, *mija* and *mijo*. Then, turn around and go do good for others. If you learn anything from your Chicana feminist mami, please learn to love yourself, love others, and be a part of bringing about justice and change. That's my legacy to you, Luna and Jude. A space like this one is the perfect place to send you this message, *ustedes quien viven en mi corazón, siempre.*

Huitzin de mi alma

A Meditation on Healing in Adoption

CORINA BENAVIDES LÓPEZ

Faith is the bird that feels the light when the dawn is still dark.
— RABINDRANATH TAGORE, NOBEL PRIZE LAUREATE, 1913

Multiple pregnancy losses affected my path toward becoming a Chicana mother of adoption. The grief I experienced turned me to ancestral medicine for healing. Burning sage, spiritual *limpias*, breathing, and taking in hot essential-oil baths of eucalyptus, peppermint, and rosemary helped nurse my soul's darkness. Therapy, meditation, and yoga helped with the anxiety attacks triggered by the losses. Today, I experience good weeks, but the anniversary months of fall and winter still bring *dolor*.

My work toward healing led my partner and me to take the long journey toward adoption. We began our search for our baby in the fall of 2010. After years of preparing financially and emotionally, we received approval for adoption in 2014. The many difficult discussions with family and friends about adoption constantly triggered my grief. I kept an altar that helped me endure the emotional demands. The altar, now a permanent pillar of spiritual strength and a protector in my home, lives across my home's entranceway as a welcoming symbol to all who enter.

The altar holds pictures of my ancestors, a *sahumador* for the *hierbas*, a *chachayote* rattle, *agua bendita*, candles, and various *calaveras*, sculptures, and art pieces. And within the altar lives a tiny altar of miniature school building blocks and miniature spiritual trinkets representing *mis angelitos*. Every day I recognize the altar and its purpose. On days I experience pain about my losses, I attempt to listen to the messages being sent. What helps me on those days is spending time at my altar. I speak to my ancestors and to *mis angelitos*, burn *hierbas*, and light candles, and I make sure to honor Karmen (pseudonym), my son's birth mother, and *her* pain and grief.

When Karmen chose my partner and me to adopt her baby, we inevitably stepped on to a spiritual path with her, represented by the lifelong bond between her, my union with my partner, and our son. This spiritual path began with choosing a gift for her to represent our bond, a small Mexican tin box with a *sagrado corazón* / sacred heart at the center, surrounded by silver *milagritos* embedded in the lid. For years, my partner and I have gifted each other sacred hearts as a symbol of our love. We purchased two boxes, one for Karmen and one for the baby, as a *recuerdo* of the strong *mujer* that carried him in her womb. His box lives on our altar.

Then, our son's middle name, Huitzin, arrived to us in an emotional moment and spiritual message, days after we had already chosen his name. Huitzin, a derivative of *huitzitzilin*, the Nahuatl word for hummingbird, was a name I dreamt for a baby boy. Depending on Indigenous spiritual philosophies, huitzins are time-traveling ancestors who return to visit us with messages that serve as healing medicine. The name held a special place on my metaphorical list of baby wishes and dreams. My dream came true.

When meeting Karmen, she explained that she chose my partner and me as her baby's parents because of a *corazonada* (a hunch in her heart). She explained that she "just knew." We explained the symbolic importance of the *sagrado corazón* in our relationship. After Karmen handed our baby over to my partner and me as she shared her message of hope and love for her baby, I felt her elder spirit take over her soul and speak to mine. The energy in the room shifted with heat, and I sense our great-grandmothers holding us in an ancestral song as we birthed a united love for our baby.

The healing I experienced the day I met my Huitzin forever changed me. I became more in tune with the messages my body signals through dreams, energy, and connections with other people. I have good and bad days, and I also have days where I sense the energy of *mis angelitos* who work hard to remind me of their presence in my *corazón*. But looking into my Huitzin's large brown eyes grounds me, and if I listen closely, I can sometimes hear the buzzing coming from him as he flaps his wings, bringing me comfort.

Welcome, Nova

Consejos for Surviving Pregnancy Loss

PATRICIA MARINA TRUJILLO

For HML

Nova. (n.) A rare celestial phenomenon involving the explosion of a star resulting in an extremely bright, short-lived [being] that emits vast amounts of energy.

My *comadre* called me one day from La Capilla de Santo Niño, in Santa Cruz, New Mexico. "Hurry, come over and help." It was time to prepare for the Santo Niño's feast day, and the chapel had to be cleaned.

"I can't, I have to get this Title V annual review in."

"This is more important, trust me."

On that day, I started a years-long journey through faith, sacrifice, transformation, and submission that I wanted to lead me to motherhood. My *maestra*, a comadre whom I see as my guide through the interconnecting realms of spirit and reality, helped me contemplate and learn to start making decisions in the direction of health and spirit, really, of life. The cleaning was a gesture to mentally prepare myself for a baby. It forced me to put down inane academic work, the silly choices I was making, and to start cleaning up. I cleaned the floor of a *capilla* on my hands and knees, this chosen labor a step in developing an embodied meditation for a change. The labor shifted into other forms of cleansing.

It wasn't just my attitude about my academic life that my comadre recognized as an impediment to health, spirit, and life. She helped me recognize the chains of grief I'd been dragging since the death of my father, in my second year on the tenure track—the energy output of always feeling like I was throwing thimbles of water onto forest fires of injustice and the out-of-balance sense of responsibility I felt for all of it. She recognized that the self-soothing I indulged in took the form of social drinking and smoking cigarettes. This invitation to prepare for feast was her gentle nudge, her free-willed intervention. She pointed at a shift in path, but it was mine for the choosing.

My path led to a pregnancy. I wish the story ended with sobs of joy and a cooing baby girl. However, for me, it led to a pregnancy loss and the death of my baby, Nova. The consejos I share below are grounded in this experience, but I acknowledge that every pregnancy is unique, each with its own relationship to the process. What worked for me might not be on your path, so I offer all insights gently and encourage you to scratch out what doesn't work for you and write in the margins what does. One of the most significant reflections about this experience is how my spiritual practice shifted and evolved during this time. In particular, I came to a full acknowledgment of how journaling is one of my spiritual practices.

For me, pregnancy included several ceremonies. My comadre led me through two temazkal, the first to open my womb to the possibility of a baby and the second to close my womb after a too-early birth. Throughout the year, I celebrated moon ceremonies with Tewa elders, and the moon marked the transition between my cycles and my pregnancy. During the blue moon in July 2015, for instance, we held ceremony at the base of Truchas Peak, during a time when my body, heart, and mind were in early acceptance of the embryo. That shining of the big blue moon juxtaposed with the silhouette of the rigid peaks helped to prepare me for my journey. On my way home from the hospital after my pregnancy loss, my partner and I stopped to pray with a group of Indigenous women who had come together from around the world for the Gathering for Mother Earth. The group prayed with me around a fire under the light of the full moon in September. I laid my face on the ground and sobbed.

The day after the September moon ceremony, there was a full lunar eclipse, and the moon faded into a pool of watered-down blood. It was an ovum in the sky, a cosmic acknowledgment of the loss. My partner and I sat outside and watched the moon fade and reappear. We cried and sang and laughed and held each other. When the eclipse was complete, a shooting star streaked down from the moon, the undoing done. It was in that moment that I knew, despite my grieving and my heartache, that every experience was connected. It is a story about how, if we are open to it, celestial phenomenon exists in our everyday lives.

CONSEJOS FOR SURVIVING PREGNANCY LOSS

1. ANYTHING YOU WANT GOES. After we left our doctor's appointment where we were told "there's no heartbeat," I couldn't bear to go home. Home, where just that morning I was holding tiny pants and saying, "Can you imagine putting these on her?" Where piles of books on hypnobirthing and self-care during pregnancy lay dog-eared and scribbled on. I am thankful for a loving partner through this process, who immediately booked a room until we could figure out our next steps. In our case, we had time to think and make decisions about how to experience the loss—this is not always the case. Ask for anything you want. I wanted powdered donuts for dinner that night. I'll never forget that meal.

2. YOU CAN CHANGE YOUR BIRTH PLAN. There's not much talk about how a pregnancy loss in the second trimester requires a birth; it's not a live birth, but you can experience it naturally, with contractions, dilation, and a vaginal delivery. Or, you can choose to have a D and C, a dilation and curettage, a surgical procedure where your uterus is scraped to remove the fetus. I experienced the pregnancy loss at sixteen weeks; pregnancy loss is considered a "miscarriage" before twenty weeks and "stillbirth" after twenty-one weeks. In the first trimester, women are often told to go home and experience the loss there. But at sixteen weeks, I was far enough along that my doctor wanted to admit me to the hospital. When I was told that labor would be induced, I could not handle it emotionally. Thinking about it now still brings me to tears. I was having such a hard time choosing a surgical intervention because it wasn't "natural." My partner helped me, he said, "You get to choose your birth plan, and any choice is right." I chose a D and C.

3. ANYTHING YOU FEEL GOES. I cried for days and days until I thought all my facial features would melt into a puddle, until I couldn't breathe. My partner and I lay in bed and cried and napped and cried some more. But, I remember laughing a lot too. Right after we found out that we lost the pregnancy, we got sent down to radiology to have another ultrasound, and while we were in the waiting room we just got goofy. In a serious moment, I said that I wanted to name the baby Nova, like an exploding star that ends. And when I said it, it came out like, "*No va.*" Then I said, "Yeah, it's also perfect because this baby *no va.* She's not going to come!" And to our surprise, we laughed and laughed and laughed some more. *Carilla* is a gift. When I look back on that time, I'm glad that our baby gave us the gift of a spectrum of emotions. I felt

grief, loss, sadness, anger, envy, confusion—you name it, I felt it. But I also felt immense love and beauty.

4. YOU CAN SAY YES OR NO TO STORIES, YOURS AND OTHERS. When you lose a pregnancy, you are welcomed into a sisterhood of unspoken grief. It feels ubiquitous, a rite of passage that allows you to share and listen to stories about immense loss that haven't necessarily been shared with you before. I felt like almost every woman I encountered all of a sudden had a story about pregnancy loss. At times, this may feel comforting and normalizing to know that pregnancy loss is more common than we think. I believe stories are healing, but you don't have to take the stories on if you are in the process of just experiencing yours. You can protect yourself and your experience. You also don't have to share.

5. GIVE YOURSELF TIME. I took a month off work to grieve. It's a privilege, and when you're a woman of color in the academy, it's interesting what shapes your privilege will take. It's a privilege to have health insurance and sick leave. My experience afforded it, and for that I want to express gratitude.

It allowed me to stay still and process my loss. It gave me the time to be with myself and let my emotions and spirit morph into different shapes and expressions. I was writing in two journals at a time: in one, the emotional experience, in the other, an extension of my pregnancy journal that labeled each week with new benchmarks in baby's development and likened her size to pieces of fruit. All the writing and expressing and thinking take time. Build relationships with your art supplies again. Giving yourself time, even an hour a day, to concentrate on your healing is important.

6. SEEK POSTNATAL CARE. You experienced birth. Probably not the birth you wanted, but your body shifted and changed. You were building things like placentas and gigantic boobs and a human being. After my pregnancy loss, my milk came in. I was shocked; the one-page flyer that I got sent home with from the clinic did not cover this. I was fortunate enough to have been working with an amazing midwife, who came to my house to check on me in the days after my D and C and helped me understand the simple fact: I experienced birth. During her visits, she did some healing bodywork with me. She gave me a pelvic and lower back massage, used cups on my back, and prepared an herbal tea for me. She encouraged me to develop a self-care plan, checking in with her or my doctor, and to allow myself to feel. Mostly, she helped me feel less crazy. That's important.

7. FIND A GRIEF DOULA. Again, in all my best-laid plans, I imagined working with
   a doula to have a baby. When I lost the pregnancy, the doulas I knew told me
   about grief doulas. Resources exist. Please seek them out. It can be hard to
   find women-of-color midwives and doulas, so you might have to look outside your circle or even online, but they are out there. Sometimes you need
   someone outside your family to steer you through the loss.

8. GIVE YOURSELF MORE TIME. The week after I returned to work, one of my favorite
   students killed himself. When I had imagined getting off the sofa and returning to work, he was one of the people I thought of getting back to. I was back
   in the sleeping-bag cocoon for a couple of days and thinking of the Sandra
   Cisneros story, "Eleven," where she describes birthdays as all the years
   stacking like Russian dolls inside of us. I think we have stacking babushkas
   of grief inside of us as well. The death of my grandmother is a doll inside of
   the death of my father, who is stacked inside of Nova, who got stacked inside
   my student. This is all to say, we never know what's going to come at us next,
   what we will be asked to hold. Losing my student after losing Nova made
   me reflect on how we are always in the process of becoming more human.
   During this time, I felt anger that is still inexplicable, and I covered more
   pages in my journal than I can remember. I'm still trying to figure out this
   particular spiral of stories, but I have to believe that it is part of the ceremony
   of spirit that makes us who we are. Becoming a human is hard; it takes time.
   Forgive yourself for not figuring it all out at once.

9. CEREMONIA. We kept Nova at home on an altar until we buried her in a clay
   bowl my friend made, alongside my grandma. Our family came in from all
   over and helped us say goodbye to our baby and to our dreams. We took a
   picture of Mom and Dad with her so she'll recognize us when we join her
   in that place of dreaming stuff. We tied a red *cinta* around her and gave her
   turquoise so her ancestors could find her.

   A few months later, two of my comadres went with me to a temazkal
   around the time Nova would have been born. When you enter the temazkal,
   you are symbolically reentering the womb, going back to your essence. For
   me, it was a ceremony to close what had been opened. Your ceremony, or
   closure, will probably take a different form, but seek it out. If it is meaningful
   to your process of healing, whatever it is, it is ceremony.

10. GETTING BACK TO IT, OUR DAILY RITUALS. When I returned to work the second
    time, I was edgy. Anyone who experiences grief knows that you live on a

different calendar than everyone else for a while. Some people experienced March 2016, I experienced Month Critter Was Supposed to Be Born 2016. You'll have to endure other people's lives going on, seeing the colleague's new baby born on the day your baby was supposed to be born, answering the curious questions about your whereabouts, and just dealing with the inane qualities of life that are magnified at these times. You'll put the ink footprints the doctor gave you after your D and C on your home altar. You will look at it daily, and you'll be thankful for proof that she really was here, even if you were the only person to experience her moonwalk inside your belly. And days will turn into weeks. And one day, something will jolt you into a new awareness; you'll know you are going to be okay. For me, it was applying for a job that I didn't get, but the application process got me back into a future-thinking mode. It was an exercise that reminded me of the joys in my work and in my life, of the art I love to create. It reminded me that I could try again and again, not just for a baby, but for life.

Chalchiuhtlicue—The Passing of One's Child

AIDA SALAZAR

When we were told that my daughter would not live because her brain damage was too severe, I heard the ocean calling us. I wanted nothing more than to take my dying baby there. I didn't know why, but in the years since her passing, I have come to believe that the spirit mother of all waters, Chalchiuhtlicue, wanted to pay witness to her little life, kiss her with her ocean's spray, and say goodbye to her. Thanks to my husband's knowledge of the San Francisco coast, we took our daughter to a remarkable cliff that overlooks Ocean Beach and adored our baby there for two magical hours. And on her birthday and on the anniversary of her death, we go to any oceanside, to perform a ritual in her absence. Because Chalchiuhtlicue is the goddess of all waters, this ritual can be performed at any water source, such as ponds, lakes, rivers, springs. She is also the goddess of fertility and the protector of women and children. We honor Chalchiuhtlicue to thank her for holding the spirit of our children in her loving arms.

First, we greet Chalchiuhtlicue by touching her waters and/or by saying something like the following:

Blessings and love, goddess mother Chalchiuhtlicue
Thank you for holding the memory
of our child (insert child's name)
safe in your waters.

We build an altar with organic found objects in our surroundings: shells, sea-weed, twigs, rocks, flowers, grasses, etc. This is an offering to Chalchihuitlicue, and most items should naturally return to the elements. We make it as elaborate or as minimal as we like, but we take our time. The building of the altar is such an integral part of calling the spirit of our child to the ocean while also revering the Goddess. It allows time for us to begin to find and process the emotions we hold in our grief. We place a picture of our child in the center. If a picture is not available, we choose a found object, a beautiful shell, for instance, and place that in the center of the altar. If we are on the sand, we write out the name of our child in the sand inside the altar. If we have sage and can burn it, we douse ourselves and the altar with its smoke. We do this at the moments we sit in front of the altar and before we leave the altar.

I spend a good amount of time crying during my time with the altar/ocean. I am free to sit with the range of feelings—loss, anger, self-pity, and guilt—each of which takes turns being prominent in my grief. Chalchiuhtlicue allows us that. But my husband and living children like to sing, and this helps pull me out of myself and reminds me that we are also there to celebrate the life of our baby and pay our respects. You can sing "Las Mañanitas" or a song you sang to your child when they lived or a song that has some meaning to you. My husband's traditions come from the Yoruba, and so he sings songs to Yemayá—the spirit of the ocean from that tradition. We take a maraca or hit rocks and make music and play in praise to the ocean and our child. We say the names of the goddess and our child and thank them, talk to them and to ourselves about whatever comes up. This is the opportunity to openly love our child though her body is no longer with us. Chalchiuhtlicue helps us invoke our child and helps us step into her memory with all the immeasurable love that we gave her in life.

We are mindful to say goodbye to Chalchiuhtlicue and to our spirit child. We recite:

Thank you, Chalchiuhtlicue
Goddess of all waters
the essence of all life.
Thank you for holding
our child (insert child's name)
in your healing waters,

your waters that wash away
tears from our heart
and open us to continue
to journey and continue to love
in the cycles of life.
May the circle never be broken.

Post-Cesarean Ceremony / Baby's
First Journey to the Heart

JENNIE LUNA

It is common knowledge that the United States is a country with one of the highest rates for cesarean births in the world. One in three births will be delivered by C-section in the United States. This number has risen dramatically since the 1970s, as more women are opting for an elective C-section, and hospitals deem this procedure as preferred over vaginal births and VBACs (Vaginal Birth After Cesarean). The rate of C-sections is exponentially higher than is medically necessary, yet lack of knowledge and education of a woman's options and rights continue to be the main barrier for women in their reproductive choices. Simultaneously, there is a dramatic rise and movement of women who adamantly oppose the medicalization of birthing and are returning to Indigenous birthing methods.

More women, particularly within the Xicanx community, are revitalizing *partera*/midwifery practices and opting for home births and doulas (labor assistants). In my practice as a doula, women come to me with the goal of having a natural, medical-free birth. While the majority of the births I have assisted have accomplished this goal, there still exist emergency incidents where a birth must end up in a cesarean birth. Many of the women who undergo this procedure, after what is often a long and arduous labor, often feel cheated of the experience of a vaginal delivery and the benefits (both physical and emotional for both mama and baby) that come along with a vaginal birth. Often, women feel as if they've failed themselves and their baby. In all births, the ultimate goal is to have a healthy mom and healthy baby. As a doula, I am trained to give all options to a mother and allow her to choose the type of birth she desires. While I encourage and advocate for a mother to birth as naturally as possible, in the end, it is every mother's choice to decide what she desires for her body and her baby. It is not my role to place judgment but rather to educate and offer my professional advice and, in the end, to carry out the wishes of the mother and support her.

The benefits are innumerable for a natural birth, and most every woman is capable of birthing vaginally, but in the case where a woman either elects for a C-section or ultimately is not able to birth vaginally due to medical complications, this post-cesarean ceremony is a way for a mom and her baby to re-create the circular closure that needs to take place for a mother and her creation. Many women feel that there was a rupture in the cycle of childbirth both for herself and for the baby and, in fact, a major operation/surgery such as the cesarean can indeed leave a mom feeling emotional pain and loss in not having experienced the birth she desired. In my training as a doula, the midwife who taught me this ceremony affirmed that this process is critical for mom and baby. This small ceremony will create the sense of closure needed for the baby that did not travel the vaginal canal to make the journey to the mother's heart. It also allows for the mother to feel the circular closure that she also did not get the opportunity to experience.

It is very important that a mom is able to experience this ritual as soon as she is able to, after recovery and medication has worn off and when she is fully aware. The cycle of birth moves circular, from the womb to the heart. A baby that moves through the vaginal canal instinctively desires to return to their mother's heart. It is the heartbeat/drumbeat that they listened to for nine months. Immediately after a baby is born, they should be given to the mom, skin-to-skin so the baby can connect and complete their journey to their mother's heart. When a cesarean takes place, the journey is ruptured for both mother and baby, but it is still possible to re-create this journey and create the closure to this life-giving ceremony of birth.

As soon as the baby is able to be united with the mother, the partner or special person in the baby's life will take the baby and gently place the baby as close to the mother's abdomen as possible, carefully holding the baby so as not to hurt the mother's incision. The special person will gently guide the baby to crawl from the womb to the mother's heart/breast. The mother will simply lie resting, arms ready to embrace her creation. Mother should allow the special person to guide the baby upward to mother's chest.

During this moment/process, someone can offer a soft song with a light drumbeat, or, if the mother is able, she can sing to her baby as she welcomes the baby to her heart. While this is occurring, a third person can use a bouquet of fresh herbs such as sage, ruda, and/or lavender to gently pat the mothers shoulders, head, and chest to create the welcome scent of these sacred medicines as the creation completes their journey in this birthing process. The scent of the *yerbas* helps the mother remain grounded as she breaths in the smell of Mother Earth and soothes her baby, letting them know that they are fine and have made it to the final step of the birthing journey, to mama's heart. The ceremony is complete once the baby reaches mother's heart/chest, as the baby has closed the circle.

The mother can then try to give the baby her breast to feed and those present can rejoice and continue to sing softly so the baby and mom may feel the celebratory experience of completing the birth process. The yerbas can be saved and dried, then buried with the placenta or the umbilical cord, whichever the mother chooses or is able to do.

Fortifying Our Spirits

A Talking Circle for Our Daughters

IRENE LARA

LISTEN

In a moment of clarity and purpose, during the summer when the busyness of the school year has melted into longer days with more space to dream and to act on our visions, I hear . . . "Gather the *tías* in support of your daughter and her friends beginning the transition into older girlhood."

I plant the date seed, October 1, a Saturday a few months from now. The first day of the month, a good day to mark a beginning. Later, I realize it will be a new moon, even more auspicious! And evidence that my ancestors made sure I was deeply listening. (*Gracias, ancestros.*)

GATHER SUPPORT

I reach out to a friend who had created a talking circle and with whom I share a similar spirituality, sexual politics, and desire for holistically supporting our daughters and youth in general. "Can you help me think about this? Can you come with your daughter and help me hold the space?"

She responds with a "Yes, of course," and reminds me about it a month later. A true organizer at heart, she initiates a Google Doc so we can keep brainstorming ideas as they emerge. Intergenerational, herbal *baños*, veggie enchiladas . . . At home or by the beach?

SET LOOSE THE INTENTION

Seizing another moment of clarity, I text some of my local *comadres*, sisters, and daughter's friends' moms to save the date for "a special circle for Belén, as she enters older girlhood," a "talking circle about growing up and guidance around what it means to discover and create one's self." When I see them next, I elaborate on the idea, built on Indigenous sensibilities that recognize this spiritually powerful life-cycle stage and our communal responsibility for one another's well-being. Inspired by the restorative cultural activist work of Mujeres de Maiz, Xilonen, and other Native ceremonial leaders and women-of-color ritualists, we can remember and reenvision our community rituals.[1] In person, I work to convey how much I value their beloved presence in my family's life. (*In Lak' ech, you are my other me.*)

THE INVITATION

On October 1, I am hosting a talking circle for Belén with her tías, a few of my comadres, and a few of her twelve-year-old friends. This is my Chicana feminist ritual for honoring where she is at in the borderlands of being an older girl and becoming a young woman on the cusp of puberty. I desire for the vibe to be self-love,

1. Many women continue to inspire and teach me about the significance of ceremony. I deeply thank the women physically present who helped with this communal ritual and those spiritually present. Xilonen, a Nahuatl word that means "young tender ears of corn," returned in the mid-1980s as a rite-of-passage ceremony for girls throughout California, in places such as Los Angeles, Sacramento, and Watsonville. It is now also organized by Aztec danza communities in places such San Diego, Isla Vista, San Jose, San Francisco, and even Idaho, either annually in the summer or occasionally when the community calls for one. According to Graciela B. Ramirez, one of the elders leading the ceremony in Sacramento, paraphrased by David Alvarez, a "Community Voice" contributor to the *Sacramento Press*, "The corn, a central crop to the Aztec and indigenous people of the Americas, symbolizes . . . a young woman yet to mature that will pass through various stages and as she weathers these stages she will be a staple to her community, a model for others to follow and pass on the seed and traditions" (Alvarez 2010).

Also see the documentary *Xilonen: Ceremony of Tender Corn* (Alba 2013) that depicts the months-long training the young girls go through, which includes learning danza, Indigenous cultural identity, and the related values of responsibility and service to one's communities as practiced by the White Hawk Circle in Watsonville, California.

positive sexuality, and having a web of support. It's a sharing of curandera *tools: for those hard periods (her moon time) and other challenging times of life. For riding/ writing through the hormonal seas of crushes and friendships. For figuring out who you are as a unique individual and as related to all of life. For expressing what you need and want (even if it goes against the tide of friends, family, society at large) and other powerful emotions. Emotions that Gloria Anzaldúa would say are cenotes of* conocimiento, nepantla *states rich with the potential for transformation. . . .*

Please simply bring your loving energy and words of wisdom to share with Belén and the rest of the girls.[2] *Self-care recipes, an empowering story, a favorite song, poem,* dicho, *prayer, etc. are all welcome. What do you wish a compassionate, non-judgmental* angelita, *nature-spirit* diosito/diosita *had come to tell you about surviving and thriving when you were twelve?*

Love,

Irene

THE DAY

My friend and her daughter arrive the evening before, armed with yerba buena from their garden. We rejoice in our friendship and shop for needed food and materials. We ease into the next morning and start cooking. My *compañero* takes our younger daughter out for an adventure, as today is for the twelve-year-olds and their *tías y mamás*. We send the girls to the backyard to harvest *romero, lavanda,* and sage, showing them how we have been taught: always ask for permission and reciprocate with tobacco, songs, words of gratitude. We create an altar with our *plantitas*, roses, water, *y la abuela-sahumeria.* Arranging them in the four directions from the Lakota tradition, we also place small squares of yellow, red, black, and white bandanna fabric on our altar for creating prayer ties later on.

I work well with a general structure while maintaining flexibility, which entails listening to the needs of the group and trusting the flow of the Spirit.

---

2. Because I didn't want to have too many more adults than young people, and because many of my close friends live far away and wouldn't be able to attend, I asked additional *madrinas* to send their prayers and words of wisdom our way. My plan is to collect them all and, along with photos and mementos from the gathering, offer them to Belén when I sense she needs a reminder of the fierce and loving women who stand with her as she discovers and carves her own path of conocimiento.

So, as folks arrive and leave throughout the afternoon, the girls play, and we eat when we're hungry. We end up creating three talking circles.

First, sitting on the rug in a circle in a sunny spot in the house, we each share what we like(d) and what is (was) hard about being twelve.

Second, speaking our prayers—what we desire for ourselves and what we desire for others—as we gently submerse our plantitas and rose petals infused with our love for ourselves and all life into a large pot over the stove for the herbal baños we brew. (I add my feminist commentary that we don't have to wait to be gifted with roses from romantic interests, we can offer *ofrendas* to ourselves, our friends, our ancestors, and Guadalupe-Tonantzin or La Gran Madre, or whatever our names for the Great Mystery that is sacred Life.)

Third, as we gather around the big table to make prayer ties joined by red yarn, the women share the *conocimientos* that have been passed on to us and that we have learned from reflecting on our paths. Everything from the power of prayer ties, the healing properties of plants, and why we create altars to gifts of poetry, story, *consejo*, and a beautiful knitted cream blanket to remind Belén to honor her gentleness alongside her strength. With intricately etched *zonaja* in hand, my comadre, a longtime *danzante*, sings her a "Mariposa/Papalotl" song, immersing us all in the Spirit of ancient sound.

Our closure is as much an aperture, taking time to go around the circle and see one another, breathing with the confidence that we have one another, our ancestors, and the ability to listen to our Spirits, as we all forge ahead, fortified.

Shaking It All Up

LAURA PÉREZ

Madre
Tierra
Tú
Yo
We are all each other's other self
Daughters
Shaking
Earth
Earth
Shaking
Daughters.
We are all earth.
We are all shaking.
We are all daughters.
Shaking it all up
The earth moves
The spirit quickens
The heart blossoms
Again, again, and again.

15

MOON MEDITATIONS

INTRODUCTION

The moon has a deep and meaningful history in the development of who we are as humans, as peoples within the larger human family, and as womxn. In a world where night is illuminated by the stars, the moon, the planets, and an occasional comet, the moon is the brightest celestial body of the evening. Reconnecting with the moon and her meaning in our lives can bring us to an understanding of our story as womxn, as people—a history that has been suppressed, decontextualized, and often demonized by Western theologies that have relegated ritual observations of the night to acts associated with evil.

Due to womxn's biological affinities with the moon's cycle, it is thought that womxn may have been the first mathematicians; they would have been the first to observe the connection between a menstruating or pregnant womxn's body and the approximately twenty-nine-day cycle of the moon. This consistent observation of the moon's cycles assisted humanity to conceptualize abstraction and to build even longer calendars of time. We know, for instance, that some of the first calendars were lunar calendars, such as that found in Chaco Canyon, New Mexico, a city planned and built according to the moon's long cycle.[1] And,

---

1. Luna and Galeana (2016) clarify the reason for the Coyolxauhqui stone to have been placed at the foot of the Templo Mayor in Mexico-Tenochtitlan. Her placement indicated the shift from the primary use of a lunar calendar to the primary use of a solar calendar.

people who settled near to where the oceans meet the land must have also noted the shifting tides in accordance with how the moon appears in the night sky.

Though many of us today refer to the moon as female, Coyolxauhqui is like all of creation in Mesoamerican cosmology, "a representation of duality and the dual nature of all life" (Luna and Galeana 2016, 19). This reiterates for us that her cycle of death and rebirth, her coming and going over the course of approximately twenty-nine days, is important not just to womxn but to all of humanity. Agriculture develops as people learned to plant according to her shorter cycles. And womxn's accumulated knowledge over the centuries allows for the planning and birthing of communities of people. This section contains an offering of song and ritual, both communal and private, for the moon that womxn have both inherited traditionally and have reclaimed, reshaped, and remade for themselves.

"Coyolxauhqui Canto" by Cristina Gorocica, a song written in offering to the moon, documents the moment of recognition when a womxn's body undergoing a metamorphoses to accommodate the growth of life is mirrored back in the phases of the moon, affirming for us our existence in time, the acknowledged connection of womxn's biology to the phases of Coyolxauhqui, the moon, "a woman engaging in cycles of menstruation, reproduction, labor and birth" (Luna and Galeana 2016, 8).

In "Full Moon Coyolxauhqui Circle," Felicia "Fe" Montes tells how she envisioned and made reality monthly gatherings of womxn coming together to share in ritual the meaning of the lunar cycle in our lives. The Coyolxauhqui Circle creates space and time for being at ease with one another, as womxn. In her second contribution, Patrisia Gonzales's "Patzin: Abuela Luna and the Cycles of la Mujer" reminds us of the directions for right living embedded within a moon ritual—from the directions for individual modes of being to our communal responsibility for "strengthening the feminine energy's protective influence on Mother Earth." Here, Patrisia lovingly offers "some moon teachings to honor this grandmother pouring her *olla* of waters from above."

In "Moon Gazing," Lara Medina offers the novitiate to Grandmother, a method to deepen our relationship with the moon, a journey she herself undertook as taught to her by a Tibetan Buddhist shamanic healer—a testament to cross-cultural regard for the healing powers of the moon!

How do we begin to rename, rethink, and reshape our understanding of the world, as we know it? We begin slowly, with a combination of observation and listening in our encounters with *la luna*. We begin by standing beneath her and taking in her light and the coolness of her rays, different from the warmth of the sun—a different kind of healing. Then we understand, and we thank her for being. Tlazocahmati Grandmother—it feels right to say it, so you say it again. Tlazocahmati Grandmother, simple, humble, and endearing because she has been there always, always, and will be there long after we are gone.

Martha R. Gonzales

Coyolxauhqui Canto

CRISTINA GOROCICA

Composed in 2000, this Coyolxuahqui *canto* came to life as both prayer and reflection. I was observing the full moon on a warm summer evening and wondering why she, *la luna,* was so physically distant or far, yet I could feel her presence internally and spiritually.

I was filled with life, about five months with my daughter, Ixchel, in my womb; pregnant and my breasts filled with mothers' milk as I was still breastfeeding my other daughter, Textli. My body was in metamorphosis, changing, growing, adapting to my baby inside me. The feelings I was encountering were of longing to feel whole again with my physical body, a time when my breasts were not swollen nor in pain, when my back did not spasm nor my womb experience pain from movement or change, when my legs and feet did not swell, when my hair did not fall out, when my freckles did not expand into large marks on my face. I was feeling the physical effects of pregnancy and breastfeeding, all beautiful and powerful moments in my life, yet at times it was difficult to accept the turmoil that my body was experiencing, even feeling guilty for feeling what I was feeling. I kept looking up at the moon with feelings of guilt and pain, wondering when these sensations would dissipate.

In my observations, the moon became her, Coyolxauhqui, the Aztec moon woman who took shape on the gray moon I was observing: her body, her breasts, the bells on her face, the dismembered bones, her legs in position to run, her arms bent, her feathered headdress, the *calaveras* on knees, arms, and back. Her presence, her image a vision, an apparition on the gray full moon. My mouth opened and started singing . . . *Coyolxauhqui, Coyolxauhqui, tú eres mujer, en la luna está tu imagen, tú eres fuerte, sangramos, damos vida, damos leche y amor, tu espíritu está conmigo, soy fuerte mujer. . . . Weyaheeya weyaheeya weyahheya heeya, weyaheeya weyaheeya weyaheeya heeya. . . .*

Unexpected and without pretense, the *canto* came to life. I grabbed the gourd that was on my porch, shook it, and sang along with it.

Coyolxauhqui, Coyolxauhqui, tú eres mujer, en la luna está tu imagen, tú eres fuerte, sangramos, damos vida, damos leche y amor, tu espíritu está conmigo, soy fuerte mujer.

Weyaheeya weyaheeya weyahheya heeya, weyaheya weyaheeya weyaheeya heeya (2x)

The canto can use a water drum, as the moon shares fertility and water with women. The canto can be sung with just *sonajas*, or rattles, and/or a hand drum. It is meant for connecting, healing, and honoring women during times of transition—menses, birth, menopause, and/or unification, as we can also feel dismembered or disconnected from society.

Aho.

Full Moon Coyolxauhqui Circle

FELICIA "FE" MONTES

For more than a decade before the Coyolxauhqui Circle in East Los Angeles was founded in 2010, it was a vision and dream in my heart and spirit to gather women on the full moon, to share, to sing, to connect. Sometimes our dreams are realized, and sometimes we womxnifest them.

After being part of a womxn's annual ceremony under the full moon in Mexico over a four-year period, I knew it was time to bring that vision to life in Los Angeles. As an MC, or *Mujer en Ceremonia* (womxn involved in ceremony and circles), I asked around to friends and siStars (spirit siStars connected to circle and spirit) if they had been part of one before, or what their own rituals were for the full moon. There were a couple home-based circles that met intermittently but nothing that I knew of within my community in the eastside that focused on Spirit and wellness of womxn. I also asked my *tías*, mentors, and *veteranas* on the Red Road if there were full-moon ceremonies, ways, and rituals that womxn could do or had gathered for. I have participated in northern Native traditional ceremonies related to the sun and other sacred purposes, some that are practiced yearly on full moons, so I sought to see womxn involved and honored in ways I believe were practiced before colonization.

The tías (aunties) and *abuelas* (grandmothers) we spoke with mainly shared about personal ceremonies like baths, full-moon water blessings, and the like. They shared the practice of keeping water under the moonlight and using that charged water to bless an altar, ourselves, our gardens, our homes. Little else was shared, and we asked permission to begin our circle.

Our Full Moon Coyolxauhqui Circle began in November 2010 at a public art plaza in East Los Angeles, City Terrace, California, called the Coyolxauhqui Plaza. In that plaza lies a large-sized replica of the ancient Coyolxauhqui disc first unearthed in Mexico City in 1978. At the first gathering, we were just two womxn, me and a friend who had been part of other womxn's circles before. We burned sage, sang songs, and were asked by a homegirl walking by if we were singing to the stars . . . to which I responded, "YES, exactly!" and that she was welcome to join us at any time. She smiled, said "cool," and walked on. From that day forward, we have continued our circle every month. We have always felt welcomed. We have our circle in various locations. It is usually in an open space across from a small community market, a library, murals, and a laundromat. Sometimes we get visitors, and people ask us what we are doing. We tell them, invite them in, and/or ask them to respect the space. So far they have all understood and seem to honor our space. Some have even bowed, said thank-you to us, and asked for a smudging.

What started as a circle of two has waxed and waned, just like the moon, to what are now circles ranging from 5 to 105 womxn, moving from the initial Coyolxauhqui Plaza to local parks and community centers, for special occasions like Womxn's Herstory Month, our annual anniversary, and as weather permits.

Over and over we have seen that our full-moon circle is needed and has built a base and example for womxn and families in our community to create a space to share, connect with one another, and transform emotions. Still, we do not think that this is successful only because of the community in East Los Angeles or because of our base circle, Mujeres de Maiz. Yes, they are all great influences, but we believe this can and should happen in all communities. Below is some information on how we run our circle, which is mainly a talking circle with ritual components. We hope it can be an inspiration to others to start their own talking circle and to continue the important healing of our communities and families.

PREP WORK

1. Identify calendar full-moon dates (we do on or around full-moon evenings).
2. Call out to friends, siStars, people you know who are interested or may want to partake.

3. Determine location, time, and needs for space. A park? Check expected weather conditions and find out if automatic sprinklers are involved. Think about security, safety, etc.

4. Share the logistics and invitations along with information on what to bring.

5. Determine roles and responsibilities of group leads (welcomer, incense/smudger, lead singer, harmony, etc.). These may vary.

OUR CIRCLE IS GUIDED IN THIS GENERAL ORDER

1. Creating the circle space and intentional space/altar.

2. Smudging/cleansing.

3. Welcoming and thanksgiving.

4. Singing the welcome song.

5. Introducing the circle: intention, vision, how it started, guidelines, etc.

6. Participating in the talking circle (share name, what you want to let go of or celebrate, listen to others).

7. Introducing special guest/presentation/teachings (if available and usually related to moon cycle, wellness, etc.).

8. Singing the closing song.

Patzin

Abuela Luna and the Cycles of la Mujer

PATRISIA GONZALES

PATZIN: NAHUATL FOR RESPECTWORTHY MEDICINE

Abuela Luna exerts a powerful force on the earth, particularly on women. *La luna* affects the tides and therefore also the waters in our bodies. Water is also associated with emotions, and human beings are significantly composed of electricity, or light, and water. As women, it is important to understand our cycles, both physical and emotional. From the moon, elders can detect rain, harvests, and seasonal occurrences. While the moon reveals herself in fours, or an eight-fold cycle, la luna's major faces of new moon, full moon, and dark moon are often described as the maiden, mother, and crone. The moon, like *la mujer*, is an astral body that goes through numerous changes in a cycle. *La luna es la reflexión cósmica* of our emotions. I offer some moon teachings to honor this grandmother pouring her *olla* of waters from above. In many ancient symbols of our ancestors, the woman's uterus is the same U-shaped figure that signifies the pot of waters of a full moon. In recent years, elders have encouraged Native peoples to gather on the full moon, when its energy exerts the greatest force on earth. Elders encourage us to honor our Abuela Luna, either through ceremony and prayer or simply by gathering our family and friends together to share a meal and friendship. This serves to strengthen the feminine energy's protective influence on Mother Earth. Because feminine energy and women have been disrespected for so long, Mother Earth's energy is out of balance. "We've been disrespecting that energy for hundreds of years—we as women," said Melinda

Garcia, a Chicana community psychologist and keeper of a moon ceremonial tradition, in a 2007 journalistic interview. Many elders also encourage us to begin to align our lives with the moon cycle. I watch the sky, check the weather pages, and keep a *Farmer's Almanac* to track the moon time or use calendars that track the moon. Many knowledge keepers hold teachings on the moon. For instance, the moon phases can be understood as such: In the four-fold phase from new moon to first quarter, energy is initiating, there is movement forward, new beginnings. From first quarter to full moon, energy builds, form takes shape and perfects itself. In the third phase, full moon to last quarter, energy is distributed and meaning revealed in the form. From last quarter to new moon, forms break down and meaning gathered in the dark of the moon is directed into the new moon. On the full moon, offer water, flowers, and stones and the sacred materials that help bring us sight by leaving them to bathe in moonlight. Based on my own meditation and intuition developed by connecting with the moon, I sometimes offer roses and pink quartz in water and drink it the next morning to nourish self-love. Pray and offer energy to Grandmother Moon. One of my Native sisters prays that the moon be kind to her on her next moon cycle, or menstrual period. Garcia says that the full moon allows us to become more aware of the "physical energies of the Earth and how it affects our bodies." The following is a general guide to align your lives with la luna.

New moon: It's the time of preparing our *semillas*—intentions, goals. The
   energy is within. Rest.
Crescent moon: The seed is attempting to move forward. Prepare for new
   projects.
First-quarter moon: New projects take form or are initiated. Till your earth,
   physically or spiritually. Clean out closets. Cut your hair for it to grow faster.
   Fast and cleanse your body.
Half moon. A time to analyze and perfect projects, plans, goals.
Full moon: Full meaning is revealed. Meditate, journal. Gather in women's
   circles or communally.
Waning moon: Meaning spreads and is reflected.
Last-quarter moon: breakdown, dissolution.
Dark moon: Track your dreams. Dreams may be strongest then.

Moon Gazing

LARA MEDINA

I first learned how to develop a relationship with Grandmother Moon, to talk to her, to tell her what I desire to manifest in my life from Dr. Raven Lee, a Tibetan Buddhist shamanic healer.

First, be truthful with yourself about what you most desire to manifest for your well-being in the world. Do this through journaling, meditation, and deep self-reflection. On the night of a new moon, sit outside (bundle up if it is cold) and deeply gaze at the moon. Express gratitude. Allow her light to enter into you. In return, send her your light so that there is a reciprocal exchange of light. When you feel the connection, talk to her. Tell her what you believe you need. Express that you remain open to her wisdom guiding your life. Sit for a while or as long as you can. Continue your gaze. Trust that she is hearing you. If your desire is truly what is best for you, her light will send it out into the universe for manifestation.

On the night of the full moon, sit outside and gaze again at Grandmother Moon. Express gratitude. Establish the connection as before, creating a reciprocal exchange of light. Reflect on your life and discern if any movement has occurred toward the manifestation of your desire. If so, give thanks! If not, tell her again what you desire, yet remain open to her wisdom guiding your life. Develop this as a monthly practice to nourish your relationship with the moon. Also, fill a glass container with water and leave it outside overnight to be blessed with moon energy. Use it throughout the month to bless yourself and your relations. Happy moon gazing!

16

SACRED SEXUALITIES

INTRODUCTION

In the Nahua world, all living beings, all existence, are understood to embody the original creative energy, endowed with both masculine and feminine qualities. These dual energies, fluid within all of us, lead us to an understanding of ourselves as a flow of energies, resulting in the equilibrium needed to maintain our world, which is vital to our survival and ability to thrive.

Knowing how to honor our sexuality is a lifelong journey for some of us. Growing into our own skins, learning to trust ourselves and our bodies, is part of this process. Learning how to honor our longings and desires, to listen to and identify those longings within our bodymindspirits, and to redefine for ourselves what works to thrive within a paradigm that does violence to our bodies and sense of self is no easy task. Within this paradigm, our alienated bodies become sites of sexual violence, and many of us often find ourselves having to heal from these traumas. And in these processes of healing, we wrestle to maintain our bodies as sites where we can glimpse our humanity, ourselves, and one another as the Divine. Being in "our bodies as sacred," then, requires effort and work on our behalf.

Feminist theologian Lauren Frances Guerra, in "The Incarnate God and Embodied Desire," affirms for us an embodied understanding of divinity, our human sexuality, and bodies as gracious gifts from the Creator. Most important, this prose meditation offers us a critique of traditional gender roles in Western-ized patriarchy that "continue to cause damage because there is little breathing room for difference." To advance this argument, we could look to the work of Sylvia Marcos (2008), Oyeronke Oyewumi (1997), and Sadiyya Shaikh (2013), who present non-Western understandings of gender and sexuality.

How we choose to process the experience of the lover and lovemaking, or not, is key for our bodymindspirits. "In Gratitude" pays homage to the deep healing power of Yemayá, the sea, to whose waters I offered my gratitude for the renewal of sexual energy I encountered with a lover, and whose waters offer a cleansing of unresolved energies or emotions, and to Eros, erotic attraction or desire, in gratitude for a love affair whose near end brought about a redemptive transformation of self. In "prayer to my Lover // Ofrenda a mi amante," yaz mendez nuñez declares her desire, situated within a "brown, queer" body, which feels "sex is a practice of connection to source." With these words yaz affirms the divine present both in herself and in her lover. These offerings remind us, as does Lauren Frances Guerra, that the ethics with which we decide to encounter one another are at stake here; we make politics when we declare our love for one another despite the many phobias associated with differently perceived ways of expressing oneself as a sexual being.

"Healing from Sexual Trauma," by María Elena Fernández, is a thoughtful communal ritual where supportive participants gather to affirm and "listen lov-ingly, without judgment," to persons seeking support and looking to address "any self-blame, shame, and anger" resulting from sexual assault.

Sexuality holds great alchemic, transformative, and regenerative power. How can we best put this regenerative energy to work? In the spirit of this text, we suggest that we must begin by decolonizing, by acknowledging the violence of the gender binary that dominates our conceptions and understandings of ourselves as sexual beings, and instead consider gender as dynamic, fluid, and constantly in motion.

Martha R. Gonzales

The Incarnate God and Embodied Desire

LAUREN FRANCES GUERRA

Latina bodies have been sanitized, deodorized, and forcibly sterilized. Black and brown bodies continue to be colonized. Machismo, which is prevalent in our communities, functions in ways that oppress and sexually repress women. All too familiar are the "double standards" for sexual behavior: boys will be boys, and good girls keep their legs closed. The need for sexual healing is urgent and long overdue. I dedicate this reflection to all the women who have come to embrace their body and sexuality, despite being told otherwise.

Human liberation in history comes in multiple forms. The Catholic Church often identifies its members in Pauline terms, as members of the Body of Christ. God becomes one of us, in flesh and blood, through the person of Jesus. That is what the Incarnation means. Believers are members of this one Body. And we have our own individual bodies. Yet rather than adopting an embodied understanding of divinity, quite the opposite has happened.

In terms of the way in which women are perceived in Christian thought, Mary and Eve come to mind. Mother Mary's virginity and obedience to God are revered as the standard by which all women are measured. She is juxtaposed with Eve, a woman whose disobedience and whose sexuality are perceived as the root of human sin. Women basically have two paths to choose from: Virgin or Whore. Good or Evil. This paradigm leaves much to be desired.

Instead of this unfair dichotomy, I seek to affirm human sexuality and our bodies as gracious gifts from the Creator. For Latinas in particular, to reject this imposed sense of bodily shame and to embrace our sexuality thus becomes a subversive act. To tap into and explore one's sexual power becomes a life-giving source. This is what Audre Lorde describes in her work as the power of the erotic. We must move away from repressing our desires and move toward a more holistic understanding of human sexuality.

To become unapologetically comfortable in one's own skin is exactly what we are called to do. Why? Without this type of liberative work, all humanity continues to suffer. Under the yoke of patriarchy, traditional gender roles continue to cause damage because there is little breathing room for difference. A myopic vision of sexuality and of embodiment ultimately inhibits human flourishing. Breaking the chains of sexual silence and gendered violence is part of the struggle for justice.

I pray that we can get to a place in which human beings, in our myriad of bodily forms, can love unabashedly. I pray that sexual expression can be a pathway to empowerment, particularly for women who have struggled to love themselves fully. Encountering divinity happens through our encounter with one another, for there is no religious experience that occurs outside the context of daily life. It is precisely in the mundane that we come to know God. It is precisely through human touch and in the fulfillment of unspoken desires that we experience the Spirit of love incarnate. Inarguably, love and sex represent that which is universal in human experience. There are no saints and no sinners. There are simply people who we meet along the journey, whose bodies must be approached as sacred. May we perceive the eternal light of the Creator and honor the flesh of the incarnate God when we engage one another. For this too constitutes our salvation and liberation.

A PRAYER FOR HEALING
To our Loving Creator . . .

Open our hearts so that we may continue to become more vulnerable with one another.

Open our hearts so that we may embrace loving partnerships in all of their
multiple forms.

Continue to help us express your love more fully in and through our embodied
selves.
Continue to help us to see your divine light when we encounter one another.

Bless each part of our body, as you have made us sacred from head to toe.
Bless us with healing and overflowing love made tangible through sexual
intimacy.

For this and so much more, we pray.

In Gratitude

MARTHA R. GONZALES

for T

I'm done writing about you for now, all done.

Tomorrow I leave, and I do not wish to take you with me, not so far away that I will find myself pining for you in half-empty verses that make no sense when you're a continent and ocean away. Before I go, I'll walk out to the Sea to offer Her my gratitude and the last of my tears. When I'm done giving thanks, I'll swim in Her soft salt water, and with Her blessing, I'll emerge cleansed and renewed, then I'll lie on the sand, let the sun curl my hair and kiss my skin for the last time this summer. I might even let myself imagine the sun's heat is you.

When just the right wind arrives, I'll blow it a soft kiss and send this love back, grateful to Ἔρως for having met you. Grateful to Ἔρως for delivering you to me so I could blossom amid both this pain and our pleasure.

prayer to my Lover // Ofrenda a mi amante

YAZ MENDEZ NUÑEZ

this is a prayer of offering to the altar of my Lover. i am offering myself up to my Lover who desires me, giving myself over to the chasm between my round, brown, gender-strange body and Her Own. this gaping wound has been slashed repeatedly by years of imperialism and forced migration, theft of land and body and family. it feels like lost language, lost dreams, sleeplessness, too-much-work for not-enough-wellness, and a creeping anxiety of islands disappearing into the sea.

when we come together, My Lover and i pursue a deep, generations-old desire and *conocimiento* that gushes over and fills that space in-between with Erotic Source . . . in hope it can hold us there, hold our children, our peoples and our ancestors there in that gash which is now Other Place.

our sex is a practice of connection to source. it is so fertile that the scent of my Lover alone is generative enough to shift my orientation toward the Creative, the Erotic, the Source of All. like a spider does, we spin webs of spirit medicine so deeply intricate and practiced by our ancestors that we need not fear where we step as we dance across it. and where i find myself worshipping the body of this brown femme Lover, i come to know deeper the face of the Divine.

this prayer is an offering of bravery to any brown queer who's scared to sex
another brown queer for what they all might see in themselves afterward.

it can be offered in sexual engagements, nonsexual engagements, and even by
one's self in masturbation. it is a prayer of the erotic and requires nothing from
the reader but their willingness to call in the Creative Spirit to the flesh of your
body/bodies.

Mother of God, thank you for this pleasure
thank you for feeding this body
quisqueya
borinken
Mother God

i hear your voice,
it sounds like my name
or waves crashing
and fires growing
that climb the walls of my inner being
licking, groping in pleasure
and want
and lust
until my body gives over to You—

thank You, for calling my name in the calm—
in the wilderness of my loss—
in the cold of knowing stolen places—
you call to me
and i know only the truth of me, and You, and the flicker of my sex's desire

in the heat of my chest i feel a clearing
my growing want,
in the dizzying desires of my soul,
my spirit knows You, and so we know a calling sound

Mother God you offer Source in me,
which i lay again down at your altar
Mother God you offer Beauty in me,
and i refract the beauty of You
and all my people
in my nakedness

allow me to
see your image in my body
allow me to
submit to you cracking me open
wider and wider
to hear your call
to give myself over to you
to be yours

and where i whisper god into Your body
let it be etched into our souls
know that god feels like You
and so god feels like Me

Healing from Sexual Trauma

MARÍA ELENA FERNÁNDEZ

This ritual is inspired by my students, who work so tirelessly to raise consciousness about our culture of sexual assault.

PREPARATION

- Select a skilled facilitator.
- Instruct each supporter to bring a flower.
- Instruct those seeking healing to bring
    - one candle
    - an object(s) that represent grief, shame, anger, self-blame, etc., whatever is applicable to the emotional burden they are carrying.
    - a protective object, such as a gem stone, crystal, amulet, rebozo, etc.

THE DAY OF THE CEREMONY

Set up a simple altar honoring the four directions.

- Include a bowl of water, matches, and a *sahumador* for burning sage or copal.
- Sit in a circle around the altar.

- Smudge everyone using sage or copal, calling on the ancestors and spirit guides to be present (performed by the facilitator).

DECLARATION OF SUPPORT

SUPPORTERS: "We are here to support you in your healing. We will listen lovingly, without judgment, to your story. We will accompany you through this ritual to grieve with you about what happened to you and to support you in shedding any shame or self-blame and in recovering trust in yourself, your sense of safety, and your ability to love and trust others in an intimate way. And we will keep everything you say confidential. We offer these flowers as a symbol of our support."

- Supporters place their flowers on the altar.

TELLING YOUR STORY, EXPRESSING AND RELEASING EMOTIONS

FACILITATOR: "It's very important to tell your story, to speak your truth. This is a safe space to share with us what you have experienced. We are here to listen with open hearts. Allow yourself to feel whatever emotions come up, to cry, to express anger or shame. When you do so, you are unburdening yourself, and this is fundamental to your healing process."

- Participants seeking healing share their story.
- When each participant has finished, they place on the altar the symbols that represent the emotions they were able to release, or were able to begin releasing, and explain these.

FORGIVING SELF, AFFIRMING GOODNESS

FACILITATOR: "We are clear that you did nothing wrong, that you trusted, that you are a good person, and that you did your best under the circumstances. It is important that you declare for yourself your goodness and your innocence."

- Those seeking healing can together declare the following, or each individually can declare their own version:

"I understand this sexual violation was not my fault. I did not give my consent. The culture we live in of male domination taught this person to feel entitled to dominate me. They did not respect my humanity as an equal or the right to my own agency. I did not deserve this."

- Those seeking healing wet their hands and rub water along hair, arms, neck, clothes, and legs and say the following:

"With this water, I release self-blame, shame, and anger. I affirm my innocence and my goodness."

DECLARATION OF AGENCY AND SACREDNESS; BLESSING FOR SAFETY AND PROTECTION

EVERYONE: "No one has the right to dominate or violate me. My body and my agency are to be respected. I have the right to choose what happens to my body. My body is sacred, and my will is sacred. I am sacred."

FACILITATOR: "We are blessed with this copal. As the smoke encircles us, we are wrapped in the protection of Mother Earth, Grandmother Moon, and Yemayá, the power of the ocean. Remember that we are part of them and that we are equally sacred. May they always illuminate our paths, speak to us through our intuition, wisdom, and discernment, and keep us safe and protected."

THOSE SEEKING HEALING HOLD OR PUT ON THEIR PROTECTIVE OBJECT: "This (amulet, rebozo, etc.) is a symbol of my sacredness and of the safety and protection that always surround me."

ENVISIONING THE ABILITY TO TRUST AND TO LOVE

THOSE SEEKING HEALING: "Although I was violated and injured in a terrible way, I know that I am healing, that I am recovering trust in myself, and that I will recover trust in others so that one day I can love and have healthy and nurturing sexual intimacy. I light this candle as a symbol of the light and hope guiding me in my healing."

NOTE TO ORGANIZER: Emphasize the confidentiality of the stories told during the ritual, including the identity of those sharing their experiences. Also be aware that the strong emotions expressed by participants or arising from unrecognized trauma in supporters may require advice from a licensed mental health-care professional.

17

PRAYER AND SONG

INTRODUCTION

The violence and criminalization toward non-Christian forms of praying are telling of the fear provoked in the church's power structure, for prayer is telling of how we constitute or interpret the world, or what the world should be. For this reason, prayer and song, when song is enacted as prayer, are powerful acts in the service of decolonization. In prayer we reconstitute our agency, lay claim to our beliefs, and acknowledge ourselves as spiritual beings. In that recognition we intentionally locate our center and realign ourselves with the world and the fabric of energy that constitutes our cosmos. Prayer, therefore, holds potential for transformation of bodymindspirit and the world.

We open this section with "The Wounded Warrior," by Sara H. Salazar, whose protagonist sits in prayer, allowing her life story to tumble "from her mouth." By letting go of what no longer serves her, she sets her prayer with intention on what she requires to move forward: "balance, clarity, and wholeness." In "On Prayer," Laura Pérez reminds us of the power of prayer when recited with intention. Pérez asks us to evaluate the meaning of prayer in our lives and the intention with which we pray and to consider our actions as acts of prayer guided by an ethics of care to effect transformation in our world.

To prayer we can also add song, when sung as prayer or as an offering. Maria Sabina, the Mazatec traditional healer, used her sung prayers to heal others. She tells in her songs of the transformation the singer, herself in this case, undergoes in the process:

> I am a woman of light, says
> I am a woman of the day, says
> I am a woman who resounds, says
> I am a woman wise in medicine, says
> I am a woman wise in words, says
> I am a Christ woman, says
> Ah, Jesus Christ, says
> I am a Morning Star woman, says
> I am the God Star woman, says
> I am the Cross Star woman, says
> I am the Moon woman, says
> (Estrada 1981, 109)

Maria Sabina, in her chants recorded by Gordon Wasson, gathers up her energy as she sings, "With words we live, with words we grow" (Estrada 1981, 176).

Womxn have a long connection with creating music for ritual purposes. In *When the Drummers Were Women: A Spiritual History of Women*, Layne Redmond (1997) illuminates a herstory of womxn, in their handling of the frame drum and additional percussion instruments, as technicians of the sacred. In "Woman Nation," Marisol Lydia Torres speaks to how songs are about movement in their becoming, generating energy, mood, and tone. The creation of this song also led to creating womxn's circles and demonstrates how womxn create community and culture. The movement generated by the song then supports how we move in the world and how we negotiate our existence within our local and global contexts, beyond nation-state and culture. We become anchored in the reality of our lives, as womxn of this planet.

"Cántico de mujer," by singer/songwriter and longtime activist Rosa Martha Zárate Macías, also lovingly called "La Señora de la Canción" for her songs, recordings, and years of vision, work, and dedication to her community, is a canticle proclaiming "that women be blessed when she options for the cause of God, the law of love"; love here being an active force that is in the first stanza equated with "justice and peace." Rosa Martha closes the canticle by thanking God for placing within her song hope.

The heartfelt and enduring "Woman Song" is offered to us by Cristina Goro-cica, yet another example of how womxn build community even when separated by prison and correctional-institution walls and, for the full-time mother, the walls of her home as well. "Woman Song" resonates because most of us know these experiences intimately, either via our own life's path or the path of a womxn dear to us.

In "I Pray: Un Rezo of Healing pa' lxs Mariconxs," we are submerged in Eddie Francisco Alvarez Jr.'s prayer of survival, healing, and dancing toward "a future of sequins, where we can all shine." We feel along with him the call of Yemayá and Oschún, orishas of magic, dancing, and sexuality!

Martha R. Gonzales

The Wounded Warrior

SARA H. SALAZAR

The wounded warrior womxn sits facing east and
her story tumbles from her mouth:
A life of seeking, straying, dancing and languishing,
of silver ribbons of grief wound around her heart.

She yearns for healing through reconnection and faith.
She sets her intention for balance, clarity, and wholeness.
She asks for forgiveness, wisdom, guidance, and strength.

On Prayer

LAURA PÉREZ

In some spiritual traditions, prayer is, above all else, intention. It is the directing of attention, of energy, toward a particular outcome, often towards loving union with whatever name and idea we have of the Creator(s), the creative energy that constitutes. But whether religious or secular will power, prayer is an invisible yet energetically real act of alignment. It is a kind of weaving of our intent toward a particular outcome, whether this be replenishment of our own flagging forces, the regular maintenance of our wellbeing and that of others, or the powerful plea for change to remedy situations of crisis. Prayer is an act of harmonization, the sewing up of tears in the fabric of being, the reweaving of new patterns for better futures, a protective rebozo.

I can't help but to feel and to think that across time and space, to create with the intention of the Greater Good is prayer by whatever name—if by this we mean a profoundly ethical act of care and a harnessing of power, acting with an awareness that all acts, including those of art, can be acts of power, rather than mere metaphors.

Excerpted from "Prayers for the Planet: Reweaving the Natural and the Social: Consuelo Jimenez Underwood's Welcome to Flower-Landia," in *Eros Ideologies* by Laura E. Pérez, 220–234. Copyright 2019, Duke University Press. All rights reserved. Republished by permission of the copyright holder. www.dukeupress.edu.

Cántico de mujer

ROSA MARTHA ZÁRATE MACÍAS

¡Dichosa mujer, la que sabe ser fiel
al quehacer de implantar la justicia y la paz!
Bendita será la mujer que hace opción por la
causa de Dios, por la ley del Amor!

1. Hoy canto a Dios del Pueblo en mi guitarra
un canto de mujer que se libera,
Dios se solidariza con mi causa y me consagra
portavoz de la esperanza.
Dios escuchó el clamor de nuestro Pueblo, se alió
al empobrecido y explotado y a la mujer libera
de cadenas, impuestas con crueldad por tantos siglos.

2. Harás justicia a todas las mujeres,
que firmes no cayeron ante el yugo,
nos das la libertad y reivindicas, oh Dios
tu semejansa originaria.
Al mal pastor que causa tanto daño, al gobernante
infiel que vende al Pueblo a todo quien oprime tu
destruyes, sin piedad del poder tu lo derrumbas.

3. Nos llamas a gestar en nuestros vientres,
mujeres y hombres nuevos, Pueblo fuerte, nos
unges servidoras, profetizas,
testigos de tu amor que nos redime.

Haz puesto en mi cantar una esperanza, soy eco
de tu amor que reconcilia, espada de dos filos sea
mi canto pregón de un evangelio libertario.

La, la, lara la. . . .
Bendita será, la mujer, la mujer, la mujer!

Woman Song

Woman, even though I cannot see you, I'd like to let you know, I am with you heart and soul, weeyaheyo

Weeyayayo Weeyayaheeyaheyaheyayo, weeyaheeya weyaheeya, weyayaheeyaheweyaho, weeyaheyoooo

Woman, even though you cannot see me, I'd like to let you know, I am with you heart and soul

Weeyayayo Weeyayaheeyaheyaheyayo, weeyaheeya weyaheeya, weyayaheeyaheweyaho, weeyaheyoooo

Woman, even though I cannot see you, I'd like to let you know, I am with you heart and soul, weeyaheyo

Weeyayayo Weeyayaheeyaheyaheyayo, weeyaheeya weyaheeya, weyayaheeyaheweyaho, weeyaheyoooo

Woman, even though you cannot see me, I'd like to let you know, I am with you heart and soul

All versus can be repeated to make counts of four or eight

Composed in 2000, this song was written as a prayer. This song is poetry with a hand drum making the sound of heartbeats. My hand drum was my new journal. And we needed a song, a woman's song to be sung with women, for women, by women. There wasn't one I knew, and I wanted to hear women singing around me, around my children, around my community.

I was working at juvenile hall in Los Angeles when I started to write this song. I thought of the young women I worked with, taught, and was able to meet and mentor. Many times, before I left work for the day, I would let them know that even though their families could not see them, even though their community could not hear them, they were in our hearts and soul. I would say this to them often, to remind them that they are not forgotten, that they exist, and that they matter.

Once I stopped working at juvenile hall, I started to realize that this song was also for all the mothers who stay home and don't get out, who may feel that they are forgotten in their communities or society. Their lives are in their homes, their four walls, sometimes feeling trapped or depressed because of all the beautiful yet hard times motherhood brings. I would wonder how motherhood could bring on such loneliness and despair yet such happiness and elation. I knew I was not alone in this and that the lyrics of this song would resonate in the hearts of women.

Singing this song with my sisters of In Lak Ech made this a reality, made the song come to life and filled my heart, their hearts, and those listening full. Women knew/know that they are here, they are present, and we are strong. Hearing this song be sung by women and voices carried through the wind fulfills the truth of the lyrics. . . . I/women are with you heart and soul.

Woman Nation

MARISOL LYDIA TORRES

In a dream
The melodies visit
The natural asks to be mimicked
To sing its beat
In an honoring
For the people
For the ancestors . . . to be made into song

At so many points in my life I have longed to share out loud what is on the tip of my tongue, and I have stopped myself short almost every time. Somehow, music and song have always pushed me to move. And I'd move, through body and dance to the music, through years of the movement for human dignity. Yet the songs wanted to push through further, not only through body and mind, but also through this sealed voice. In ceremony, in dream, in the in-between of night and day, melodies would reveal themselves. Even in the daily drudge of hours through traffic, songs would ask to be sung. Finally, I sang out. And the songs gifted me. And I was gifted with a circle of womxn, In Lak Ech, with whom I could share the melodic language of these prayers and hopes, out loud.

"Woman Nation" was written for all womxn, so that we could recognize all the gifts we have. We give life to this world in immeasurable ways. As I chose the phrasing for this melody, I thought of my sisters, my *primas*, my friends and of the life we have lived, the heartaches and struggles we've cried together through, the times we have felt so alone or felt we just couldn't get through another day, and of the absolute joys we have shared and experienced together. I never want them to accept that they are less than anything or anyone; I never want them to accept less than they deserve. What I desire for my sisters, primas, amigas, womxn of the world is to walk with their heads up, rejoice in their gifts, lift their voices without fear, and to know they—we—make up part of an ancient lineage, a "nation" of womxn creators, healers, lovers, movers, laborers, badasses who have changed the face of our worlds throughout time and will continue to do so, because it is in our nature, in our DNA. It is who we are; it is etched into the imprint of our hands and in the curve of our walk.

The following song was written in 2007:

Woman Nation
Lift up your heads
Lift up your voice
You give life in countless ways
So lift up your voice
Lift up your heads

With love, your sister

I Pray

Un Rezo of Healing Pa' Ixs Mariconxs

EDDY FRANCISCO ALVAREZ JR.

Do I pray? How do I pray? What is a prayer? Lingering questions loom as
fiberglass shards of Catholicism enter and exit my body, and
the holy water feels good, so good on my forehead, and
the wounds, as I do the sign of the cross.
I kneel. Then I dance.
A prayer is what I make of it, through hands joined in ceremony and
contemplation, through naked bodies joined in ecstasy and in prayer.
I pray honoring *los 41*
y los 49 in Orlando, lost to senseless violence, *también.*
I pray for their souls. I pray because I know they were in sacred space, in sacred
    moments of queer world making. I pray to honor their strength to be who
    they were.
In my art making, my writing, my walks on the beach, altar building, I pray, *rezo*
    por ellxs,
for the 108 trans women of color murdered in 2016, *rezamos por ellxs,*
por los 43 de Ayotzinapa, tambíen.

I pray *por los mariconxs que no llegarón, que quisierón llegar, que nunca podrán.*
    Por aquellos con los que bailé, jugué, por aquellxs que me enseñarón a ser
    como soy, be who I am; I pray for them.

I pray to them, through my dancing, my gesturing body pointing up and down,
   side to side, toward something different, a future of sequins, where we can all
   shine, I pray.

I pray to my queer ancestors,
I pray, not always kneeling, like I was taught by the Catholic Church,
but on the dance floor like I learned from my drag sisters and
my kin in *jotería*.
I pray among religious iconography,
Madonna's "Like a Prayer," adorned in sequins and glitter,
It feels like a prayer when I am naked with you as one,
our bodies and souls in holy trinity,
a Sagrado Corazón portrait:
la Virgin de Guadalupe, votive candles, incense,
empty glass of wine, when we make love, when we are bare,
naked bodies of two men, brown men, queer bodies, we pray.

I pray when faced with the power of Yemayá and Oschún,
their waters and powers calling me,
I am afraid, but walk to them
the spirits of my Cuban, Mexican and queer ancestors touch me gently,
nudge me forward toward the waters.
A water-sign child, I was born to nurture: born after crossing rivers and borders,
   I crossed the border in my mom's womb as she crossed the mountainous
   terrain of the U.S.-Mexico border, through tunnels, desert, and fear, she
   survived, we survived.
That was the beginning
of my *nepantlerismo*,
of my journey.
My mother prayed all along the journey
for her child and herself
to be safe, that she not succumb
to the fear
the cold
the violence of the border.
She had been denied reentry and now her son,

soon to be born would be denied entry to the sacred world, but he was born sacred, and she knew it, her queer son was sacred. I am sacred. She prayed that he was well, that he would be strong, spending hours with her Vicks VapoRub drawing fingers below his nostrils, to make sure he was well

She prayed.

I pray.

18

RELATIONSHIP WITH LAND AND PLANTS

INTRODUCTION

For the last 526 years, the world has been approached as an endless resource commodified for profit.[1] The raping of Africa and the Americas, the regions' people and natural resources, fueled the growth of capitalism. "The statistical reality is that the rational, logical, capitalist, consumerist, industrial, and 'enlightened' West is the main cause of climate change" (Yugar, Tavárez, Barrera 2017, 168) Through ceremonial practices, prayers for the land are intended to heal her. Our environmental crisis has resulted in an existential crisis; mending this breach in our relationship with land and plants requires that we continue to take steps toward coming back into balance with our ecosystem.

From the reciprocal relationship we share with land and plants is born an awareness of our own life's ephemeral existence. For millennia, people have made sense of their own mortality in connection to the agricultural cycles. In "The Earth Moves," Laura Pérez brilliantly affirms this holistic movement that includes life and death within its cycle.

"Encontrándome" brings us to the understanding of the bruja as that person who knows how to balance one's material life with the immaterial realm that holds our possibility, our "part of becoming." Berenice Dimas's advice speaks to

---

1. For visual reflection, see plate 7, *De maguey* by Jessica L. Rocha.

the reciprocal relationship we share with plant life and, based on her own bond with *plantitas*, offers a path for engaging in a reflective, grounding relationship/ bond with the earth that can withstand the daily. She reminds us of knowledges passed down in the home, namely, how to make the most of your life when economics are tight and there is a mistrust of Western medicine. Her call to stand with the environment and affirm our relationship with and dependence on plants, even if we have not always acknowledged that relationship, is based on her following truth: "*Las plantas* have always known me. They have known me more than I've known them."

In "Letter to Eva," Theresa Yugar reminds humanity that we have lost our way from our original gift, or mandate, to be "good stewards of all creation." Maritza Alvarez, in "Growing Maíz," beautifully shares her spiritual experience in returning to this mandate in planting and tending to corn seeds gifted to her "from the Diné and Hopi territory." From her observations and careful tending of the seedlings, which Alvarez refers to as "a beautiful ceremony," to watching the corn push through the ground in "their growing process with the tassels and silks hairs," to the pollination that follows, this most ancient of rituals informs our understanding of ourselves, our own process of growth, and our interdependence and relationship with plants.

Martha R. Gonzales

The Earth Moves

LAURA PÉREZ

The Earth moves
Continuously
Movimiento
Movimiento
Es vida
Es muerte
regeneración
constante circulación de energía
De movimientos
And we, not like, but *are* tiny creatures, swarming the Earth.

Our ancestors, many ancestors
Spoke of energies crisscrossing, weaving this planet,
Coursing through us, broken into and reshaped into all manner of beings.
Us too, energies in *movimiento*.

Encontrándome

BERENICE DIMAS

bruja tip to self:

offerings are important on your path of becoming.
offer.
offer often.
offer abundantly.
offer.
feed that which is guiding your way.

> *Mis maestras, mis ancestros y mis guías me recuerdan*
> *siempre se empieza con agradecimiento . . .*

Queridas Plantitas,
Gracias.
You have always been there,
taking care of me.
Gracias.
You have always known me.
Gracias.
I remember that Mama *confiaba en ustedes.*
She would go to you,

pray over you.
Mama trusted you to heal me.
Gracias.
You were always there,
willing,
available,
accessible,
and able to take care of me when she could not.
Gracias.
You have always been there
and now I understand.

Abuelitas plantas sagradas,
Gracias.
Gracias por su amor,
por su calor,
por su medicina,
por dar su esencia,
por ayudarme a sanar.
Gracias, Abuelitas.
Gracias por cuidarme,
por no abandonarme.
Gracias, Abuelitas.
Gracias por ayudarme a encontrarme a mi misma.
Gracias, Abuelitas.

bruja tip to self:

no matter what happens next,
grow and Love plants.
they will love us,
help us grow,
and heal us back.

The medicine that we need is all around us.
All we have to do is learn to recognize it.

Las plantas have always known me.

They have known me more than I've known them.

Han sido my faithful healers.

My Companions.

My *Sanadoras.*

My Friends.

Las plantas have always known me.

One thing I remember clearly about my childhood is that I hardly got sick. I fractured my arm once (or twice) while being a *traviesa* and hanging off monkey bars. *Mama nos hacía sopa de zanahoria, espinacas, hongos.* She made us *caldos.* She gave us *tecitos.* Although she was far away from her homeland, she still practiced with us what she had learned from her mom. Mama used food and herbs as preventative care for her family. Mama knew that they were our best medicine. When we got a cough, she made us her famous *jarabe* that had been passed down from my grandmothers to her. She boiled half a can of Coke, added a spoon of oregano, and let it simmer until it turned into a syrup. She would say a prayer and give it to us. When I was little, I didn't ask questions. I simply took everything she gave me. When I was a teenager, I remember thinking it was funny that she used Coke, a cola drink, to help get rid of our cough. Mama used to tell me that her mama was resourceful and even turned something so toxic like Coke into medicine. It was cheaper than water in Mexico, so they learned how to do many things with it. Mama would give us *cucharadas* of that *jarabe* and it worked every time. She called it her "Mexican Robitussin" but *más* better. When I got a fever, I knew that she was going to give me her *baño de alcohol con sal,* bundle me in blankets, give me tea, and have me sweat out the fever overnight. She said, "*Aver ven,*" and would touch my forehead. Then she would say, "*Déjame tocar tus pies.*" I already knew that if my feet were cold, I would need the *baño.* If they were warm, she would go into the kitchen and find something to give me to help the *calentura* go down. I always woke up feeling better. Other days *me decía,* "*Mija, sal y tírame . . .*" *orégano, hierbabuena, epazote,* or *verdolagas.* Mama trusted her plants more than doctors. The plants always helped us. Healed us. Her relationship with plants was trustworthy; it was consistent, and it supported her by taking care of us. *Yerbas y remedios caseros* also allowed Mama to save money, especially from going to places that she did not trust to really take care of our health. As a single mother of three, plants were her support. So, when I think about my journey with the plants, I ask myself "When did they become fundamentally part of my life?" And I go back to my childhood. I go back to my mama. I go back to all those memories, those times in my life when I benefited from the relationship that Mama already had with plants. My relationship with plants and *remedios* started long ago.

bruja tip to self:
trust your medicine.

> *I used to think I did not know trust,*
> *until I reunited with plants again.*

My relationship with plants has significantly changed over time. I went through a phase as a teenager where I became really numb. Numb to my connection with the natural world. Numb with myself and my body. I cut off that relationship I had with them. I stopped connecting with my plant friends. I stopped being myself. With so many changes happening around me, it was the easiest thing for me to do.

I was "weird" to hear leaves talk to me. To feel when plants or trees were sad because they did not have water. It made me think I was "crazy." So I blocked them off. I even stopped drinking my mom's remedies because they would communicate with me there, too. "*Me llamaban.*" "*Me contaban chistes,*" but I ignored them. I even argued with Mama about taking the teas. I threw *berinches* when she wanted to give me *caldos, sopas, tecitos, baños de alcohol* whenever I got sick. I cut it all off.

I did get sick, and I did feel pain, because, well, that's part of life. So I started taking Advil when I felt pain. When I didn't want to feel at all. I took them without Mama knowing sometimes. I took them a lot. I got good at being numb. At school, I found spaces in crowds with people who were not like me. I surrounded myself with people who were not always genuine or nice to me. I made friends with them even though some of them did not care about me. I knew that, but it was easy for me. It kept myself busy from actually being myself. From feeling all that was around me. All that was trying to get my attention. All that knew me. Despite my disconnection, nature and plants called to me. Sometimes, it was confusing and scary. I did not know how to talk about it. I did not know who to talk to about it. I never told Mama. I was too scared. So, I ignored the plants. What I realized was that the more I ignored them, the more they called to me.

Healing my relationship with plants is the path I'm currently on. It took many years to return to them, but here I am, finally acknowledging them as my first friends. The ones that have loved me unconditionally. The ones that have taught me how to trust again. Plants show me that I know trust and that my body knows trust, because I know them.

Our relationship is not to plants,
our relationship is with plants.

Letter to Eva

THERESA YUGAR

Dearest Eva (Life),

I write this letter to ask your forgiveness for my complicity in the denigration of our natural world. Sadly, we humans have lived our lives indifferent to the negative effects of our human footprint on all sentient and nonsentient life-forms. To be insensitive to any Life is to denigrate all Life. At this point, we cannot go back. We must learn from our mistakes and develop a positive legacy of environmental sensitivity.

We have forgotten who we are. We have forgotten our Story. This Story began billions of years ago when God birthed the cosmos, our own galaxy, the Milky Way, and the universe of our sun and planets. God made man and woman in God's image and likeness. There were no inequalities, or hierarchies, between humans and nonhumans. Humans were called to be good stewards of all creation. Earth was a gift to us. Humans chose to exploit the gift, rather than to understand it and share it.

In my times, some prophets have warned against ideologies that justify the exploitation of the planet. It is my intention to become a prophet like them, one who is an activist and an educator. Those prophets I emulate include environmentalists Rachel Carson and David Orr; environmental scientist Carolyn Merchant; physician Helen Caldicott; physicist Vandana Shiva; historian Lynn White; journalist Paul Hawkins; ecofeminist theologian Sally McFague; liberation theologians

Rosemary Radford Ruether and Ivone Gebara; writer Arundhati Roy; religious leaders Pamela Brubaker, David Loy, Sharon Delgado, and Linda Vogel; social critic John Robbins; economist and businessman David Korten; and Buddhist monk Phrakhru Pitak Nanthakhun.

Listen to me, humans. Generations, past and present, have preferred gain at the expense of all Life. Western ideologies have stripped religious symbols of the sacred. I tell you that all Life's many forms are SACRED. Our bodies are a microcosm not only of Earth but also of the Cosmos. Our minds have been colonized and indoctrinated by a Western philosophical tradition as well as by religions that in God's name have distorted their sacred scriptures. We need to remember that Earth is a living organism who preserves our past, sustains our present, and promises our future. To kill Her is to kill us. Responsibility to Her echoes our responsibilities to God.

This letter is to implore us to remember who we are and where we came from. In God, all creatures are one, whether from diverse continents or of varying races or species, whether male or female. God moves in all life-forms. Hold onto this TRUTH. Rejoice in the beauty of creation. Nurture your sensitivity to all Life. It is time to change our attitudes toward Life on Earth. If we choose not to, EARTH will be lost. We dare not let that happen.

Growing Maíz

MARITZA ALVAREZ

Growing corn has been an extremely spiritual experience for me. From the moment I had the seed in my hand to putting it in the ground, I tried in my way to pay respect, knowing how ancient they are. I talked to the seeds. I prayed to the seeds—I had them on my altar prior to planting. These seeds in particular were gifted to others and myself from the Diné and Hopi territory. They shared their manner of growing the corn and planting it. So I wanted to pay my respects and do it in that way, for the corn has that memory. I had to put them in bundles, as that is what they are used to. I imagined like just for a person who is being displaced, it is an adjustment. So I tried to make the adjustment as comfortable as possible for them. I placed them in a circle and close to one another. My relationship with them is like that.

When I planted them, I sang to them as I put each in the ground. I made twenty-six holes and placed four seeds in each hole. Every hole I sang to. I had to. The seeds were babies. Every morning I sang. Sound is vibration, and I knew they would hear it and feel it. I sang whatever came to me. Whatever tone came out. A hum or words. When I saw them coming out, my heart was so happy. They were pushing through in these grounds that were very different for them.

I planted on the new moon, as the new moon is the darkest moon and that is where life begins, in the dark. In the dark you have to push through to the light. Every time I watered I had to thank the elements. At one point, I saw that some of the leaves were tearing. I asked my teacher, but then I listened to my instincts and knew that they had to push through the challenges. I just needed to sing more and let them know they would be fine. And they were. It is symbolic of how we must often push through life and trust. And go through life with song and prayer. And dance, as the wind is needed for the pollen to fall on the hairs. The other life, the bugs, also came to help. And my dog, she was involved too. She would go out there and greet the corn!

Seeing their growing process with the tassels and the silk hairs and the pollen falling on the silk hairs. I was told that every hair is a kernel. So that is how the kernels form. So when the pollen floats and drops on those hairs . . . that is incredible. It is about observation. I feel so good to have the opportunity to observe the entire process.

My advice is that it requires a lot of tending and it is a beautiful ceremony to be a part of. It is an honor. We hold so much energy in that seed. It requires gentleness, daily attending, even if it is just looking at them. Now they are like teenagers! They want to be alone, but I am still here for them!

19

SPIRITUAL ACTIVISM

INTRODUCTION

The many revolts against colonization and slavery in the Americas demonstrate that rebellions and movements for social justice have paired action and prayer, or spirituality, together.[1] The Dalai Lama has said that prayer is not enough. We cannot rely on prayer alone because that would be blaming God for the troubles humans have created here on the planet. We must also act in accordance with our prayer, as reflected in the activism of Gloria Anzaldúa, Dolores Huerta, Rosa Martha Zárate Macías, Cherríe Moraga, Celia Rodriguez, Maria Berriozabal, Yolanda Tarango, and many others. Anzaldúa, through her writings, directed our attention to spiritual activism as a commitment to social change propelled by a spiritual consciousness or a spiritual vision (Anzaldúa 2002; Keating 2005). Spiritual activism results from the process of self-awareness within the context of an unjust society, self-reflection that moves one to participate in collective struggle for social change. In this section, "The Scriptures of Lydia Lopez" and "The Peace Walks of Dolores Mission Parish" are two powerful examples of spiritual activism based in local communities.

In "The Scriptures of Lydia Lopez," Jacqueline M. Hidalgo offers us a sum-mation of the importance of Lydia Lopez, who "individually crafted and made

---

1. For visual reflection, see plate 9, *A Rose in My Heart* by Patricia Rodriguez.

meaningful" a set of scriptures "that work for her" and that "are communally situated." From the inception of her activism on the "picket lines of the 1960s," Lopez began crafting for herself "her own 'book.'" She recognized enacting service to others as an ethic of her Christian home. In "The Peace Walks of Dolores Mission Parish," as shared with Jennifer Owens Jofré, we learn about the work mothers have done in the community of Boyle Heights, Los Angeles, over the last thirty years to promote peace and to assist in alleviating and healing from the gang violence that claims the lives of young people in the neighborhood.

Protecting oneself spiritually to be well enough to be of use in the struggle for social justice is necessary for doing one's part in the larger daily struggle to thrive in our world. Sandra M. Pacheco offers us a glimpse of what many of us felt, and continue to feel, regarding the decision made by the Electoral College in 2016. "The Day After the Election" documents the actions taken to protect the body and spirit with prayer and herb cleansing from the venom of "white supremacist, capitalist, patriarchal hate."

"The Dharma and the Dragon Girl" by Patrisia Gonzales is a beautiful offering from the Nichiren Buddhist tradition, which is accepting and encouraging of womxn. The "little dragon who became a Buddha just as she was" offers us the important ways in which womxn affirm their will. Patrisia explains for us the meaning of human revolution within Buddhism as "a transformative movement inside our being when we are put into a revolution of positive growth." Key here is that in this growth a person "can transform their anger that is harmful and make it work toward good, such as developing a sense of justice—with wise acts," highlighting once more that prayer and action coincide powerfully to transform a life of anger into one of service.

In "Misa Mujer / Mujerista Mass," Patricia Pedroza González, activist and teacher, contributes a self-authored liturgical mass/ritual designed for womxn. Patricia's ritual celebrations are created "as wise, living, and healing practices and rescripted narratives to name women's power, honor women's blood and women's bodies." Communal ritual celebrations offer sustenance and nourishment for our commitments to social justice.

Martha R. Gonzales

The Scriptures of Lydia Lopez

JACQUELINE M. HIDALGO

Lydia Lopez has been an activist, a mother, a community leader, and a woman of deep Protestant Christian conviction, who explained that "faith and social justice are so connected in my book." This statement from our October 2013 interview underscores how Lopez's Christian activism takes root from the ongoing construction of her own "book," a set of scriptures that work for her and that are communally situated but individually crafted and made meaningful. Her lifelong and ongoing negotiation of personal scriptures models a political-religious praxis wherein one's own scriptures serve as both a challenging and a comforting mirror for daily struggle.

As someone who went to college and moved away from her family and working-class Whittier neighborhood—a neighborhood bulldozed for I-605, an interstate highway—Lopez's activism was a political and spiritual path back to herself. Meeting Christian leaders on the Los Angeles Chicano picket lines of the 1960s, she took the first step in crafting her own book: she recognized that not all religious leaders had to look or behave like the Baptist ministers of her childhood. Some of them could model a faith more reminiscent of her father's, deeply theological but also strongly committed to serving others. And religious leadership could look like her grandmother, bringing soup and juice as sustenance to those on the picket lines. While committed to the struggle for justice, her next step was to find a place where she belonged. She attended a mariachi Mass at the Episcopal Church of the Epiphany, which actively supported facets of the Chicano movement by helping the Brown Berets get started and by providing space to print *La Raza* magazine. Epiphany's Aztec dancers and *papel picado* in the sanctuary helped Lopez to see that her faith and her culture could be combined. Epiphany was a sacred space because it provided a home for Lopez as a Chicana Christian. Recognizing that homing sensation as sacrality was another step in making her unique book.

Yet life, including religious life, is ever about struggle, and Lopez continually sought and interpreted the diverse "texts" that made up her book. Lopez was challenged by a liberationist reading of traditional Christian scriptures, such as Matthew 25:40, about serving "the least of these." Such service requires an epistemic humility. As Lopez affirms, "it's also humbling when you realize that what you do, you don't do because of yourself; that there's the Holy Spirit, there's God, there's things that have to get done." Precisely because she actively fought for justice, however, she had to reach beyond traditional scriptures to embrace other traditions and practices that spoke to her world. For instance, Gustavo Gutiérrez's theological writings or Saul Alinsky's organizational model became other forms of scripture because they made sense of her daily work. The dinner conversations she had with her mother could also be a scriptural site through which she was challenged and in which she came to make sense of the world. What made any source scriptural was the imaginative space it facilitated, a sacred space that helped her to transform herself and the world.

Lopez's "book" demonstrates that one can participate in the wellsprings of Christian traditions while not having to read those traditions through the same eyes that institutional, and often white, heteropatriarchal authority figures have done. One can embrace diverse scriptural perspectives while not bowing to any one of them as a final authority.

The Peace Walks of Dolores Mission Parish

How One Community Moves Toward Healing from Violence

AS RITA CHAIREZ AND RAQUEL ROMAN OF
DOLORES MISSION PARISH HAVE SHARED WITH
JENNIFER OWENS JOFRÉ

Dolores Mission Parish sits on the corner of Gless and Third Streets in Boyle Heights, California, a small Latinx community, many of whose members trace their roots to Mexico and El Salvador. This community not only has struggled with the realities of gang violence that can wound the lives of those who live and worship there, but it also has taken communal steps to heal from that violence. The leaders of this parish—lay Latina Catholic women and white male priests— engage with the reality of this violence in ways that promote healing. Initiated by the lay Latina leaders of the parish in the early 1980s, *las caminatas por la paz* (the peace walks) contribute significantly to the work toward peace in the neighborhood. Mothers who had lost their children to gang violence began to work with Father Greg Boyle, SJ, then pastor of Dolores Mission, toward peace in the neighborhood, and las caminatas por la paz were an important first step in that direction. Since then? These walks take place during the summer, when the violence in the neighborhood calls for a response from the community with most urgency. They begin in the sprawling plaza outside the small church, where the community gathers to distribute a banner that bears the name of the parish and the candles that guide their steps as the sun begins to set over the skyscrapers of downtown Los Angeles. The choir leads songs of peace as the women of the parish, often mothers and grandmothers, make their way through the streets of their neighborhood to the site where one of their neighbors has been murdered. There, one of the priests says Mass as an act of service, an act of healing. The message they share with those who have caused the wounds, both literal and physical, is that there is another way forward in making peace with themselves, with one another, with their community, and with their God. In doing so, they reclaim the space on which the person was murdered as holy ground, and they speak of healing through their ritual actions. In doing so they remember that *la Morenita* (Our Lady of Guadalupe), knew what it was like to lose a child to violence, whether it is state-sanctioned or otherwise. Sharing their pain with one another and with la Morenita, while sending out a message of unconditional love, offers them and their community acts of healing and hope.

While conducting participant observation and in-depth interviews at Dolores Mission, I came to a deeper understanding of the devotion to *la Morenita* (Our Lady of Guadalupe) that members of the community practice, and I came to know this communal ritual, *esas caminatas por la paz*, these peace walks.

The Day After the Election

Protecting Body, Mind, and Spirit

S A N D R A   M .   P A C H E C O

WEDNESDAY: NOVEMBER 9, 2016

I wake up exhausted from staying up late the night before to watch the coverage of the elections. I remain in disbelief at who the Electoral College has elected to be the next president of the United States. Slightly numb, I begin to read the rapid, frantic posts on Facebook as people collectively release their pain, anger, and frustration. My body is activated; every cell in my being knows what is coming our way. The remnants of intergenerational trauma that reside in my body know the emboldened hate that is to come. I experienced it recently, in the time leading up to the election. Sitting at a restaurant in Oakland, California, enjoying breakfast with a friend I had not seen in months, our conversation in Spanish was abruptly interrupted by a white man sitting at the table next to us. He yelled at us to "speak English" and to "go back where you came from." With the election results, more of this is to come, and worse. I cry today, not for myself, but for my ancestors, all our ancestors who endured hatred and violence. I cry for all who will be targeted in this new era. At my home altar, filled with pictures of my ancestors, I cry more. I light the candles. I hear my grandmother's words, "*no te dejes*." Her unconquerable spirit runs through me. Yes, I got this.

I walk out to my garden with my *sahumador* and prepare the copal. As the charcoal disc heats up, I spread my arms out to the side and look up toward the sun, "*Gracias, Creador.*" I turn to face sacred mountain Tuyshtak, now known as Mount Diablo. I give my respects. I touch the ground and honor the Ohlone ancestors of Sogorea Te and Ohlone land that I live on. I cut roses with permission and take them to my Virgen de Guadalupe, "*cuidanos, por favor.*"

Sahumador now ready, I add copal and I offer smoke. I begin by smudging my body from the top of my head to the soles of my feet. I walk over to my *plantitas* and with permission ask for support from the "Grandmother plant," which we also call *pericón* or *tagetes lucida.* The Grandmother plant is one of the most powerful healing plants. She helps all plants near her to grow strong and she teaches them how to offer their best medicine. I ask permission of her and cut some branches and thank her. I cut enough to use now and to keep with me today. I draw the Grandmother plant to my face and deeply breathe into my lungs the intense scent, making her part of my body. I thank Creator and the Grandmother plant again for the medicine.

I use the Grandmother plant over my face, neck, head, arms, chest, abdomen, and legs, like I would with a washcloth, to clean my body and spirit. Like a powerful sponge, the Grandmother plant pulls the toxic energy from me. I am reminded that this is not mine to carry and to open up so the plantita can pull the *veneno* of white supremacist, capitalistic, patriarchal hate that has landed on my spirit heavier than usual. I feel the tears return and let them be. I finish and offer the now spent plantita back to La Madre Tierra.

I go inside and prepare a tea and get ready for work. I will need to care for my adrenal system today, so I mix nettles, tulsi, oat tops, oat straw, and mint. For my heart, I will add hawthorn berries. I add the mix to boiling water and turn off the flame and cover the pot. While the tea seeps until it is at room temperature, I tend to my usual morning routines. After showering, I protect my body energetically using *agua florida* and yarrow. I will need more than usual today. I select my clothes. Today will definitely be a huipil day, a long huipil with an underskirt and my Tejana boots. Beneath my huipil I will wear my red woven *faja* around my waist to protect my vulnerable center, the *ombligo.* I select a necklace that has a mini *nicho* pendant with a picture of my grandmother, Doña Mague, the strongest woman I have known. I select earrings gifted to me by Alcatraz Occupation veteran Shirley Guevara of the Mono tribe, during our occupation of Sogorea Te. I put on my Huichol-beaded cuff bracelet with images of white flowers for healing. I put on my silver bracelet made by a Taos elder—one of the last preserving the tradition of sand casting. And last, I put on my rebozo from Chiapas. My body will be my altar as I move in the world today.

I return to the kitchen to drink my tea and sit by the window to watch the humming birds. I think of Huitzilopochtli, the "humming bird of the south." I hold on to the complex mythology as a shield. It's almost time to get on the road. I grab my work bag and prepare it. A bottle of Sage Shield spray made by one of my herbalist teachers, Atava Garcia Swiecicki, goes in it to use when needed in place of copal. I pack a yarrow tincture I made to use for creating energetic boundaries. I tie the remaining branches of the Grandmother plant to the strap on my bag. Her medicine will continue to help during challenging meetings. I walk toward the door and glance one more time at my home altar, the flame of the candle reminding me that I am deeply connected to the Divine, to Creator, to Cosmos. The pictures of so many strong women who came before me remind me that I also carry their intergenerational wisdom, love, and strength. I open the door and smile to myself. I got this. We got this.

The Dharma and the Dragon Girl

PATRISIA GONZALES

Every day on the Hiaki waters, I make medicine offerings to the sea at sunrise, asking permission to enter. During my training as a scuba diver in the Sea of Cortez, I softly offer Buddhist morning prayers. As I step off the boat and plunge into the sea, I enter into its fathoms encouraged by the little Dragon Girl in the ocean who finds the dharma in the original waters of life. I talk to the water beings of my Native ways. Like the dharma or Buddhist spiritual law, my Native ways help me to honor the ocean powers. I go inside the sea to see differently, just like my two spiritual practices that have opened my eyes . . .

I aligned with the dharma after my father died, too young, in pain in the fetal position, officially from a heart attack but underneath from alcoholism and shell shock trauma from World War II and the Korean War. I found the "wheel turning" spiritual law when I wanted to understand why some people suffer more than others. I started practicing in Camden, New Jersey, with African American Buddhists in the fourth-poorest city in the country. I found that Nichiren Buddhism (notably, there are thousands of schools of Buddhism, with great variations) provided a profound but accessible system to explain suffering and how to transform karma, the effects and causes that lead to happiness or to suffering. For thirty years I have chanted *nam-myo-ho-renge-kyo*, which loosely translates as "faith in the mystic (or wonderful) law." It is "mystic" in that our minds cannot fathom its power and mystery. Through a dynamic practice of chanting, we align with this dharma, or law, through the vibrational meditation that invokes the resonance of the universe and the impulse of life to give. A thirteenth-century sage, Nichiren Daishonin founded this school of Buddhism in Japan, and many of the founder's writings were written to women. Nichiren based his study on the Shakyamuni Buddha's teachings that said women were equal to men. At that time, the teachings had become distorted, and women could only find enlightenment if they died and were reborn a man. Deep within the Buddhist stories was that of the little girl dragon who became a Buddha, just as she was. This female being did not have to change form to become a Buddha—all beings share the same spiritual potential.

Lay Buddhists embraced this Buddhism, as survivors of Hiroshima and nuclear destruction. Later, war brides brought Nichiren Buddhism to the United States. As a community, we work toward nuclear disarmament and peace. Daily prayers are offered for peace and the happiness of all life. We pray for peace that results when each person becomes happy through elevating their life condition and experiencing their own "human revolution" from within. Human revolution refers to a transformative movement inside our being in which we are put into a revolution of positive growth. For us, "happiness" is an unshakable strength that is not swayed by external factors and that emerges as we bring forth our Buddha nature—goodness, respect, kindness, compassion, wisdom, courage, and clarity. In our form of engaged Buddhism, a person with an angry nature, once their Buddha nature emerges, can transform their anger that is harmful and make it work toward good, such as developing a sense of justice, with wise acts. The Buddha is the Universe itself, not some guy with a fat belly.

As an Indigenous woman, Buddhism aligns with some of my key Native beliefs and with spiritual law. The "mystic law" coincides with my teachings on the Great Mystery, an existence that is not explainable or captured in words, yet its power is experienced. Other corresponding values include believing in oneness of the self and the environment and oneness of the mind and the body. The environment reflects human thinking, including our unconscious thoughts about ourselves and others. We must discipline our minds, our thoughts, yet what stirs in our heart is most important. Rather than the Christian god, we adhere to a spiritual law of the universe, one of multiple fields of causes and effects that function in an intricate web of "dependent origination." Everything is created in relation to others and other causes, similar to my ancestral Spider-woman teachings that personify the web of interrelationship. These spiritual laws are laws of justice, strict in their consequences. All causes are imprinted in life and at the right time manifest as positive or negative effects. Nothing in life escapes them. My Native ways and my Buddhist teachings share multiple understandings of sending prayers across time, back and forth across seven generations. These different spiritual systems share a respect for women and the female and different genders.

From these thirty years of chanting and praying to/through the breaking points, chanting through rage, tears, amazement, and wonderful struggles to transform my karma in all aspects of my life, I want to share prayers and guidance that may help others pray. Many of these guidances have been given to me by Buddhist elders, many of them women leaders in our community of practitioners, and my mentors Daisaku Ikeda and Nancy Mallory, who raised me in Buddhist faith.

> *Pray to make new causes that will lead to your happiness. Chant (pray) intently, delving into the depths of your life.*
> *Pray, I want to make a different cause. Determine: I pray not to make causes that lead to unhappiness. I pray not to harm myself or others with my thoughts, words, or actions.*
> *Pray to open the path to your dreams.*
> *Pray to be in harmony with your environment and pray for the environment to support you.*
> *Pray for the truth to be known.*
> *Pray to open your eyes, to see with the Buddha's eye, meaning from the depth of the wisdom of the universe.*
> *Pray to open your heart and release judgment, while maintaining discernment.*
> *Pray for protection: pray to tap into the power of life, the power of the universe and for the protective forces to inhabit your life and that of others.*
> *Pray to experience the limitless potential that gives impulse to all of life (the Buddha nature of the universe).*
> *Pray to see the worth of your lives and that of others, even when they are in conflict with you.*
> *Pray to harmonize your hearts and minds with others, even those you disagree with, that the Buddha nature in you bring forth the Buddha nature in your environment and those around you.*

Shake up the universe with your prayers; permeate your karma to sever your chains of suffering.

Pray to see value in every suffering and every struggle and to not be defeated. For we suffer when we do not believe we can change the pattern, path, and trajectory of our lives.

As an Indigenous woman, I have integrated living with my Native ways and with my Buddhist teachings. It is important to have a spiritual foundation. My spiritual life is not a grab bag of teachings. I am grounded in teachings that are thousands of years old. The Buddhist teachings evolved in a way that they can be shared publicly. My Native teachings are secreted to protect them against exploitation. I know how to act based on different systems of spiritual protocols. Additionally, as a Kanaka Maoli Buddhist practitioner once told me, these traditions are separate or distinct, but they become one in me.

. . . Deep in the ocean on one dive, the fingers of the ocean grab my waist and pull me out to sea. My diving partner loses sight of me. I am totally alone and no one knows exactly where I am in the ocean. I ask the ocean powers for permission to leave, and I chant in my mind, and the story of the Dragon Girl keeps me unshaken. With those prayers, the grasp of the riptide loosen, and my partner finds me. In one of our returns to shore at the end of the dives, several hundred dolphins surround the boat. A dive instructor notes he has never seen so many approach at once. They are the envoys of the water beings and spiritual laws.

Misa Mujer / Mujerista Mass

PATRICIA PEDROZA GONZÁLEZ

Sunday morning meetings were times for Catholic *Misa*/Mass for my grand-mothers. I loved going to *la misa* with my grandmothers, yet I never really liked what was said within the ritual. But oh how I admired the faces of both my grandmothers as they sang their faith! My work now, as an activist and teacher, has grown over the years, and I have created spiritual rituals to expand and embrace the faith I have, a legacy from my grandmothers but within recon-structed liturgical celebrations that name womxn's power and honor womxn's blood and womxn's bodies.

The following guidelines for what I call a *Misa Mujer,* or *Mujerista* Mass are flexible and can be accommodated to what is comfortable for those participat-ing. The various spoken parts can be printed and distributed as desired.

A circle of chairs is arranged and an altar set in the middle on a small table with the following:

- a transparent bowl with water
- flowers and different kinds of seeds
- a bell and a basket with bread to share
- red juice and a chalice or glass

The group will need a facilitator, or *sacerdotisa*, and speakers to lead at specific parts of la misa. The speakers should represent the diversity of womxn who are present and be there to honor womxn and their power, participate in a time to heal, and celebrate community among womxn.

Sacerdotisa:

Queridas hermanxs:

Antes de iniciar nuestra celebración, tomemos unos minutos para reconocernos, mirándonos a los ojos, aprecien la belleza de los y las aquí presentes. Reconozcamos en nuestros rostros, nuestra historia, nuestros ancestros, nuestra fuerza y nuestra vulnerabilidad.

Tomemos un momento para escuchar la intención de esta eucaristía,

que hoy día, vaya esta energía para la causa que más se necesite en nuestra comunidad.

SPEAKER 1: *Ofrecemos esta misa mujer por las necesidades de nuestra comunidad:*

(Speaker reads the petitions or intentions collected from participants.)

(After the petitions are read, everyone repeats.)

EVERYONE: *¡Qué las bendiciones sean!*

SACERDOTISA: *Para continuar nuestra misa mujer cada persona aquí presente diga su nombre en voz alta.*

(Todos/as dicen su nombre, se escuchan las palabras como en un *coro*.)

SACERDOTISA: Our life began in water and it flows upon the earth . . . making earth fruitful. Water, fertility, and flexibility. We choose you as the symbol of this celebration.

(Sacerdotisa sumerge sus manos en el agua y en forma suave rocía gotas de agua a su alrededor y del altar.)

EVERYONE: We celebrate! Through the water we celebrate our lives and passions.

(Sacerdotisa reparte algunas de las semillas entre las participantes mientras recita esta parte.)

SACERDOTISA: *Las ideas se diseminaron por mi cuerpo y lo fertilizaron con semillas de creatividad, creciendo la flor y el canto para honrar a mis hermanas mujeres, honrar a mi madre tierra y a la energía que ella nos da.*

La energía que nos ayuda a seguir con los ciclos vitales, iluminar los ciclos obscuros, e integrar las fuerzas masculinas y femeninas que se encuentran en cada uno y una y que se manifiestan con el latido del corazón, centro de amor.

SPEAKER 2: ACKNOWLEDGMENT OF SELF-DENIAL
I confess, here, before each of you.

I confess to hiding my dreams and hopes. I confess that I don't believe in myself or make decisions according to my insights. I swallow my opinions and deny my needs when faced with the neediness of others. I confess that I am insecure, closed off within myself in ignorance. I confess that I am guilty of rivalry, abandonment, envy, and competition in my relationships with womxn, my sisters.

(El grupo espera unos segundos en silencio antes de continuar.)

SPEAKER 3: *Madre Nuestra*
Do you know what the sound of universal love is? I've heard so many sounds of love from the ocean and nature, from the earth, but there is also the powerful sound to call our mother: Mama, Mama, Mama!

SACERDOTISA: Let us pray,
Madre nuestra que estás en los cielos,
Quiero que vuelvas antes de que las mujeres olvidemos como ayudarnos las unas
    a las otras
Madre nuestra que estás en los cielos, no te olvides de nosotras.
Cuando hablaste de que las mujeres somos iguales, también alzó su mano la mujer
    indígena silenciosa quien se resistía a anular su propia voluntad.
Nuestras voluntades como mujeres no son respetadas, por el contrario son ahogadas
    y aplastadas. Nuestras voluntades se encuentran separadas, aisladas.
Madre nuestra ayúdanos a recordar que la división destruye y la unión fortifica.
Madre nuestra ayúdanos a caminar con nuestros conflictos y
convertirlos en colaboraciones entre nosotras.
Our Mother in heaven . . . you are present everywhere, on earth as in heaven.
(Speaker 3 shares with participants the seeds that represent the agricultural cycles.)

SPEAKER 3: CELEBRATION OF CYCLES
There is a time to plant.
There is a time to reap.
There is a time to conceive.

There is a time to birth.

I mark the cycle of womxn, I speak my wisdom.

SPEAKER 4: *Credo*

Creo en la madre y la hija.

Creo en el amor entre mujeres, de la madre a la hija, de la abuela a la nieta, de la tía a la sobrina.

Creo en el espíritu de amor que se derrama por la tierra fertilizándola con vida y esperanza.

I believe in peace on earth based on justice and where all children are treated equally.
   I believe in Mother, her child and the spirit of solidarity.

(Before sacerdotisa recites the next part, she rings the bell, calling for the moment of blessing the bread and juice.)

SACERDOTISA:

Antes de nuestra consagración, hablemos entre nosotras, las que están en el cielo, las que estamos aquí, las que están en prisión, las que están desaparecidas, las exiliadas, las ricas, las pobres, las prostitutas, las mudas, las mujeres lisiadas, las santas en todas.

Tenemos en nuestros cuerpos la sangre de las mujeres asesinadas. Womxn tortured by repressions all around the world.

No nos quedemos encerradas en las puertas del silencio.

Now we will talk, as womxn among ourselves. Let us not be shut away behind the doors of silence. We take the risk with all our hearts, breaking down those divisions among us.

(Sacerdotisa rings the bell again.)

SPEAKER 5: LITANY TO OPENING DOORS

(Speaker 5 asks these questions.) (Everyone answers.)

Who will open this door? To the silence about incest, the silent crime.

Who will open this door? *A mi dolor por la violencia.*

Who will open this door? My compassion, acts of love will disarm.

(Sacerdotisa pours the red juice in the chalice.)

I take in my hands this chalice that contains the blood of womxn who have died giving birth without proper assistance and in clandestine abortions.

I take in my hands this chalice that contains the menstrual blood issuing from the uterus, the nest of life.

Drinking this blood, I plant the seed of awareness, seed of the desire for transformation by means of magic, sexuality, and positive, generous, enthusiastic vision.

SACERDOTISA: OFFERING

We celebrate the end of violence against womxn, the end of discrimination against Indigenous womxn, who suffer double discrimination.

We celebrate the victories of womxn who struggle for dignity in the workplace and for decent wages.

We celebrate the love of the lesbian and transwomxn who desire to live their relationships in the open.

We celebrate the end of isolation and shaming of the prostitute.

We celebrate, fiber by fiber, the body of the womxn who is a mother, and also of the womxn who is not.

We celebrate our physical pleasure without guilt, the right of a womxn to grow old with dignity.

We offer in this celebration the future, like a burst of light, the energy and the desires of each womxn here present.

EVERYONE:

Today I bless my search and my growth.

Today I bless my speech.

Today I plant the seed of healing; I plant habits that purify.

Today I plant the seed of my vocation. I plant the seeds of spiritual creative discipline.

Today I plant the seed of my freedom.

Today I plant reflective speech and sincerity of expression.

Today I bless my creativity, our creativity.

SACERDOTISA: COMMUNION

Hermanas compartemos este pan y sangre bajo el amparo de la providencia. Recordemos dar de comer a quien tiene hambre porque en el dar está el recibir.

(Sacerdotisa drinks the red juice symbolizing the blessed blood. After she finishes the drinking, she rings the bell. Once ringing stops, speakers share the chalice and bread in little pieces with all participants.)

EVERYONE SPEAKS: CLOSING

Hail womxn

Hail womxn, full of grace.

Blessed womxn: together we all are transgressors.

Hail womxn, we are true life that inhabit the earth and inherit the planet.

Together now, here today.

We are the owners of our lives!

(Sacerdotisa toma una flor, la sumerge en el agua y en forma suave rocia con gotas de agua a las participantes, como cuando se recibe agua bendita en la eucaristia.)

SACERDOTISA:

Vayamos en paz y sigamos con el compromiso de seguir adelante honrando y respetando a nuestras hermanxs mujeres,

Benditas y benditos seamos. Amén.

20

SPIRITUAL PEDAGOGY

INTRODUCTION

Religious education was utilized as a tool in the European colonial projects throughout the Americas. The education of Indigenous peoples by Catholic priests, missionaries, and Christian ministers within the walls of religious institutions was intended to eradicate the Indigenous cultures of children and young adults and to root out "evil," a process accompanied by violence. Often, what was being eradicated was the Indigenous value placed on education, the learner, and the learning process itself. Most importantly, the value of education in developing the personality or agency of the learner. In the twentieth century, Paulo Freire wrote that educators could counter the banking model of education by engaging in dialogue, for dialogue is the foundation to becoming more fully human. This requires love, humility, faith in humankind, trust, hope, and critical thinking (Freire 2014). Freire's notion of humanity involved "a deeper reflective interpretation of the dialectical relationship between our cultural existence as individuals and our political and economic existence as social beings" (Darder 2009, 568).

Teaching takes time. It takes time to prepare our lessons, beginning with the creative process of designing the syllabus and choosing with care and consideration the materials we will be incorporating to fulfill the needs of the institutions we work within as well as attaining the end goal of assisting to transform hearts and minds. How we teach matters. How we transmit information and how we find ways for students to understand the material matter.

This chapter offers reflections from educators who intend their classrooms to be liberatory educational spaces that further the process of decolonizing our histories, our minds, our spirits, and our bodies; spaces that speak truth to power. In "A Pedagogy of Ofrendas: The Altar as a Tool for Integrating Social Justice in the Classroom," Norell Martínez proposes that we create sacred space "by embodying the meaning of an altar in our educational work," thereby creating "an altar-like pedagogy that turns the classroom into a sacred space where we nurture our students' bodymindspirit," and that when "we view our work as educators as an *ofrenda*, we are creating a sacred space in the classroom because we acknowledge that learning itself is sacred."

Lara Medina, in "A Spiritual Pedagogy," offers various techniques for integrating "nonsectarian spiritual practices" in the classroom, whether it be an indoor classroom or outdoor campus space. Lara's contribution acknowledges that this work can be challenging, but the challenges "can be overcome with persistence and commitment to a more holistic way of learning."

In "Decolonizing Spirit in the Classroom con Anzaldúa," Susy Zepeda, who self-identifies as a queer, "detribalized" Xicana Indígena, discusses the ways Anzaldúa's spiritual borderlands have inspired her pedagogy to engage with colonization and decolonization to create and open space for Indigenous forms of spirituality, ceremony, and sacredness with Xicanx, Chicanx, and Latinx students. Susy's practice in the classroom exemplifies what Antonia Darder calls "teaching as an act of love." Love as an act "rooted in a committed willingness to struggle persistently with purpose in our life" toward what Freire called "our 'true vocation': to be human" (Darder 2009, 567).

Martha R. Gonzales

A Pedagogy of Ofrendas

The Altar as a Tool for Integrating Social Justice in the Classroom

NORELL MARTÍNEZ

Altares have been used throughout time and across cultures to create sacred spaces, spaces of prayer and ritual, and sites of offering and memory or to connect with our ancestors. While altars in the material form are crucial components in these practices, I propose that we can also create a sacred space by embodying the meaning of an altar in our educational work. This is a valuable form of integrating social justice into the classroom, particularly for those of us who work with disadvantaged students.

This idea came to me after reading Laura E. Pérez's (2007) book *Chicana Art: The Politics of Spiritual and Aesthetic Altarities*. She uses the concept of altars to describe Chicana visual art that is not necessarily in the form of an altar but rather art as offerings on an altar where "the material and the still disembodied are invoked" (6). Pérez explains that traditionally altars have been spaces where one "invokes, mediates, and offers homage to the unseen but felt presence in our lives, whether these be deities, ancestors, or the memories of our personal, familial, and collective pasts" (7). She states that Chicana artists use the altar to acknowledge, make visible, and pay respect to that which is visually, socially, and culturally invisible. If Chicanas can create altar-like art, I believe that we can create an altar-like pedagogy that turns the classroom into a sacred space where we nurture our students' bodymindspirit, where teaching is acknowledged as a sacred ritual of raising consciousness, and where we pay homage to and connect with the history of our ancestors' struggle and resistance.

Below I discuss three ways we can create a sacred learning space by embody-ing the altar in our teachings. Explaining to students the significance of the altar-making tradition could further illuminate the classroom as an *ofrenda* in the making.

ALTAR AS OFRENDA. Because the altar itself functions as an ofrenda, we re-create this element in the act of teaching. The mental and emotional energy we put into preparing our lessons, the pedagogical tools we use in creating an equitable and just space, and the passion we have for raising consciousness are our ofren-das to our students. We give this offering because it promotes healing for our students (and for ourselves) and because part of teaching from a social justice perspective is helping students unlearn dominant narratives of race, class, and gender inferiority. When we view our work as educators as an ofrenda, we are creating a sacred space in the classroom because we acknowledge that learning itself is sacred. Likewise, we teach our students that the work they are doing, the knowledge they produce in our classroom, is their ofrenda.

ALTAR AS INVOCATION AND MEMORY. The altar is a site of invocation, as Pérez states, of the socially and culturally invisible. It is a site of recuperation, recovery, or memory for those who are not "seen" or who are "dead" in the eyes of many, those who are "not fully within social discourse"—the ethnic "minority," the Latina/o, the sexually "queer" (125). The altar can serve to invoke people from marginalized communities who have gone unacknowledged, whose pain has been ignored, whose bodies have been abused, or who have made important contributions yet have not been given proper homage. Hence, altars can be political acts of cultural resistance. We practice this element in the classroom by invoking those who are "unseen" in the readings we assign. We make the invis-ible visible and pay them homage when we share their work and contributions to social movements. We also put this concept into practice by validating the experiences and cultural knowledge students bring into the classroom. This is especially important with disadvantaged students who are often not validated in educational spaces. We engage with material that reflects their experiences.

ALTAR AS SACRIFICIAL SLAB. Altars have served in some cultures as sites of death. The altar as "sacrificial slab," as Pérez calls it, signifies violence and annihilation or that which has been sacrificed against one's will (114). The altar, then, can sym-bolize for some the cycles of life (summoning) and death (sacrifice). When we invoke the altar as a sacrificial slab in the classroom, we point to the ugly side of history, a history that is not often told in K–12 public education, a history that tells of the unfathomable forms of violence that perpetrators of colonialism, racism, and homophobia enacted on our ancestors. We shed light on those whom capitalist, patriarchic, homophobic, and other violent systems have hurt or "sacrificed." Practicing this element of the altar in the classroom means that we create a sacred space, a safe space, a healing space for our students as they make sense of and understand these systems of oppression.

Ultimately, from a social justice perspective, our goal as instructors is to raise consciousness among our students, which requires a transformation, a sort of "death" of regressive ways of thinking, so that students can then go out and create change in the worlds in which they live.

A Spiritual Pedagogy

LARA MEDINA

Integrating spirituality into a traditional Western educational setting is a challenge, but one that can be overcome with persistence and commitment to a more holistic way of learning. Nonsectarian spiritual practices can be shared with students of all disciplines. I teach meditation techniques in general education history courses to help students release their anxieties and ground themselves in gratitude and compassion. When teaching Chicanx history, we critically examine the impact of Christianity on our history of colonization and consider the unique spirituality of Mexican Catholicism. We also explore the return to Indigenous spirituality that began during the Chicano movement and connect it to current spiritual, cultural, and artistic expressions.

In my classes directly related to spirituality and religion, we gather in a circle and review Chicanx religious history, then we explore spirituality as reflective of our relationship to self, others, the natural world, and the Source of life and death, or the Great Mystery. Honoring students' feelings about religion, which are frequently estranged, is key to nurturing their interest in studying religion from a feminist, queer, and culturally specific lens. The freedom to question inherited religious beliefs offers spiritual liberation.

I also introduce Mesoamerican spiritual concepts and values such as Tloque Nahuaque, In Lak' ech, Ometeotl, huehuehtlahtolli, tonalli, teyolia, tlamatinime, in xochitl in cuicatl, in ixtli in yollotl, and the "mother of all medicine," the temazkal.[1] Emphasizing the values within these concepts—our sacred interconnectedness to all of life, divine duality, reciprocity, fluidity, balance, movement, and guidance from the ancestors—helps students to apply these spiritual "laws" to their own lives. At times, I have the luxury to hold class outside on a patio or on a grassy area. Smudging students with sage and/or copal aids in experiencing a spiritual practice. I always extend the smudging as an invitation, which, at times, a few students do not accept.

Teaching students how to create communal sacred space by creating a sacred center in the middle of the circle on the ground solidifies my intention that we are in the circle as co-learners and even co-teachers and that learning itself is a sacred process. Symbols of earth, air, fire, and water, in their corresponding directions, along with greenery and perhaps flowers placed in a circle on a special cloth are sufficient. The burning sage or copal can be placed in the center if class is held outside. Students sharing their responses to the readings reinforces the significance of their voices. Connecting the topics to their own experience is always encouraged.

When funding is available, I invite traditional healers, *curanderas*, to class to share their life story and the knowledge systems embedded in their holistic healing practices. I also teach students how to conduct self-limpias using plant medicine and about creative journaling for maintaining consistent well-being.

These are small but significant steps that can be taken to dismantle sterile learning environments with students sitting in static rows of chairs expecting to be "fed" information. As educators committed to decolonizing Western education, we have to teach to the whole person, to the bodymindspiritnature consciousness.

---

1. Tloque Nahuaque: our sacred interconnectedness to all of life
   In Lak Ech: the reflection of ourselves in others
   Ometeotl: divine duality both male and female
   Huehuetlahtolli: the wisdom of the ancestors representing traditional teachings
   Tonalli: our divine fire within connecting us to the sacred fire of the sun
   Teyolia: our spiritual energy located in our hearts that lives on after death
   Tlamatinime: the wise ones who teach profound truth through poetry and the
      art of language
   in xochitl in cuicatl: the arts expressing beauty and truth
   in itxli in yollotl: the spiritual character of a person
   Temazkal: sweat ceremony

Decolonizing Spirit in the Classroom con Anzaldúa

SUSY ZEPEDA

Anzaldúa's opening of the spiritual borderlands has inspired my pedagogy to engage with colonization and decolonization, to open space for Indigenous forms of spirituality, ceremony, and sacredness with Xicanx, Chicanx, and Latinx students. I utilize the writings of Gloria Anzaldúa in my teaching because her ceremonial writings are path openers. I usually introduce and frame courses with her essay "Now Let Us Shift . . . The Path of Conocimiento . . . Inner Work, Public Acts" or her now classic text *Borderlands / La Frontera: The New Mestiza*, and/or I assign "Speaking in Tongues: Letter to Third World Women Writers" from *This Bridge Called My Back*. I begin by telling my students about her life trajectory and how even though her *nepantlera* writing and theorizations are central to the formation of women-of-color feminisms, the theorization and study of the multiple manifestations of borderlands (material and nonmaterial) and their many dimensions in our lives, Xicana spirituality, decolonization, and what it means to be *una de las otras*, Gloria Anzaldúa, the dyke Chicana philosopher, was met with an intense amount of resistance from academic colonial heteropatriarchal logics and practitioners of this violence. I also share that Gloria transitioned to the spirit world at the age of sixty-two from complications of diabetes.

Usually, students respond with anger at learning of her life struggles, next to expressing deep curiosity and compassion for her life story, and identification with some form of her path, rooted *palabras*, and transformative imagination.

By sharing her story and struggles, Gloria gives me permission to create a space of *sanación*, healing for my students and me, to be unbounded in our generosity, love, and respect for one another and the learning process as we grow and transform. Reflection and dialogue are key in this space. Tezcatlipoca. Obsidian mirror.

In my Chicana/o Theory course, we begin by questioning who is given the privilege of being called a theorist or philosopher. Soon after, the students articulate that they, too, are theorists—that their lived experiences have value, as do the lives of their family and community members, and that they are carriers of knowledge. This becomes clearer as we read *This Bridge Called My Back* and dialogue about "theory in the flesh" while sitting in a circle. We disrespect no one, including ourselves, even when we have betrayed our spirits. We value our palabra, admit when we are wrong or have misspoken, offer our regrets to the earth, to the fire, we enter the classroom with open hearts, and we share in vulnerable ways that allow us to heal our traumas, including the violence imposed on us by university structures. We recognize the white walls that were never meant for our voices or imaginations but that now in our classroom we disrupt with our collective presence and ancestral wisdom.

In many ways, the vision of *This Bridge* provides a guided path to come home to oneself, to bring your whole self home again, to call your spirit back by looking at the pain, fear, and trauma in the face. To check in and ask: How do you keep yourself well? How do we fully connect our hearts and minds when we are constantly experiencing and/or witnessing violence? We start to ask ourselves: How do we build a collective world where we can all be sustained?

On the day we discuss section VI, *otros mundos*, we begin class with a guided meditation. I ask students to close their eyes and begin taking deep breaths. I ask them to imagine the world we currently inhabit. I then invite them to visualize water (i.e., river, ocean, lake) or a form of light (like the sun) so they can cleanse. Finally, I ask them to visualize *otro mundo* (another world), a different world from the one we currently inhabit. I ask them what it feels like, looks like, who is there. This is followed by a short write-up. In this way the radical feminist vision of *This Bridge* inspires a decolonial, feminist, critical pedagogy of reading the world through the third eye—visual imagination—to see possibilities of justice and transformation beyond the material world.

To close out the course, I have students read sections of *This Bridge Called My Back* over the span of three weeks. We spend time reading aloud passages to illuminate what is meant by "theory in the flesh." The students immediately relate their own stories—which have usually been silenced or gone unnoticed—to the words and experiences of racism, colonialism, and heterosexism spoken of on the pages of *This Bridge*. I encourage dialogue among their stories and ideas so they feel connected to the process of creating theory through connection, community, and multiplicity instead of through isolation.

Anzaldúa's teachings furthermore facilitate the presence of the sacred in intellectual spaces as well as the awareness that we are embodied beings who are remembering ourselves as Indigenous people. In my Decolonizing Spirit seminar, we create a circle and altar every time we meet; we honor the original peoples of the land and the four directions. On occasion, I bring fresh herbs into the classroom, such as basil, rosemary, or sage. I offer these to align bodymindspirit, to bring a harmonious vibration back to the body and to allow for an alignment with the earth and the cosmos. In conversations with other *colegas* who teach in this manner, we have discussed how Gloria was a trailblazer for this form of intervention and knowledge, in creating pathways of healing and spirit in the academic world and classrooms. We have wondered whether us building a network of people and doing the work at this time to create transformative and meaningful classrooms were part of her prayer. Even if we are in different departments or institutions, we know **we are many** who offer our hearts to this *trabajo* of lifting our students to be their higher selves in their writing, stories, and visual forms of expression.

Gracias a la Gloria.
Tlazohcamati, Ometeotl.

21

TALKING CIRCLES

INTRODUCTION

For many Indigenous peoples, gathering together for the purpose of listening to one another's concerns, challenges, and joys traditionally takes place in the form of a circle, a talking circle. A circle mirrors the patterns of the universe and allows energy to flow equally among the participants. Talking circles provide the ritual place and time to "hold space" for one another and to listen without judgment. Talking circles are sacred circles that should begin with prayer around a sacred center. Opening prayers petitioning guidance from the directions, the elements, the ancestors ensure the strength and safety of the circle. Talking circles offer the opportunity to heal as we hear ourSelves through our own words and in the words of others. For womxn, talking circles break imposed silence and encourage us to speak our truths.

The poetry of Sara H. Salazar blesses the opening of this section with imagery accessing the healing power of listening to one another and recognizing our own pain in "the story of the wounded warrior womxn." Trini Tlazohteotl Rodriguez's reflection of her path to facilitating talking circles illuminates the value of these spaces to help us recognize "that we are all sacred. That we are all worthy." Trini shares about the different kinds of talking circles, which are based on the needs of those gathered as well as basic protocol. And Ann Hidalgo reflects on her digital experience with a circle of womxn in Santiago, Chile, who first began to gather in circles to create their own ritual outside of patriarchal spaces. The circle inspired their journal *Con-spirando*, which Ann edited and digitally archived, inspiring her to compose a song in honor of the Chileana circle, "a place of healing . . . and solidarity [that] can inspire dreams of a better future."

Naomi H. Quiñonez blesses the closing of this section with her poem "Circles of Women," an expression of her deep knowledge of the power of womxn gathering in circle "so that [we] may wake to dreams of [our] own designs . . . and piece together new truths from the discarded fabric of old pain."

Lara Medina

The Curandera Listens . . .

SARA H. SALAZAR

*The curandera listens to the wounded warrior womxn's story
with her whole body—her bones, her heart, her hands, her teeth, her skin.*

*She remembers that the story of the wounded warrior womxn is her story, too
It is also the story of her ancestors.
She feels the pain of the warrior womxn as if it were her own and
re-members a bittersweet history of celebration and conquest,
culture and colonization, land and loss.*

*The curandera recognizes the hollow echoes of susto that reverberate from
the warrior womxn's heart and knows that her susto is not hers alone,
Her susto resides deep within the threads of her lineage.
The wounded warrior's healing begins today but will take a lifetime to mend.*

From Past to Present

The Healing Power of Talking Circles

TRINI TLAZOHTEOTL RODRIGUEZ

I was introduced to Indigenous practices relatively late in my life, but I am grateful to have incorporated their healing essence into my life ever since.

In 1983, I was living in Chicago and was active as a Chicana editor of a national newspaper advocating for the rights of undocumented workers. By 1988, I was married to an equally politically active editor/writer/poet, Luis. Our lives revolved around seeking systemic change. Then something happened to remind us we had to do more than just change the world—we also had to change ourselves.

Shortly after Luis and I married, his thirteen-year-old son from a previous marriage, Ramiro, came to live with us. I was pregnant, and that same year, our son Ruben was born. Suddenly, we went from being busy newlyweds to being busy full-time parents. Inevitably, Ramiro's anger and long-held feelings of abandonment, loss, and betrayal surfaced, and he turned to gang activity to "belong." Stepping up as a father, my husband turned to community and cofounded an organization, Youth Struggling for Survival (YSS), to embrace our wayward son and his friends. By 1994, Luis's seventeen-year-old daughter, Andrea, also moved in with us. I was forty-one, once again pregnant, and that year, our son Chito was born.

Disowned at the age of twenty-one, I still had my share of personal struggles. My husband had his own traumas too. We all needed healing.

Thankfully, with all the challenges came blessings.

It was through this YSS youth work that our family was introduced to Mexica Indigenous elders, sweat lodges, and healing circles. We participated in and adopted these practices, bringing these young people to them for all of us to heal from our respective wounds. We brought these practices with us when we moved back to California in 2000, and they have served us well.

Along this path, I was spiritually adopted by a Navajo Nation Diné family, who have shared their beautiful ways with me. My father, roadman Anthony Lee Sr., and his wife, Delores Lee, have always been profoundly generous Diné teachers, while also encouraging me to reclaim my own Indigenous roots. This quest has led me to many teachings, which I do my best to honor when conducting women's sweat lodge ceremonies and also when facilitating healing circles for community members. Healing circles are more than talking circles, if conducted well.

The age-old concept of the circle-spiral permeates Indigenous beliefs and practices. It reflects the understanding that the universe functions according to set principles, laws, and values, which we must align with in order to live in harmony and grow. Original peoples observed that all life was circular. The planets, sun, and moon are circular, the rising and setting of the sun follows a circular pattern, birds build their nests in circles. The circle and circular movement can be found throughout nature.[1] Gathering in a circle reminds us that we are interconnected to one another, the earth, the sky, and to every other being. It reminds us that we are all sacred. That we are all worthy. And that when we open our hearts to Creator Spirit—outside and inside us—we can face anything with more wellness and clarity to move forward and continue developing.

Healing circles can be held in many settings and for many purposes, such as to consider a problem or uncertainty in a relationship, be it family, community, organization, society, etc. Participants come to offer their piece of truthfulness to help create the collective wisdom that will be discerned. The intent is not to make strong arguments or to convince others of right or wrong, rather it is to become still and quiet so that all can be heard. When truth is spoken on an issue, it is heard and sits well with the circle. Healing circles lend themselves to almost any situation or topic.

---

1. Inspired by the teachings from the Dancing to Eagle Spirit Society (2008). This is a society to advance Native American healing and spiritual principles for people who self-identify as two-spirit. See also Mehl-Madrona (2014) and "How to Conduct Talking Circles" (Coyhis 2012)—a presentation by elder Don Coyhis as part of a series of workshops for twelve-step recovery programs.

My experience is with facilitating healing circles, in which a decision might not have to be made, but the participants merely need to share about their lives and their challenges for release and/or clarity. When someone asks me to do this, the person requesting the circle explains why they want one. Invited participants are asked to prepare to attend by refraining from ingesting alcohol or other substances that intoxicate the body and mind, including sugars, in the days leading up to the talking circle. This helps everyone to be their most clear, authentic, present self.

Healing circles embody this intention: We come together to cocreate a safe place where tough issues can be faced by listening and sharing in a circle of support, truth, and compassion. The entire circle can gain from the beauty and empowerment of this experience. It is medicine for us all.

Briefly, the basic healing circle protocol for facilitating is as follows: Form a circle for everyone to be seated. Create a sacred center with a simple offering, including medicinal plants. Welcome everyone. Use sage or copal to cleanse participants' energy. Offer an opening prayer. Remind everyone that the circle is sacred and what we see and hear stays there. Introduce the subject matter. Pass the talking stick or other symbolic item, such as a crystal or stone, to the left for participants to speak their truth until everyone has spoken. Explain to participants that listening without reacting is key to a healing circle so that everyone can connect with their own wisdom as well as the collective wisdom.

Above all, a healing circle requires that we speak from the heart. We must all slow down, be present, speak honestly, be authentic, listen, and reflect deeply. In our fast-paced world, where distractions and fears often compel us to keep moving with no clear direction, grounding ourselves and regaining perspective with the help of healing circles can go a long way to making our lives and our world better.

The power of healing circles is immense. This ancestral gift is a blessing that can help us face the challenges of today.

En este círculo

ANN HIDALGO

In 1991, a group of women in Santiago, Chile, began gathering monthly to celebrate *ritos* (rites) of their own creation to celebrate their spirituality outside
of patriarchal spaces. These women resolved to create a space in which they
could freely express how they experienced the sacred in their lives. The following year, the group began publishing *Con-spirando: Revista Latinoamericana de
Ecofeminismo, Espritualidad y Teología* (Con-spirando: Latin American Journal
of Ecofeminism, Spirituality and Theology). Like the rites, the journal became
a space in which the women explored and reflected on elements of their daily
lives that connected them with the sacred. In addition to feature articles written
by women in various Latin American countries and translations of works by
relevant authors from around the globe, each issue included artwork, poetry,
and a brief description of one of the group's rites.

In 2014, I began working on a digital archiving project for the journal, scan-
ning and digitally editing each page of the first thirty issues of the journal. As the
months progressed, the thousands of miles between my desk at a library in California and Santiago, Chile, seemed to melt away. Members of the Con-spirando
Collective who were frequent contributors to the journal became my teachers
and friends, even though I have never met most of them. I composed this song
in their honor. It reflects what I have experienced of their lived spirituality, conveyed through their writings and art. This is a tribute to my teachers and friends.

The song introduces the concept of a circle ritual in which women share stories of their experiences and encounters with the sacred in their lives. "*En este círculo*" (In this Circle) acknowledges that everyone has a story to tell and invites participants to share their stories, dreams, joys, and sorrows in the circle of wisdom and love. Just as feminist theologians rigorously analyze scripture and religious traditions to distinguish elements that are life giving from those that are oppressive, this song invites women to consider their inherited traditions—religious, cultural, and social—to identify which are helpful and which are harmful. The circle is a place of healing in which tears can be shed and where conversation, laughter, and solidarity can inspire dreams of a better future.

En este círculo

Ann Hidalgo

A - bue-la, a - mi-ga, com-pa - ñe - ra,   Cuén-ta-nos de tu vi-da: Las his - to-ri_as y los

sueñ-os   Que a - ni - man   tus dí - as.   To - das tra-e-mos   cuen-tos De_a-le -

grí_as y su-fri-mien-tos   Pa-ra com-par-tir en es-te cír-cu-lo   De sa-bi-du-rí-a_y

de ___ a - mor.

To verses   Final ending

Verse 1

En es-te cír-cu-lo es-cu-cha-mos el pa-sa-do, Dis-tin-guien-do ver-dad-es de men-ti-ras, Re-co-gien-do per-las de sa-bi-du-rí-a, Y cor-tan-do las re-des que a-tra-pan.

Cuen-tos nos en-se-ñan quien-es so-mos y cre-an lo que que-re-mos ser. De las his-to-rias de las gen-er-a-cion-es He-re-da-mos fuer-za, es-pe-ran-za_y fe.

Verse 3

En es-te cír-cu-lo ce-le-bra-mos jun-tas, Soñ-an-do un mun-do me-jor. La un-ión es más pro-fun-da Que lo que nos pue-de se-par-ar. Con-ver-san-do sur-gen las i-de-as; Ri-en-do bro-ta la in-spi-ra-ción. De nues-tro tiem-po com-par-ti-do Na-ce la co-mu-ni-dad de a-mor.

Circles of Women

NAOMI H. QUIÑONEZ

Circles of women surround me.
They brush sorrows
off my shoulders
like dust
and sprinkle moon water
on my face
so that I may wake to dreams
of my own designs.

Our circle is a round mouth
laced in red lipstick
and laughter.
Half-moon smiles spill out
candlelight, sage smoke
copal.

We speak heartbeat
to one another's
unique palpitations
small vibrations
gather as one.

We remember
the bruised
broken faces
that reside in our fears.

We sort out futility
from power
and piece together new truths
from the discarded fabric
of old pain.

We see the greatest lies
intermingled
with the highest truths

We hold flesh
to moonlight
and hear
the muffled sounds
of wounds healing.

We utter the sacred songs
written into the hands
of the four directions.

A circle of small moons spinning
into a smoking vortex
we invoke La Diosa.
A hallow throat opens
and swallows us.

We are the entrails of Mother Earth.
Fires lap at our heels
winds howl like restless coyotas.
Rivers of sweat roll down our stomachs
our feet root
in a mulch of earth and bones.

Dis-ease drains out of
wounded hearts and weary bodies
into the loving earth.
We heal, we heal, we heal.
We are planted in a mixture
of earth and bone and memory.

We tell our stories
sing our songs
bless and cleanse
and invoke.

Spirit of the East
place of new beginnings
your winds brush our faces.
Carry our prayers
to the universe
bring us wisdom
on your wings.

Spirit of the South
we invoke your vitality
ignite our red-flame passion
fuel our desire
for justice and love.

Spirit of the West
slack our thirst
for knowledge
refresh our spirits
with cleansing waters.

Spirit of the North
Nuestra Madre Tierra
we honor you
press our foreheads to the earth

take in your energy
and ground in compassion.

Circles of women surround me
they brush sorrows
off my shoulders
like dust
and sprinkle moon water
on my face
so that I may wake to dreams
of my own designs.

22

EVENING PRAYERS

INTRODUCTION

Night, I Thank You
I thank you for your coolness
for the safety and comfort you provide
for welcoming me in
for illuminating Grandmother Moon and
Her siblings, the Stars
I thank you for the medicines
and the ceremonies you guard.

Just as we greet the day, we also greet the evening.[1] We greet the coming of the night. We greet the evening as the sun sinks into the horizon, that liminal moment when day changes to night. I've greeted the dusk from the hills of Northeast Los Angeles, have watched the sun go down over the city, across the Pacific, thanking Creator and Tonatiuh for another day, and then I've waited to welcome the night.

---

1. For visual reflection, see plate 11, *Full Moon in Daylight* by Linda Vallejo.

We privilege the productivity of the daylight hours and shun the night. We've become accustomed to denigrating the activities of the nighttime hours, of the dark. Having grown up Catholic, I was taught to fear the dark and to associate things of this world considered malignant with the night. What a simplistic and misconstrued way to understand the world; particularly because evil and malignancy roam the world in broad daylight, causing economic despair, dropping bombs. It is fair to say that one cannot make the argument that night itself is evil.

Night is the time when we can see the moon and the stars, when we can observe the depth of the heavens and our cosmos. It is the time that brings on discovery, not just of the evening but of ourselves; for as we turn upward, we turn inward and come to realization about our place within the bigger picture. For this reason, creation has provided us medicines to pray with during nighttime, such as *hikuri*[2] of the northern Mexican desert and the Saint Children[3] found in the sierras of southern Mexico, in Oaxaca. From these medicines evolved ceremonies for healing, for the night is for healing, holding a deep transformative potential for us within its fold.

We arrive at a full circle in this chapter, honoring the transition from day to night, when we take our longest rest. The night is for regeneration of the body through sleep and, yes, dreams. Here we address our night rituals for protecting and guarding our sleep. For night can also be an ambivalent time as it provides the space for the disembodied spirits to come out and mingle. I keep a doll *de dos colores* my *padrino* asked me to procure and dress to protect against the *pesadillas* and spirits disturbing my sleep. On a little dream altar by my bed she sits alongside a set of crystals in a seashell, white rosary beads, and a small plaque declaiming a prayer to Asklepios.

In "Ángel de mi guardia," María Figueroa shares cherished memories of her grandmother and of learning by observation the importance of a nightly prayer ritual, prayers for oneself and "prayers of protection and love for *la familia*." In teaching her children this simple prayer that calls on our spirit guardians to watch over us while we sleep, Figueroa recalls the ancient Mexican belief in the *nahual* and the *tonal* and the importance of caring for the spirit self while sleeping.

In "Descansando en paz," Jerry Tello leads us on a nighttime meditation to help ease us into a peaceful rest, a path for acknowledging "the challenges and

2. The Wixárika (Huichol) term for peyote.
3. The name by which María Sabina lovingly called the mushroom (Estrada 1981).

joys of the day" and for knowing "it is not important to carry them further." For that is the promise of a new day, that we can begin again. Instead we express gratitude for all that is as we are guided into "a restful sleep."

Grace Alvarez Sesma graces the ending of this chapter, of this volume, with "Tlazocahmati Tatita Sol," an endearing prayer thanking our radiant star, our sun for illuminating and making possible the day, asking with "a good heart" that Tatita Sol take with him, as he sets, "all that no longer serves the highest vision" of herself.

Martha R. Gonzales

Ángel de mi guardia . . .

MARÍA FIGUEROA

Ángel de mi guardia
Dulce compania
No me desampares
Ni de noche ni de dia

When I was a little girl, eight or nine years old, *mi abuelita* Josefina taught me a special prayer for protection. A special prayer to help me end my day and rest my little body and mind. Like most children, I learned through observation. I learned from the actions of my elders, *los mayores,* and often practiced what they did. Mi abuelita would bring down the covers from her bed, crawl into their comforting warmth, and kneel in the center of the bed. In the venerated kneeling position, *se persinaba,* as she murmured the words accompanying the sign of the cross so as to ask permission and acknowledgment from the spirits to continue. *Persinaba las cuatro direcciones,* turning her fingers into *cruzes,* and motioning her blessing and prayers in all directions. In a faint whisper, like the ones heard during all-night *velorios,* I could hear her pray for all her children, grandchildren, and extended relations. These were her ways, and soon, they became mine.

So at the young, impressionable age of nine years old, I began, like her, crawling into my bed, kneeling in the center, turning my nine-year-old *deditos* into *crucecitas,* and signing/blessing in the four directions. I remember using my bedposts as directional markers to guide my prayer. I don't remember for whom I prayed, but if I had learned from *la mayor,* it was probably first for myself, while prayers of protection and love for *la familia* followed. My abuelita lived with us for only a short period of time before moving to Arizona, but in these few years, there were many valuable and lifelong prayerful teachings I learned from her. Mind you, my abuelita Josefina was not the stereotypical "chocolate abuelita." She was a tougher, rough-around-the-edges type of abuelita. *Era la que te queria y daba amor indio.* It was a tough Indigenous love, informed by her love for *lucha libre,* her survival tactics, and her bodily strength. After all, it was she who crossed *la frontera de Juárez* and El Paso daily, collecting food scraps to feed her children. It was she who raised four children as a single mother, one stricken with polio from the age of nine. Her strength endured in her body and in her spirit. So it was never on her accord that she sat me on her lap to teach me the bedtime prayerful ways, although in retrospect, I think she always knew I was observing and learning.

Once my prayer was complete, the left palm, as body, met the right palm, as mind, and together in prayer form, as spirit, I would begin, "*Ángel de mi guardia / ducle compania / no me desampares / ni de noche ni de día.*" This was the nightly ritual, and one that made me feel protected. She'd tell me that we all had *un angelito* to watch over us. That guardian angel was our protector and our guide. This I trusted, and because it seemed right, I would invoke my guardian angel nightly.

Fast-forward thirty-two years. In my early forties, I am a single mother of two beautiful children. I am a traditional Aztec dancer, a sundancer, a teatrista, and a community college professor. My life is abundant to say the least! So as a multimodal momma, the evenings with my *xinatchlis* (seeds), Cuauhtemoc Victorio and Esperanza Tonantzin, are sometimes stressful. On the "good" nights, when calm sets in on the home front, my children crawl into the warmth of their beds, nestled by their *cobija's* embrace, and begin their prayer. Unlike my grandmother, who never prompted or seemingly interfered with my prayer, I often prompt my children with "Okay, say your prayers." And they do.

Like my abuelita Josefina's whispering murmur, I can hear my Esperanza's voice, "*Ángel de mi guardia. . . ,*" and down the hallway, I can hear Cuauhtemoc loudly and intentionally call on his guardian angel as well, ". . . *no me desampares . . .*" Many teachings return to me when parenting my children. Often, through storytelling, *mis semillas* have learned the ways of *el amor indio* and how they serve to invoke physical and spiritual *conocimientos.*

Descansando en paz

JERRY TELLO

- As we prepare to allow our bodies to rest, let us take a deep breath and reflect on our day . . .
- The many things we did, the challenges and the joys.
- As you breathe deeply, allow your body to settle . . . Allow your thoughts and feelings to be released through your breath so your body can rest.
- These were today's lessons and it is not important to carry them further.
- Honor your body, allow yourself to rest. Also express gratitude for the wonderful things that happened today, those who greeted you, those you served.
- Feel the gratitude for another day of life.
- Recognize that the Creator, the angels, the ancestors, and the loving universe are prepared to guide you through a restful sleep so that your bodymind-spirit can rest.
- Offer good intentions for all your relations.
- We complete this day and close this sacred circle.

Adapted from "Peaceful Rest: Nighttime Meditation: Descansando en Paz." *Sacred Circles: Honoring the Ancient Traditions of the Ancestors*/CD Jerry Tello, Susana Armijo, Citlali Arvizu Carmelo, and Xavier Quijas Yxayotl.

Tlazocahmati Tatita Sol

GRACE ALVAREZ SESMA

Tlazocahmati Tatita Sol for this day now ending, knowing that for others another day is just beginning. I greet your sacred duality, Grandmother Moon, with offerings of smoke and prayers that all obstacles, inner and outer, may be removed for the healing and well-being of all those with whom I share my medicine, in person and in spirit. As you set, please take with you all that no longer serves the highest vision of myself so that I may be of service and a blessing to all creation. I say these words with a good heart and for the benefit of All Our Relations.

REFERENCES

Alba, Consuelo, dir. 2013. *Xilonen: Ceremony of Tender Corn.* Veremos Productions.

Alvarez, David. 2010. "Xilonen." *Sacramento Press*, August 2, 2010. https://sacramentopress .com/2010/08/02/xilonen/.

Anzaldúa, Gloria. 1987. *Borderlands / La Frontera: The New Mestiza.* San Francisco: Aunt Lute Books.

Anzaldúa, Gloria. 1999. *Borderlands / La Frontera: The New Mestiza.* 2nd ed. San Francisco: Aunt Lute Books.

Anzaldúa, Gloria. 2002. "Now Let Us Shift . . . The Path of Conocimiento . . . Inner Work, Public Acts." In *This Bridge We Call Home: Radical Visions for Transformation,* edited by Gloria Anzaldúa and AnaLouise Keating. New York: Routledge.

Anzaldúa, Gloria. 2015. *Light in the Dark/Luz en lo oscuro: Rewriting Identity, Spirituality, Reality,* edited by AnaLouise Keating. Durham, NC: Duke University Press.

Anzaldúa, Gloria, and AnaLouise Keating. 2000. *Interviews/Entrevistas.* New York: Routledge.

Aponte, Edwin David. 2012. *Santo! Varieties of Latino/a Spirituality.* New York: Orbis Books.

Armijo, Susanna, Cítlali Arvizu Carmelo, Xavier Quíjas Yxayotl, and Jerry Tello. 2010. *Sacred Circles: Honoring the Ancient Traditions of the Ancestors.* Sacred Circles. CD.

Avila, Elena, with Joy Parker. 2000. *Woman Who Glows in the Dark: A Curandera Reveals Traditional Aztec Secrets of Physical and Spiritual Health.* New York: Jeremy P. Tarcher/Putnam.

Barrios, Carlos. Maya Teachings, January 2, 2015.

Barrón Druckrey, Eleanor. 2008. *Corn Woman Sings: A Medicine Woman's Dream Map.* New York: iUniverse.

Brownworth, Lars. 2009. *Lost to the West: The Forgotten Byzantine Empire that Rescued Western Civilization.* New York: Crown.

Bruchac, Joseph. 1993. *The Native American Sweat Lodge: History and Legends.* Freedom, CA: Crossing Press.

Buenflor, Erika. 2018. *Cleansing Rites of Curandersismo: Limpias Esprituales of Ancient Mesoamerican Shamans.* Rochester, VT: Bear and Company.

Calvo, Luz, and Catriona Rueda Esquibel. 2015. *Decolonize Your Diet.* Vancouver: Arsenal Pulp Press.

Caraza, Xánath. 2015. *Ocelocíhuatl.* N.p.: Mouthfeel Press.

Caraza, Xánath, and Sandra Kingery. 2014. *Sílabas de viento / Syllables of Wind.* Lawrence, KS: Mammoth.

Caraza, Xánath, and Sandra Kingery. 2016. *Donde la luz es violeta / Where the Light Is Violet.* Lawrence, KS: Mammoth.

Caraza, Xánath, Rafaela Enríquez Mejía, Sandra Kingery, and Stephen Holland-Wempe. 2012. *Conjuro.* Lawrence, KS: Mammoth.

Carrasco, Davíd. 1990. *Religions of MesoAmerica: Cosmovision and Ceremonial Centers.* New York: Harper and Row.

Carrillo, Ricardo A., Isaac Alvarez Cardenas, Evelyn Crespo, Ramon DelCastillo, Berta Hernandez, David Hoskins, Concepcion Saucedo Martinez, Samuel Martinez, Sal Nuñez, E. Padron, Jerry Tello, and Eliseo Cheo Torres. 2017. *Cultura y Bienestar: Mesoamerican Healing and Mental Health Practice Based Evidence.* Self-published, CreateSpace.

Castillo, Ana. 1996. *Goddess of the Americas / La Diosa de las Américas: Writings on the Virgen of Guadalupe.* New York: Riverhead Books.

Castillo, Ana. 2014. *Massacre of the Dreamers: Essays on Xicanisma.* Rev. ed. Albuquerque: University of New Mexico Press.

Ceseña, María Teresa. 2009. "Creating Agency and Identity in Danza Azteca." In *Dancing Across Borders: Danzas y Bailes Mexicanos,* edited by Olga Nájera-Ramírez, Norma E. Cantú, and Brenda M. Romero, 80–94. Urbana: University of Illinois Press.

Coffman, Franklin A., and T. R. Stanton. 1977. *Oat History, Identification, and Classification.* Washington: Agricultural Research Service, U.S. Department of Agriculture.

Coyhis, Don. 2012. "How to Conduct Talking Circles." Youtube. https://www.youtube.com/watch?v=3RdIX7UM4ks.

Dancing to Eagle Spirit Society. 2008. "The Talking and Healing Circle." http://www.dancingtoeaglespiritsociety.org/circles.php.

Darder, Antonia. 2009. "Teaching as an Act of Love: Reflections on Paulo Freire and His Contributions to Our Lives and Our Work." In *The Critical Pedagogy Reader,* 2nd ed., edited by Antonia Darder, Marta P. Baltodano, and Rodolfo D. Torres, 567–578. New York: Routledge.

Deagan, Kathleen, and José Maria Cruxent. 2002. *Columbus's Outpost Among the Tainos: Spain and America at La Isabela, 1493–1498.* New Haven: Yale University Press.

de las Casas, Bartolomeo. 2011. "A Brief Account of the Destruction of the Indies. In *Born in Blood and Fire: Latin American Voice,* edited by John Charles Chasteen. New York: W.W. Norton.

de la Torre, Miguel Ángel. 2004. *Santeria: The Beliefs and Rituals of a Growing Religion in America.* Grand Rapids, MI: W. B. Eerdmans.

Delgadillo, Theresa. 2011. *Spiritual Mestizaje: Religion, Gender, Race and Nation in Contemporary Chicana Literature.* Durham, NC: Duke University Press.

Delgado Bernal, Dolores, C. Alejandra Elenes, Francisca Godinez, and Sofia Villenas, eds. 2006. *Chicana/Latina Education in Everyday Life: Feminista Perspectives on Pedagogy and Epistemology.* Albany: SUNY Press.

Deloria, Vine, Jr. 2006. *The World We Used to Live In: Remembering the Powers of the Medicine Men.* Golden, CO: Fulcrum.

Durán, Fray Diego. 1971. *Book of the Gods and Rites and the Ancient Calendar.* Translated by Fernando Horcasitas and Doris Heyden. Norman: University of Oklahoma Press.

Elizondo, Virgilio P. 1980. *La Morenita: Evangelizer of the Americas.* Forward by Patrick F. Flores. San Antonio: Mexican American Cultural Center.

Estrada, Álvaro. 1981. *María Sabina: Her Life and Chants.* Translated by Henry Munn. Santa Barbara, CA: Ross-Erikson.

Facio, Elisa, and Irene Lara, eds. 2014. *Fleshing the Spirit: Spirituality and Activism in Chicana, Latina, and Indigenous Women's Lives.* Tucson: University of Arizona Press.

Fiesta de Maíz. 1993. Brochure, privately printed.

Figueroa, María. 2014. "Toward a Spiritual Pedagogy Along the Borderlands." In *Fleshing the Spirit: Spirituality and Activism in Chicana, Latina, and Indigenous Women's Lives,* edited by Elisa Facio and Irene Lara, 34–42. Tucson: University of Arizona Press.

Four Worlds Development Project, Lethbridge. 1986. *The ANISA Model of Education: A Critique. Issues in Native Education.* Alberta, Canada: Four Worlds Development.

Fox, Matthew. 2000. *Original Blessing: A Primer in Creation Spirituality Presented in Four Paths, Twenty-Six Themes, and Two Questions.* New York: Jeremy P. Tarcher/Putnam.

Freire, Paulo. 2014. *Pedagogy of the Oppressed.* 30th anniversary edition. New York: Bloomsbury.

Garciagodoy, Juanita. 1998. *Digging Days of the Dead: A Reading of Mexico's Dias de Muertos.* Boulder: University of Colorado Press.

Gaspar de Alba, Alicia, and Alma López. 2011. *Our Lady of Controversy: Alma López's Irreverent Apparition.* Austin: University of Texas Press.

Goizueta, Roberto. 2002. "The Symbolic World of the Mexican American Religion." In *Horizons of the Sacred: Mexican Traditions in U.S. Catholicism,* edited by Timothy Matovina and Gary Reibe-Estrella, 119–38. Ithaca, NY: Cornell University Press.

Gonzales, Patrisia. 2003. *The Mud People: Chronicles, Testimonios and Remembrances.* San Jose, CA: Chusma House.

Gonzales, Patrisia. 2012a. "Calling Our Spirits Back: Indigenous Ways of Diagnosing and Treating Soul Sickness." *Fourth World Journal* 11 (2): 25–39.

Gonzales, Patrisia. 2012b. *Red Medicine: Traditional Indigenous Rites of Birthing and Healing.* Tucson: University of Arizona Press.

González-Wippler, Migene. 2007. *Santeria: The Religion.* 2nd ed. Woodbury, MN: Llewellyn.

Grosfoguel, Ramon. 2013. "The Structure of Knowledge in Westernized Universities: Epistemic Racism/Sexism and the Four Genocides/Epistemicides of the Long 16th Century." *Human Architecture: Journal of the Sociology of Self-Knowledge* 11 (1): 73–90.

Hạnh, Thích Nhất. 1974. *The Miracle of Mindfulness*. Boston: Beacon Press.

Hạnh, Thích Nhất. 1992. *Touching Peace: Practicing the Art of Mindful Living*. Edited by Arnold Kotler. Berkeley, CA: Parallex Press.

Hendrickson, Brett. 2014. *Border Medicine: A Transcultural History of Mexican American Curanderismo*. New York: New York University.

Hernández-Ávila, Inés. 2006. "Ometeotl Moyocoyatzin: Nahuatl Spiritual Foundations in Holistic Healing." In *Teaching Religion and Healing*, edited by Linda L. Barnes and Inés Talamantez, 127–38. New York: Oxford University Press.

Herrera, Juan Felipe. 1974. *Rebozos of Love / We Have Woven / Sudor de Pueblos on Our Back*. San Diego: Toltecas en Aztlán.

Hill, Louis Paul. 2001. "Understanding Indigenous Canadian Traditional Health and Healing." PhD diss., Wilfrid Laurier University.

hooks, bell. 1994. *Teaching to Transgress: Education as the Practice of Freedom*. New York: Routledge.

hooks, bell. 2003. *Teaching Community: A Pedagogy of Hope*. New York: Routledge.

Hyatt, Sydney. 2012. "Martin Manalansan on 'Queer Dwellings: Migrancy, Precarity and Fabulosity.'" *Toronto Review of Books*. Podcast audio, October 12, 2012.

Iféwarinw, Oyasuúru. 2018 "Priest of the Ifa Tradition." Presentation at Pacific School of Religion, Berkeley, CA, August 7, 2018.

Isasi-Díaz, Ada María, and Yolanda Tarango. 1988. *Hispanic Women: Prophetic Voice in the Church*. New York: Harper and Row.

Keating, AnaLouise. 2005. "Shifting Perspectives: Spiritual Activism, Social Transformation, and the Politics of Spirit." In *EntreMundos/Among Worlds: New Perspectives on Gloria E. Anzaldúa*, edited by AnaLouise Keating, 241–54. New York: Palgrave Macmillan.

Kellogg, Susan. 2005. *Weaving the Past: A History of Latin America's Indigenous Women from the Prehispanic Period to the Present*. New York: Oxford University Press.

Kelly, J. N. D. 2000. *Early Christian Doctrines*. 5th rev. ed. London: Continuum.

Klor de Alva, Jorge. 1993. "Aztec Spirituality and Nahuatized Christianity." In *South and Meso-American Native Spirituality: From the Cult of the Feathered Serpent to the Theology of Liberation,* edited by Gary H. Gossen and Miguel León-Portilla, 173–97. New York: Crossroad.

Kroger, Joseph, and Patrizia Granziera. 2012. *Aztec Goddesses and Christian Madonnas: Images of the Divine Feminine in Mexico*. Farnham: Ashgate.

Laframboise Sandra, and Karen Sherbina. 2008. "The Medicine Wheel." Dancing to Eagle Spirit Society. Accessed May 2012. http://www.dancingtoeaglespiritsociety.org/medwheel.php.

Lara, Irene. 2014. "Sensing the Serpent in the Mother, Dando a Luz la Madre Serpiente." In *Fleshing the Spirit: Spirituality and Activism in Chicana, Latina, and Indigenous*

Women's Lives, edited by Elisa Facio and Irene Lara, 113–34. Tucson: University of Arizona Press.

León-Portilla, Miguel. 1992. *Fifteen Poets of the Aztec World.* Norman: University of Oklahoma Press.

López Austin, Alfredo. 1988. *The Human Body and Ideology: Concepts of the Ancient Nahuas.* Vols. 1 and 2. Salt Lake City: University of Utah Press.

Lorde, Audre. 1996. "Poetry Is Not a Luxury." In *Sister Outsider*, 36–39. Rev. ed. Berkeley, CA: Crossing Press.

Luna, Jennie, and Martha Galeana. 2016. "Remembering Coyolxauhqui as a Birthing Text." *Regeneración Tlacuilolli: UCLA Raza Studies Journal* 2 (1): 7–32.

Magaña, Sergio. 2014. *The Toltec Secret: Dreaming Practices of the Ancient Mexicans.* Carlsbad, CA: Hay House.

Maldonado-Torres, Nelson. 2014. "AAR Centennial Roundtable: Religion, Conquest, and Race in the Foundations of the Modern/Colonial World." *Journal of the American Academy of Religion* 82 (3): 636–665.

Marcos, Sylvia. 2008. "*Raíces espistemológicas Mesoamericanas: La construcción religiosa del género.*" In *Religión y Género*, edición de Sylvia Marcos. Madrid: Editorial Trotta.

Marcos, Sylvia. 2009. "Mesoamerican Women's Indigenous Spirituality: Decolonizing Religious Beliefs." *Journal of Feminist Studies in Religion* 25 (2): 25–45.

McCampbell, Harvest. 2002. *Sacred Smoke: The Ancient Art of Smudging for Modern Times.* 2nd ed. Summertown, TN: Native Voices.

Medina, Lara. 1998. "Los Espíritus Siguen Hablando: Chicana Spiritualities." In *Living Chicana Theory*, edited by Carla Trujillo, 189–213. Berkeley, CA: Third Woman Press.

Medina, Lara. 2004. *Las Hermanas: Chicana/Latina Religious/Political Activism in the U.S. Catholic Church.* Philadelphia: Temple University Press.

Medina, Lara. 2006. "Chicanos and Religion: Traditions and Transformations." In *Teaching Religion and Healing*, edited by Linda L. Barnes and Inés Talamantez, 139–55. New York: Oxford University Press.

Medina, Lara. 2011. "Nepantla Spirituality: An Emancipative Vision for Inclusion." In *Wading Through Many Voices: Toward a Theology of Public Conversation*, edited by Harold J. Recinos, 279–94. Lanham, MD: Rowman and Littlefield.

Medina, Lara. 2014. "Nepantla Spirituality: My Path to the Sources of Healing." In *Fleshing the Spirit: Spirituality and Activism in Chicana, Latina, and Indigenous Women's Lives*, edited by Elisa Facio and Irene Lara, 167–85. Tucson: University of Arizona Press.

Mehl-Madrona, Lewis. 2003. *Coyote Healing: Miracles in Native Medicine.* Rochester, VT: Bear.

Mehl-Madrona, Lewis. 2014. "Introducing Healing Circles and Talking Circles into Primary Care." *Permanente Journal* 18 (2): 4–9. https://www.ncbi.nlm.nih.gov/pmc/articles/PMC4022550/.

Meissler, Reinhild Emily. 1993. "Medicine Wheel: An Ancient Symbol in Modern Society." PhD diss., University of Montana. Accessed: https://scholarworks.umt.edu/cgi/viewcontent.cgi.

Menchaca, Martha. 2001. *Recovering History/Constructing Race: The Indian, Black, and White Roots of Mexican Americans*. Austin: University of Texas Press.

Mesa-Bains, Amalia. 1993. "Altarmakers: The Historic Mediators." In *Ceremony of Spirit: Nature and Memory in Contemporary Latino Art*, edited by Amalia Mesa-Bains, Victor Zamudio-Taylor, and Arturo Lindsay, 5–7. San Francisco: Mexican Museum.

Miranda, Deborah A. 2010. "Extermination of the Joyas: Gendercide in Spanish California." *GLQ: A Journal of Lesbian and Gay Studies* 16 (1–2): 253–84.

Montour, Louis T. 1996. "The Medicine Wheel: Understanding 'Problem' Patients in Primary Care." Paper presented at the Fifth Annual Meeting of the Native Physician Association, Canada, Ottawa, Ontario.

Moraga, Cherríe. 1993. *The Last Generation: Prose and Poetry*. Boston: South End Press.

Morales, Francisco. 2001. "Baptism." In *The Oxford Encyclopedia of Mesoamerican Cultures: The Civilizations of Mexico and Central Americas*. Vol. 1, edited by Davíd Carrasco, 78–9. New York: Oxford University Press.

Muñoz, Susana, and Lourdes Portillo, dirs. 1989. *La Ofrenda: The Days of the Dead*. San Francisco: Xochitl Films.

National Latin@ Network. 2016. "31 Facts About Domestic Violence in the Latin@ Community." National Latin@ Network. Accessed March 22, 2019. https://enblog.nationallatinonetwork.org/31-facts-about-domestic-violence-in-latin-community/.

Ortiz de Montellano, Bernard R. 2001. "Human Body," In *The Oxford Encyclopedia of Mesoamerican Cultures*. Vol. 1, edited by Davíd Carrasco, 23–4. New York: Oxford University Press.

Oyewumi, Oyeronke. 1997. *The Invention of Women: Making an African Sense of Western Gender Discourses*. Minneapolis: University of Minnesota Press.

Palmer, Colin A. n.d. "Africa's Legacy in Mexico: A Legacy of Slavery." Smithsonian Learning Lab. Accessed October 26, 2016. http://www.smithsonianeducation.org/migrations/legacy/almleg.html.

Pandermalis, Dimitrios, Stamatia Eleftheratou, and Christina Vlassopoulou. 2015. *Acropolis Museum Guide*. Edited by Stamatia Eleftheratou. Translated by John Leonard. Athens: Acropolis Museum Editions.

Pasztory, Esther. 1997. *Teotihuacan: An Experiment in Living*. Norman: University of Oklahoma Press.

Pérez, Laura. 2007. *Chicana Art: The Politics of Spiritual and Aesthetic Altarities*. Durham: Duke University Press.

Puche, Mari Carmen Serra. 2001. "The Concept of Feminine Places in Mesoamerica: The Case of Xochitécatl, Tlaxcala, Mexico." In *Gender in Pre-Hispanic America*, edited by Cecilia F. Klein, 255–283. Washington, D.C.: Dumbarton Oaks.

Raju, C. K. 2012. *Euclid and Jesus: How and Why the Church Changed Mathematics and Christianity across Two Religious Wars*. Penang, Malaysia: Multiversity and Citizens International.

Rassias, Vlassis. 2000. *Demolish Them*. 2nd edition. Athens: Anichti Poli Editions.

Redmond, Layne. 1997. *When the Drummers Were Women: A Spiritual History of Women*. New York: Three Rivers Press.

Rendón, Laura. 2009. *Sentipensante (Sensing/Thinking): Pedagogy: Educating for Wholeness, Social Justice, and Liberation*. Sertling, VA: Stylus.

Ripper, Velcrow. 2009. "What Is Spiritual Activism?" Accessed January 2012, https://fiercelove.wordpress.com/what-is-spiritual-activism/.

Ritskes, Eric J. 2011. "Connected: Indigenous Spirituality as Resistance in the Classroom." In *Spirituality, Education, and Society: An Integrated Approach*, edited by Njoki N. Wane, Energy L. Manyimo, and Eric J. Ritskes. Rotterdam: Sense Publishers.

Roberts, Lynn, and Robert Levy. 2008. *Shamanic Reiki: Expanded Ways of Working with Universal Life Force Energy*. Lanham: O-Books.

Rodríguez, Roberto "Cintli." 2014. *Our Sacred Maíz Is Our Mother: Indigeneity and Belonging in the Americas*. Tucson: University of Arizona Press.

Román, Estela. 2012. *Nuestra medicina de los remedios para el aire y los remedios para el alma*. Bloomington, IN: Palibrio.

Ruiz, Don Miguel. 1997. *The Four Agreements: A Toltec Wisdom Book*. San Rafael, CA: Amber-Allen.

Sanchez, Victor. 2004. *The Toltec Oracle*. Rochester, VT: Bear.

Senate Joint Economic Committee. 2016. "The Economic State of the Latino Community in America." United States Congress. Updated July 2016. https://www.jec.senate.gov/public/_cache/files/c80b26fc-9d13-4537-a7a3-aa926e483cdf/the-economic-state-of-the-latino-community-in-america-july-2016-update-final-with-appendix-table-.pdf.

Shaikh, Sadiyya. 2013. *Sufi Narratives of Intimacy: Ibn Arabi, Gender, and Sexuality*. Cape Town: University of Cape Town Press.

Somé, Malidoma Patrice. 1993. *Ritual: Power, Healing, and Community*. New York: Penguin/Arkana.

Somé, Malidoma Patrice. 1999. *The Healing Wisdom of Africa: Finding Life Purpose Through Nature, Ritual, and Community*. London: Thorsons.

Talamantez, Inés. 1993. "Images of the Feminine in Apache Religious Tradition." In *After Patriarchy: Feminist Transformations of the World Religions*, edited by Paula M. Cooey, William R. Eakin, and Jay B. McDaniel, 131–45. Maryknoll, NY: Orbis Books.

Ten Fingers, Tony. 2014. *Lakota Wisdom*. Self-published: CreateSpace.

Townsend, Camilla. 2006. *Malintzin's Choices: An Indian Woman in the Conquest of Mexico*. Albuquerque: University of New Mexico Press.

Trotter, Robert T., and Juan Antonio Chavira. 1997. *Curanderismo: Mexican American Folk Healing*. Athens: University of Georgia Press.

Turner, Kay. 1986. "Home Altars and The Arts of Devotion: Texas-Mexican Expressions of Faith." In *Chicano Expressions: A New View in American Art*, edited by Inverna Lockpez, 40–48. New York: INTAR Latin American Gallery.

Van Praagh, James. 1997. *Talking to Heaven: A Medium's Message of Life After Death*. New York: Signet.

Valdez, Luis. 1994. "Pensamiento Serpentino: A Chicano Approach to the Teatre of Reality." In *Early Works: Actos, Bernabé, Pensamiento Serpentino*. Houston: Arte Público Press.

Walker, Matthew. 2017. "Why Your Brain Needs to Dream." *Mind and Body.* Greater Good Magazine, October 24, 2017. https://greatergood.berkeley.edu/article/item/why_your_brain_needs_to_dream.

Wangyal Tenzin Rinpoche. 2012. *Awakening the Luminous Mind.* Carlsbad, CA: Hay House.

Warner, Marina. 2013. *Alone of All Her Sex: The Myth and the Cult of the Virgin Mary.* Oxford: Oxford University Press.

Watts, Edward J. 2017. *Hypatia: The Life and Legend of an Ancient Philosopher.* Oxford: Oxford University Press.

Williams, Walter L. 1986. *The Spirit and the Flesh: Sexual Diversity in American Indian Culture.* Boston: Beacon Press.

Yugar, Theresa A. 2014. *Sor Juana Inés de la Cruz: Feminist Reconstruction of Biography and Text.* Eugene, OR: Wipf and Stock.

Yugar, Theresa A., Juan A. Tavárez, Alan A. Barrera. 2017. "The Enlightened West and the Origins of Climate Change." *Journal of Feminist Studies in Religion* 13 (2): 167–170.

CONTRIBUTORS

Margaret "Quica" Alarcón (Xicana) works in mixed media, painting, drawing, printmaking, *papel picado*, and publishing with decades of community activism with Mujeres de Maiz. She holds a BFA in illustration from the ArtCenter College of Design in Pasadena, an MA in education from National University School of Education, and an MFA in studio arts from California State University, Los Angeles.

Pedro Alvarado (Xicano) is a queer student and scholar at Northwestern University. Originally from San Diego, California, Pedro seeks to heal himself and others through artistic expression and community building.

Eddy Francisco Alvarez Jr. (Chicanx-Cubanx), PhD, is an assistant professor in the departments of Women, Gender, and Sexuality Studies and University Studies at Portland State University. His work has been published in *TSQ*, *Aztlan*, and *Bilingual Review/Revista Bilingue*.

Gloria Enedina Alvarez (Chicana) is an award-winning poet, intermedia artist, playwright, librettist, translator, and curator. She cofounded several artist organizations and mentored generations of artists. Publications include *emerging en un mar de olanes*, *la excusa/the excuse*, a spoken word cd, *Centerground*, and numerous anthologies and periodicals.

Grace Alvarez Sesma (Kumiai, Yaqui, Chicana) is a practitioner, student, and teacher of *curanderismo*. She considers this path to be one of lifelong learning and is committed to being of service to the best of her ability to her community and to the areas where she is invited to share her medicine. www.curanderismo.org.

Maritza Alvarez (Two-Spirit Xicanx), filmmaker and photographer, finds her familial footprints in the serpent and deer trails of Xalisco and Sonora, in the *papalotl* winds of Michoacán, in the ocean fronts of Comondú, Baja Sur. Her matrilineal clans guide her to defy patriarchal constructs and to sow dream bundles of medicine to harvest and share.

Issa Linda Arroyo (Xicana) resides in Los Angeles. After a near-death experience, which allowed her to reflect on her life, she decided to consciously walk the path *de las guerreras de la luz*. This battle of self and continuous-learning experience has led her to become a *danzante, zauhmadora,* and *temazcalera.*

Corina Benavides López (Chicana), PhD, is assistant professor of Chicana/o studies at California State University, Dominguez Hills. As a fem-crit, educational scholar, she promotes transformative and emancipatory scholarship on how systems of oppression impact Chicanx and people of color in the United States. She gives thanks to her ancestors for their blessings.

Norma Elia Cantú (Xicana/Coahuilteca), PhD, is the Norine R. and T. Frank Murchison Endowed Professor in Humanities at Trinity University and the author of the award-winning *Canícula: Snapshots of a Girlhood en la Frontera* (1995) as well as numerous other publications. A scholar of the U.S.-Mexico borderlands, she is a folklorist whose academic and transnational spiritual-activist work spans five decades.

Xánath Caraza (Mexicana, Chicana, Indígena) writes for *La Bloga, Seattle Escribe, SLC,* and *Monolito.* For the 2018 International Latino Book Awards, she received first place for *Lágrima roja* and *Sin preámbulos / Without Preamble* in "Best Book of Poetry in Spanish" and "Best Book Bilingual Poetry" categories. *Syllables of Wind* received the 2015 International Book Award for poetry.

Yadira Cazares (Tejana-Mexicana) is an artist and owner/founder of Galería Beso Maya in Oakland, California. She is a graduate of the California College of the Arts (CCA). As a community activist with more than a decade of social work service, Yadira paints, connects, heals, teaches, curates, and immerses herself in art and her local community.

Yreina D. Cervántez (Xicana Indígena), MFA, is a visual artist who has contributed to the discourse on an ever-evolving Chicana/o aesthetic through her art, teaching, and community activism over the last forty years. She is a professor in the Department of Chicana/o Studies at California State University, Northridge. Yreina has exhibited her work nationally and internationally at universities, museums, galleries, and community organizations.

Heidi M. Coronado (Maya/Guatemalan/Latina), PhD, is an assistant professor in the counseling department at California Lutheran University. Her research focuses on the educational experiences of Latinx students in both K–12 and higher education. As a scholar and practitioner, she integrates critical race theory pedagogies, Indigenous epistemologies, and contemplative practices in creating healing spaces for self and community exploration and empowerment.

Martha P. Cotera (Chicana), PhD, is a nationally recognized feminist historian, independent scholar, and archivist. She authored the seminal *Diosa y Hembra: The History and Heritage of Chicanas in the U.S.* and more than one hundred writings on civil rights, feminism, and Latina/o history. Her scholarship, leadership, and civic activism have earned numerous accolades.

Maria Elena Cruz (Chicana of Wixarika [Huichol] descent born in Northern California), PhD, is a sociocultural anthropologist specializing in Indigenous and Mexican American oral stories and *testimonio* in the U.S.-Mexico borderlands. She currently serves as the director of the TRIO program at San Jose State University.

Jackie Cuevas (Xicana) teaches Latinx literature at University of Texas, San Antonio. She is the author of *Post-Borderlandia,* cofounder of Evelyn Street Press, and a member of the Macondo Writers Workshop.

Karen Mary Davalos (Chicana), PhD, is trained in cultural anthropology. She is currently a professor of Chicano and Latino studies at the University of Minnesota, Twin Cities. She has authored four books about Chicana/o art and launched a major initiative, *Mexican American Art Since 1848.*

Neomi De Anda (Tejana), PhD, is an assistant professor of religious studies at the University of Dayton. She holds a PhD in constructive theology. Her research interests include Latinas and Latin American women writers in religion 1600–1900, theology and breast milk, and partnership with the Hope Border Institute.

Celeste De Luna (Tejana) is a printmaker from the lower Rio Grande Valley of South Texas. De Luna works in collaboration with the community in Brownsville, Texas, as a cofounder of the socially engaged arts collaborative Las Imaginistas and is a lecturer at the University of Texas Rio Grande Valley.

Esther Díaz Martín (Mexicana) is an assistant professor of Latin American and Latino studies and gender and women's studies at the University of Illinois at Chicago. She writes about the intersection of gender politics and sound in popular Latina/o culture. Her work is published in *Chicana/Latina Studies*, *Diálogo*, and *Spanish and Portuguese Review*.

Berenice Dimas (Xicana) is a queer writer, community-based herbalist, health educator, wellness *promotora*, and full-spectrum birth doula. Find out more about Berenice's work by visiting her website www.berenicedimas.com and her Instagram pages @hoodherbalism y @brujatip.

Ofelia Esparza (Chicana/Indígena Mexicana), artist and educator born in East Los Angeles, is known nationally and internationally for her Day of the Dead *ofrendas*. In 2016, CSULA conferred Ofelia an Honorary Doctorate Degree of Humane Letters and in 2018 she received the National Endowment for the Arts National Heritage Fellowship, the nation's highest honor in folk and traditional arts.

Rosanna Esparza Ahrens (Chicana) is a graphic artist and *altarista* (altar maker) born and raised in East Los Angeles. She is the daughter of renowned altar-maker Ofelia Esparza. Together with her mother they own and operate TONALLI STUDIO, a place of creative wellness located in the heart of East L.A. Rosanna's vision is to heal a community through art and mindful awareness.

Elisa Facio (Chicana), PhD, held a doctorate in sociology from the University of California, Berkeley, and received tenure at the University of Colorado, Boulder.

She also taught at Eastern Washington University and Sonoma State University. Elisa received numerous awards for her teaching and academic work. She cofounded Mujeres Activas en Letras y Cambio Social (MALCS). Her spirit remains with us all.

María Elena Fernández (Chicana Mexicana), based in Los Angeles, is the daughter of Mexico City immigrants. A professor of Chicana/o studies at California State University, Northridge, she also writes poetry, first-person essays, cultural journalism, and solo performance. She has written, performed, and toured nationally the autobiographical solo show *Confessions of a Cha Cha Feminist*.

María Figueroa (Chicana Indígena of Wirarika lineage), PhD, is a *maestra*, *danzante*, *teatrista*, and *poeta* who teaches English composition, literature, and humanities at MiraCosta College. Recalling her foremother's gifts of storytelling and *dichos* as healing proverbs for the soul, María courts words into a gentle metaphoric dance to highlight historically underrepresented women's experiences and generational knowledge.

Emilia Garcia (Chicana) is an artist/artivist whose work is centered on the beauty of Chicana/Latina culture, who we are and where we come from. Emilia's work conveys images that speak of strength and love through family and celebration all the while focusing on the spirit of women. Her work is exhibited nationally and internationally.

Atava Garcia Swiecicki (Xicana/Diné/Polish/Hungarian) is an herbalist, healer, and teacher and founder of the Ancestral Apothecary School of Herbal, Folk, and Indigenous Medicine in Oakland, California. Atava is informed by the healing traditions of her Mexican, Polish, Hungarian, and Navajo ancestors. Atava's websites are www.ancestralapothecary.com and www.ancestralapothecary school.com.

Jacqueline Garza Lawrence (Yaqui, Chichimeca, Pueblo, Chicana) is a spiritualist, substance abuse counselor, and advocate for the underserved. Born in Southern California, Jacqueline was raised by her grandmother and mother with traditional teachings about the healing customs of her family's Indigenous ancestors of Central Mexico. Her Indigenous roots bring a richness to her work that is exemplified in her presentations and writing.

Patrisia Gonzales (Kickapoo/Comanche and Macehual), PhD, is the author of *Red Medicine: Traditional Indigenous Rites of Birthing and Healing* and *Traditional Indian Medicine*. She is a baby catcher and has collaborated with Macehual knowledge keepers since 1991. She descends from three generations of bonesetters, herbalists, midwives, and traditional doctors.

Martha R. Gonzales (Xicanx) was raised in East Los Angeles, earned her bachelor's degree in philosophy and literature from University of California, Santa Cruz, and her doctorate in literature from University of California, San Diego. She lectures in the Ethnic Studies Department at Glendale Community College, Glendale, California.

Omar Gonzalez (Xicanx-Pueblo/Tigua Ysleta del Sur) is a poz, pochx, putx Pisces from El Paso, groomed by fierce Xicana and Black lesbian activists in Austin and later by fierce *mujer* scholars at California State University, Northridge. He has recently completed his PhD on the work of John Rechy in the Department of Chicana/o Studies at the University of California, Los Angeles, under the guidance of Dr. Alicia Gaspar de Alba.

Cristina Gorocica (Mexicana/Chicana/Maya) is the daughter of Luis and Teresa Gorocica from Merida, Yucatan, Mayab. Cristina is a mother of two beautiful daughters, a dedicated educator, leader in education, a *danzante Azteca Conchera*, and a yoga practitioner. She is a founding member of *In Lak Ech* and *Mujeres de Maiz*.

Lauren Frances Guerra (Guatemalan-Ecuadorian), PhD, was raised in Los Angeles. She earned her doctorate in systematic theology from the Graduate Theological Union, Berkeley. She is currently a visiting assistant professor in theological studies at Loyola Marymount University, Los Angeles.

Inés Hernández-Ávila (Nez Perce/Tejana), PhD, is a professor of Native American studies at University of California, Davis, a scholar, a poet, and visual artist. She is one of the founders of the Native American and Indigenous Studies Association (NAISA). Her research focuses on contemporary Indigenous expressions of personal/collective autonomy and creativity for social justice.

Alan Hicks (European American) is a lifelong community activist with a BA in journalism and Latin American studies from California State University, Los

Angeles. He is a former board member of Barrios Unidos, former president of the Springfield Grange, chair of the annual Watsonville Peace and Unity March, and current board member of the Watsonville Film Festival.

Ann Hidalgo (Cuban American), PhD, specializes in Latin American theology and feminist and decolonial theory. Her doctorate is in religion, ethics, and society from Claremont School of Theology. She studies liberation theology liturgies and musical practices that empower marginalized communities. Ann is currently the acquisitions librarian at Claremont School of Theology.

Jacqueline M. Hidalgo (Costa Rican), PhD, is an associate professor of Latina/o studies and religion at Williams College in Williamstown, Massachusetts. She is the author of *Revelation in Aztlán: Scriptures, Utopias, and the Chicano Movement* as well as various articles and essays.

Naya Armendarez Jones, (African-American and Xicana), PhD, is a Blaxicana geographer and ceremony keeper with Texas roots. She lifts up African American and Xicanx healing through research, spiritual activism, and art. A longtime meditation guide, her current community work uses ritual to explore food-related racial trauma. She writes about joyful activism. www.nayajones.com.

Patricia Juárez / Chicueyi-Coatl (Mexica-Tenochca) is the founder and leader of Calpulli Huey Papalotl, a cultural and educational Danza Mexica circle whose purpose is to cultivate Anahuacan ceremonies, tradition, and culture within the existing Native/Chicanx groups of Northern California. She is also the founder of two Calmecac, or Nahuatl, higher educational institutions.

Irene Lara (Xicana), PhD, is a women's studies professor at San Diego State University. Her teaching, scholarship, activism, and mamihood are inspired by Indigenous knowledge, Anzaldúan thought, *curandera* praxis, and living in the borderlands. She's the coeditor of *Fleshing the Spirit: Spirituality and Activism in Chicana, Latina, and Indigenous Women's Lives* and *Women in Culture: An Intersectional Anthology of Gender and Women's Studies.*

Rossy Evelin Lima (Afro-Mexican) is a linguist, a writer, and a translator. Her most recent poetry book is *Migrare Mutare*. She received the Latino Book Award in 2014 and 2016. Lima is founder of the Latin American Foundation for the Arts, FeIPoL, and the Sin Fronteras Book Fest and has presented at TEDx.

Alicia Enciso Litschi (Chicana) is a psychologist in Austin, Texas. Alicia has a private therapy practice and believes that healing the mind is inseparable from healing body, soul, heart, and community. She gardens whenever possible and delights in building *altares* to the Sacred Feminine in all Her forms.

Marta López-Garza (Xicana), PhD, is a professor in gender and women's studies and Chicana/o studies departments at California State University, Northridge. She co-facilitates Revolutionary Scholars, an organization of formerly incarcerated students and is a cofounder of Civil Discourse and Social Change, a campus-wide initiative combining education, community involvement, and sustained activism. Her scholarship focuses on formerly incarcerated womxn.

Dora Xochitl Lopez-Mata (MeXicana) holds an MA in Chicana/o studies from California State University, Northridge. She is the at-large representative for Mujeres Activas en Letras y Cambio Social (MALCS) with research interests in testimonios, fat studies, and spirituality.

Jessica Lozano Rodriguez (Chicana/Tecuexe/Caxcana) is a PhD candidate in the Department of Anthropology at University of Washington, Seattle. She is a medical anthropologist who works with rural communities in Mexico concerning issues of health, health-care systems, traditional and alternative medicines, and agency. She is a daughter of the river god Chan and a student of his healing mysteries.

Jennie Luna (Xicana/Caxcan), PhD, is a practicing doula and a traditional Mexica dancer. Her article "La Tradición Conchera: The Historical Process of Danza and Catholicism" was awarded the 2014 Antonia I. Castañeda prize by the National Association for Chicana and Chicano Studies. She is an assistant professor in Chicana/o studies at California State University, Channel Islands.

María Elena Martínez (Chicana), MEd, worked in bilingual education for thirty-four years and on education/electoral reform in the Texas Chicana/o movement. María Elena studies shamanism, having trained with Zapotec *curandera* Doña Enriqueta Contreras, and is a spiritual elder within Alma de Mujer Center for Social Change.

Norell Martínez (Xicana fronteriza), PhD, is an assistant professor at San Diego City College in the Department of English. Her research focuses on bruja knowledge in the creative work of Chicana, Indígena, and Afro-Latina women in the era of neoliberal capitalism. Norell is cofounder of Mujeres de Maiz Fronterizas in San Diego, a chapter of Mujeres de Maiz, based in East Los Angeles.

Maria Eva Mata (Mexicana) was born and raised in Michoacán, Mexico. She migrated to the United States in 1999 and is a former farmworker. In fall 2016, she created an *ofrenda* for California State University, Northridge's Dias de los Muertos in collaboration with her daughter, where she displayed her *bordados*.

Lara Medina (Xicanx) was raised in the San Francisco Bay Area, earned an MA in theology from Graduate Theological Union in Berkeley, California, and a PhD in history from Claremont Graduate University. She is a professor in the Chicana/o Studies Department at California State University, Northridge.

yaz mendez nuñez (Caribeñ@a) is a queer brown southerner who lives, loves, and hustles as altar boi to the Divine in the legacy of their *borinken* and *quisqueyan* ancestors. their political and spiritual commitments are to enthusiasm, integrity, joy, and authenticity.

Claudia A. Mercado (Xicana) is a multimedia artist in Los Angeles. Her practice and ever-evolving *conocimiento* of spirituality began with her grandmother's humanitarian Indigenous ways and has evolved into a diversity of explorations and artistic collaborations with collectives such as In Lak Ech, Mujeres de Maiz, and in northern and southern ancestral *ceremonias*. www.7serpentfilms.com.

Felicia "Fe" Montes (Xicana Indígena) is an artivist, educator, performer, and practitioner of the healing arts based in East Los Angeles. She co-founded Mujeres de Maiz and In Lak Ech and created Urban Xic and La Botanica del Barrio and is a graduate of the University of California, Los Angeles; California State University, Northridge; and Otis College of Art.

Melissa Moreno (Chicana, descendent of Otomi and Blackfoot People), PhD, teaches and researches in ethnic studies, multicultural education, and Chicano/Latino studies. She is cochair of the Indigenous Caucus for the National Association for Chicana and Chicano Studies (NACCS), a member of Mujeres Activas en Letras y Cambio Social (MALCS), and serves on the Ethnic Studies Advisory Committee for the local school district.

alba onofrio (Latinx), MDiv, a.k.a. Reverend Sex, is a southern Appalachian first-gen Latinx queer femme evangelist theologian *en la lucha* with QTPOC folks as a spiritual healer and bruja troublemaker, hustling to subvert systems of domination, combat spiritual terrorism, and reclaim Guad, as well as eradicate shame and fear wherever they are found.

Jennifer Owens Jofré (Bolivian-American), PhD, recently completed her doctorate at the Graduate Theological Union in Berkeley, California. Through a Louisville Institute postdoctoral fellowship, she currently serves as visiting professor of constructive theology at Austin Presbyterian Theological Seminary in Texas. Her dissertation explores the implications of devotion to Our Lady of Guadalupe for Mariology and for ministry.

Sandra M. Pacheco (Chicana/Mexicana/Indígena), PhD, is a professor of interdisciplinary studies at the California Institute of Integral Studies. Her teaching and research focuses on Chicana/Latina/Indígena feminisms and spirituality. Sandra cofounded Curanderas sin Fronteras, a mobile clinic dedicated to serving the health and well-being of Chican@/Latin@/Indígena communities through the use of *curanderismo*.

Patricia Pedroza González (Mexicana), PhD, is an associate professor of women's and gender studies and American studies at Keene State College in New Hampshire. Her research interests are women-of-color epistemologies, embodiment, and spirituality. Originally born in Morelia, Michoacán, Mexico, she is a practitioner of art performances and feminist pedagogy.

Irene Perez (Chicana) is an artist and muralist based in Oakland, California. She is a *verterana* artist of the Chicano movement and was a core member of Mujeres Muralistas begun in 1973, a collective of Chicana/Latina artists whose work significantly inserted issues of gender into the Chicano mural movement. Irene's image of Coyolxauhqui breaking free from patriarchy is an iconic image that helped shape Chicana feminist consciousness.

Laura Pérez (Xicana), PhD, is a professor of ethnic studies at the University of California, Berkeley. She has curated Latina/o performance art and feminist and Latinx multimedia art exhibitions and is the author of *Chicana Art: The Politics of Spiritual and Aesthetic Altarities* and *Eros Ideologies: Writings on Art, Spirituality, and the Decolonial.*

Elvira Prieto (Chicana), EdM, is from California's Central San Joaquin Valley, where she worked with her family in the fields. She is an assistant dean of student affairs and associate director of El Centro Chicano y Latino at Stanford. Elvira's writings retell *testimonios* with the intention of creating spaces of light, love, and healing.

Gloria Quesada is from Corpus Christi, Texas. She is an active member of Alma de Mujer Center for Social Change in Austin, Texas, where she assists with programming and initiatives related to social justice issues, spiritual activism, the environment, and healing and youth and women's development.

Naomi H. Quiñonez (Chicana), PhD, has written three books of poetry: *Hummingbird Dream*, *The Smoking Mirror*, and *Exiled Moon*. She holds a doctorate in history and is the editor of *Invocation L.A.* and *Decolonial Voices*. She has received a Rockefeller Fellowship and an American Book Award and is featured in Notable Hispanic Women.

Lilia "Liliflor" Ramirez (Indigenous Chicana Mexica) is a cultural arts educator who integrates Nahua cosmology in her aesthetic experimentation to address spiritual, political, and social questions. She brings knowledge of her Indigenous roots to bear in her work that dignifies the everyday people of Los Angeles, particularly women.

Jessica L. Rocha (Xicana) is interested in the ways the individual and community reclaim identity, history, culture and empowerment explored in the tradition of aesthetic representations of the Chicana feminist experience. She studied art history at California State University, Long Beach, with an emphasis in contemporary art.

Patricia Rodriguez (Chicana) received a BA in art from the San Francisco Art Institute and an MA from Sacramento State University. She is cocreator of Mujeres Muralistas 1970–1985, the first Chicana/Latina mural group, and served as a curator for the Mission Cultural Center for Latino Arts in San Francisco for ten years. Her current artwork is monotype prints and box constructions.

Trini Tlazohteotl Rodriguez (Xicana Indígena) is the cofounder of Tía Chucha's Centro Cultural, a cultural center/bookstore transforming community through ancestral knowledge, the arts, literacy, and creative engagement. A former bilingual educator and newspaper editor, she writes, speaks, and works

for personal and collective healing and systemic social change. http://www
.tiachucha.org/, http://hummingbirdcricket.libsyn.com/.

Estela Román (Mexicana Indígena) completed her studies in sociology at the
Universidad Nacional Autónoma de México and her MA in international studies of peace at the University of Notre Dame, Indiana. Since the age of nineteen
she has trained in health care using Mexican Indigenous methods of healing.
She is recognized internationally as a *curandera*.

Brenda Romero (Chicana, Mexican-American), PhD, is a professor of ethnomusicology at the University of Colorado, Boulder, serving as chair of musicology from 2004 to 2007 and 2017. She holds a PhD in ethnomusicology from the
University of California, Los Angeles, and bachelor and master degrees in music
theory and composition from the University of New Mexico.

Mónica Russel y Rodríguez (Xicana), PhD, is a cultural anthropologist at Northwestern University where she serves as associate dean in the College of Arts and
Sciences. She is affiliated with the Department of Anthropology and the Program
of Latina and Latinos Studies. Her focus is on Chicana feminist theory.

Aida Salazar (Xicana) is an Oakland-based writer. Her debut novel *The Moon
Within* is centered on a Xicanx first moon communal ritual. Her bio picture book
Jovita Wore Pants features her great-aunt Jovita Valdovinos, Mexico's Joan of Arc.
She also wrote,*By the Light of the Moon*, the first Chicana-themed ballet in history.

Sara H. Salazar (Chicana), PhD, is a second-generation from rural Illinois and
a first-generation college graduate. She is core faculty in the School of Under-
graduate Studies at the California Institute of Integral Studies (San Francisco).
Her poetry is dedicated to Marina and Mateo.

Luis Salinas, a.k.a. Luis Cihuatl, is a queer two-spirit *danzante* artist currently
working on their master's degree in Chicanx studies at California State University, Northridge.

Brenda Sendejo (Chicana/Tejana), PhD, is a feminist anthropologist who
examines embodied knowledges, spiritual activism, and the Chicana feminist
movement in Texas. She developed the concepts methodologies of the spirit and

mujerista ethnography and directs the intergenerational Latina History Project, which documents Chicana feminist thought and praxis in Texas since the 1960s.

Claudia Serrato (Purhépecha/Huasteca/Xicana) has been an active member of the growing Indigenous food movement for over a decade. She cooks with grass-roots and prominent Indigenous chefs and consults on Indigenous-centered food initiatives. Serrato's doctoral studies inform her public scholarship on the importance of returning to one's cultural heritage cuisines.

Jerry Tello (Tap Pilam Coahuiltecan) is an internationally recognized authority in family strengthening, therapeutic healing, cross-cultural issues, and moti-vational speaking. He is the author of children's books, professional publica-tions, culturally based curricula, motivational CDs, and other media. Jerry has received numerous awards, including the Ambassador of Peace Award and Pres-idential Crime Victims Service Award.

Marisol Lydia Torres (Xicana—Mexican/Nicaraguan), MFA, is a visual art-ist, performer, and writer, beginning in theater in 1996 with ChUSMA (1996–2007). Marisol is a cofounder of Xicana-Indígena poetry and song group In Lak Ech (1997–present) as well as Xicana comedy theater troupe Las Ramonas (2007–present). As a visual artist, Marisol works as a painter, muralist, and papier-mâché sculptor.

Theresa Torres (Chicana), PhD, is an associate professor at the University of Missouri, Kansas City, in the departments of sociology and Latinx and Latin American studies. Her expertise is in Latinx studies, immigration, race, and ethnic relations and spirituality. She published *The Paradox of Latina Religious Leadership in the Catholic Church*.

Modesta Barbina Trevino (Chicana Indígena) is a retired bilingual educator of twenty-seven years from Austin, Texas. She was involved in education reform and the cultural arts during the Chicano movement and was a member of the arts collective, Mujeres Artistas del Sudoeste, organizing their 1979 Conferencia Plastica Chicano.

Patricia Marina Trujillo (Chicana), PhD, is the director of Equity and Diversity and an associate professor of English and Chicana/o studies at Northern New

Mexico College. Trujillo is the creative writing editor of *Chicana/Latina Studies: The Journal of Mujeres Activas en Letras y Cambio Social* and board member of the Northern Rio Grande National Heritage Area, NewMexicoWomen.org, and Tewa Women United and is a faculty adviser to the ¡Sostenga! Farm.

Linda Vallejo (LatinX, ChicanX, IndigenX) creates art investigating contemporary cultural, spiritual, and social issues. Her solo exhibitions include Texas A&M University, UCLA Chicano Studies Research Center, Lancaster Museum of Art and History, and Califonia State University, San Bernardino. She studied danza with Las Flores de Aztlan, presenting in cultural centers, universities, and Native American and Chicano ceremonies. She supports Southern Door Lodge.

Jocelyn Vargas (Chicana) is a first-generation daughter of immigrants, was born to a single mother, and was predominantly raised by women. She is the first in her immediate family to pursue higher education, and she currently attends California State University, Los Angeles, majoring in social work and minoring in psychology.

Sybil Venegas (Chicana) is an independent art historian and curator. She is one of the first art historians to historicize Chicana art and is recognized as an early scholar in Chicana feminist art history as well as the cultural politics of *Días de los Muertos* ceremonials in Chicano/Latino communities.

Linda Villanueva (Cherokee/Apache and Raramuri) is a licensed clinical social worker. She has worked for the Los Angeles County Department of Mental Health, serving children and families for more than thirty years and was a member of CALMECAC, a Chicanx spiritual activist circle of teachers and mental health professionals in Los Angeles, working with urban youth for more than two decades, from 1970 to 1995.

Liliana Wilson (Latina) is a visual artist born in Chile. She is best known for her intricate drawings with surrealistic renderings. Liliana's history of artistic expressions is the subject of *Ofrenda: Liliana Wilson's Art of Dissidence and Dreams*, edited by Norma E. Cantú.

Theresa Yugar (Peruvian/Latinx), PhD, teaches at Loyola Marymount University in the Women's Studies Department. Her doctorate is from Claremont

Graduate University and her master's degree is from Harvard University in women's studies in religion. She is the author of *Sor Juana Inés de la Cruz: Feminist Reconstruction of Biography and Text*.

Rosa Martha Zárate Macías (Mexicana/Caxcana), is a singer and composer, popular educator, community organizer, and liberation theologian. She is also the cofounder of Librería del Pueblo, a community-based organization in San Bernardino, California. She is a member of the coordinating team in the binational movement seeking justice for 4.6 million laborers during the Bracero Program, 1942 to 1964.

Susy Zepeda (queer, detribalized Xicana Indígena) is an assistant professor in the Department of Chicana/o Studies at the University of California, Davis. Her research and teaching are in Xicana Indígena spirituality and women-of-color feminist methodologies. As part of the Santa Cruz Feminist of Color Collective, they published "Building on 'the Edge of Each Other's Battles': A Feminist of Color Multidimensional Lens."

INDEX

of umbilical cords, 72; psychotropic, 188–89

poverty rate for "Hispanics," 6n

prayers: to ancestors for guidance, 131; danza as prayer in motion, 113–16; danza ceremonial trajes as wearable, 117–19; effect upon dreams, 163–64; M. Gonzales on evening, 391–93; for healing, 308–9; honoring directions and elements as form of, 32; to lover, 311–13; M. Gonzales on prayer and song, 319–21; and memory, 142–43; morning, 17, 22–30; for nuclear disarmament and peace, 355; to sacred directions, 17; for spirit plates, 253,

Prieto, Elvira, 256, 261

pregnancy loss, 273–80

queerness, 306; Anzaldúa influence upon Zepeda's teaching, 372–74; danza as liberation for, 109, 110–12; dreams as aid to "coming out," 156, 163–64; influence upon altars, 48; joteria, 88–90, 134, 331; and prayer, 306, 311–13, 330–33

Quesada, Gloria, 244, 248–49

Quiñonez, Naomi H., 376, 387–90

radical wholeness, 263

Ramirez, Lilia "Liliflor", iv

rape, 11, 85–86, 193; of people and natural resources, 333

Red Road, 6, 86, 164

Reiki, 124

rituals: for baños de limpia spiritual, 177–81; Fiesta de Maíz, 205–8; first-moon ceremony, 200–201, 210–16; as gateways to healing, 169–70; for gender fluidity, 200, 205–10, 208–10; for leaving home ceremony, 217–18; Rite

of Passage for young woman, 202–4; talking circles, 287–89

Rocha, Jessica, 333n, Plate 7

Rodríguez, Jessica Lozano, 193–96

Rodriguez, Patricia, 120, 132, 345n, Plate 9

Rodriguez, Trini Tlazohteotl, 375, 378–80

Román, Estela, 50, 51, 158, 170–71, 182, 188–91, 235

Roman, Raquel, 349–50

Romero, Brenda, 226, 230–31

rosary, 89, 392

Russel y Rodrgíuez, Mónica, 61, 68–70

Sabina, María, 319–20

sacred cardinal directions. See cardinal directions

sacred center (axis mundi), 37

Sacred Cosmic Energy/Energies, 118; Centéotl, 205–6; Chalchiuhtlicue, 246, 281; Coatlicue, 11, Cihuateteo, 153; Coyolxauhqui, 11, 168, 173, 197, 294, 296–97; Ehecatl, 182; Grandfather Sky, 239, 241; Grandfather Sun, 214; Grandmother Moon, 16, 18, 66, 174, 175, 214, 215, 301–2, 303, 316, 397; Great Mystery, 6–7n; Huitzilopochtli, 108, 353; Ixchel, 61; Omecíhuatl (creator of universe), 144; Tlazolteotl, 74, 77, 189–90; Xilonen, 205–6, 288; Xochiquetzal, 108

sacred sexualities: affirming divine presence in oneself and lover, 306, 311–13; healing from sexual trauma, 314–17; human liberation and, 307–9; M. Gonzales on, 305–6

Sacred Source, 169

sacred spaces: classroom as, 366, 367–69; creating in home, 18, 40–46, 55–58; Medina on, 37–39; role of Our Lady of Guadalupe in, 47–49; shrine of self-realization, 44